·ALEXANDER POPE·
Poems in Facsimile

·ALEXANDER POPE·
Poems in Facsimile

An Essay on Criticism (1711)

The Rape of the Lock (1714)

The Dunciad Variorum (1729)

Epistle to Arbuthnot (1734)

An Essay on Man (1734)

Introduction by Geoffrey Day

SCOLAR PRESS

This edition first published 1988 by
SCOLAR PRESS
Gower Publishing Company Limited
Gower House, Croft Road
Aldershot GU11 3HR, England

British Library Cataloguing in Publication Data
Pope, Alexander, *1688-1744*
  Alexander Pope : poems.
  I. Title
  821'.5

ISBN 0 85967-752-4

Printed in Great Britain by Athenæum Press Ltd, Newcastle upon Tyne

Publisher's note

The texts are reproduced from the editions cited in the introduction. The format of this Scolar edition is that of the largest text, *Epistle to Arbuthnot*; the other four texts have also been reproduced in their original size and have been centred on the type area of the *Epistle*.

Introduction by Geoffrey Day

An Essay on Criticism

Griffith 2
Foxon P806

This reproduction made up from copy in Edinburgh University Library, Shelfmark Df 5.73, with final advertisement leaf taken from copy in Bodleian Library.

Collation of perfect copy: 4o: π^1 A-E^4 F^2 G^1, [\$2 signed (– A1, F2)]

Pagination of perfect copy: 24 leaves: [2] *1-3* 4-43 *44* [2]

No watermark

Catchwords lacking A2^b, C2^b; F1^{a-b} *Such*/ Who

The pair π1 and G1 were used as wrappers with the result that one or both often discarded.

Entered in the Stationers' Register on 11 May 1711.
The annotation '3 — 20' on the half title of this copy shows it to be the twentieth item of the third consignment of books from Stationers' Hall to Edinburgh University.

   There are two variant title pages to this work. The one reproduced here is the more common. The other reads: 'London: Printed for W. Lewis in Russel-Street, Covent-Garden.' In his introduction to the Scolar Press facsimile of 1970, David Foxon argues that Lewis, having been a long time friend of Pope, was the publisher, and the short imprint was used on copies for his own stock and for distribution by Pope himself: the longer imprint indicated copies for the general trade. Neither title page is a cancel: neither has priority.

   On 19 July 1711 Pope wrote to Caryll, 'Tonson's printer told me he drew off a thousand copies in his first impression' (Sherburn I 128).

The Rape of the Lock

Griffith 29
Foxon P941

This reproduction from a copy in Edinburgh University Library, Shelfmark JA 644/9

8°: (frontispiece +) A^4 B-D^8 (+ 5 plates)

28 leaves: [8], *1* 2-48 (misprinting 29 as '26', 44 as '45' and 45 as '44'. The separately inserted engravings are not included in this pagination).

Watermark: IM; not in Heawood

Catchwords lacking C8^a, D5^b, D6^b, D7^b

Title red and black. *RAPE/ LOCK./* POEM./ Mr. POPE./ *LONDON:/* BERNARD LINTOTT,/ in red.

Six copper engravings by Claude Du Bosc (1682-1745 ?) from designs by Louis Du Guernier (1677-1716).

A two canto version, 'The Rape of the Locke' with its own title page was printed at the end of *Miscellaneous Poems and Translations. By several hands* and was published 20 May 1712, the copyright having been sold to Lintott for £7 on 21 March 1711/12. On 20 February 1713/14 Lintott paid a further £15 for the additional material for this edition and copyright was entered on 2 March. Further major revision occurred for the 1717 *Works*.

Sales were brisk. Pope wrote to Caryll on 12 March 1713/14 that it had 'in four days time sold to the number [of] four thousand, and is already reprinted' (Sherburn I 214).

The Dunciad Variorum

Griffith 212

Foxon P773

This reproduction of British Library 642.K.2(1).

$4°$: (engraved title +) a-b^4 B-I^4 K^4 (–K1, 2 + K1.2) L-0^4 P^2 Q-X^4 Y^1 [\$2 signed (– a1, F2, K2, Q2)]

88 leaves, pp. [*1*] *1-2* 3-16 [*2*] *1-2* 3-16 [*2*] *1* 2-6 9-21 *22* 23-26 *27* 28-29 [*3*] *1* 2-53 *54* 55-79 *80* 81-84 *85-86* 87-118 cxix-cxxiv [*2*]

Watermark: S; not in Heawood.

Reissue of Griffith 211, Foxon P771, with additional leaf *Y1* at end.

The cancel leaves K1.2 printed together with P2 apparently as the result of a decision to eliminate a couplet: line numeration throughout the poem is consistent with this sole exception, there being only five lines between that numbered 158 (K2^b) and that numbered 165 (K3^r). Jonathan Richardson Junior's annotations of the 'Second Broglio MS' (see Mack p. 141) would suggest that the excised couplet appeared after line 152, and may have read:

> Pearls on her Neck, & Diamonds in her Hair.
> And her fore Buttocks to the Navel bare.

Richardson's record differs from the couplet as printed in the various 1728 editions and issues of *The Dunciad* (Griffith 198-204; Foxon P764-770):

> Pearls on her neck, and roses in her hair,
> And her fore-buttocks to the navel bare.

The circumstances of publication of *The Dunciad Variorum* were made deliberately confusing by Pope. The 'A. Dod' of the title page is Mrs Anne Dodd whose name had also appeared on the title page of the 1728 *Dunciad,* but when Lawton Gilliver filed a Chancery bill in 1729 to prevent publication of a pirate edition Mrs Dodd swore an affidavit that she had had nothing whatever to do with the poem and her evidence was accepted by the court (P.R.O. C 11/2581/ 36). The use of Dodd's name together with the wording of the 'Advertisement' would support the theory that Pope was intending the reader to consider the publication unauthorised. The confusion was compounded by the fact that the assignees of the poem were Edward Harley, second Earl of Oxford, Lord Bathurst and Richard Boyle, third Earl of Burlington; and that Harley's amanuensis was employed to transcribe the variorum notes and the letter purporting to be by William Cleland, but possibly by Pope. Harley was moreover involved in the distribution of the poem (see Sherburn III 25-26). The secrecy was necessitated by the decision to print in full the names of the dunces, and the assigning of the poem to the three noblemen could well have been to minimise the possibility of legal action. So successful was Pope's manoeuvring to protect himself that, according to Arbuthnot (Sherburn III 37), his action to prevent piracies of the poem failed as he was unable to 'prove any property'. Pope's carefulness in this matter was such that he did not admit the authorship until the publication of the poem in the second volume of the 1735 edition of his *Works,* though paradoxically he is named in Cleland's 'Letter to the Publisher' here.

According to John Dennis the poem was printed by J. Wright. This reissue was advertised in the *Daily Post* of 10 April 1729 as published by Lawton Gilliver and Anne Dodd thus continuing the fiction of her involvement, was entered in the Stationers' Register on 12 April, and had been published by 8 April 1729.

An Epistle from Mr. Pope, to Dr. Arbuthnot

Griffith 352
Foxon P802

This reproduction from Bodleian Library M3. 19 Art. 17, followed by reproduction of 'Epistle VII to Dr Arbuthnot' from the Edinburgh University Library copy of *The Works,* 1735, Volume II.

Folio: A^2 B-F^2

12 leaves: [4] *1* 2-20 (misprinting 20 as '30').

Published 2 January 1734/35, with copyright entered to Lawton Gilliver in the Stationers' Register.

The Bodleian copy was owned by Edward Harley, second Earl of Oxford, and bears his annotations, many of which are identifications. There are substantive revisions: 'Fanny' is substituted for '*Damon*' (C2^b), and on D2^b a couplet is interlineated:

To Bards reciting he vouchsaf'd a Nod And snuff'd their Incence like a gracious God

This couplet is to be found in a holograph fragment preserved in the Pierpoint Morgan Library, reproduced and transcribed by Mack (pp. 438-39). Harley also adds a defence of Pope's attack on Addison (D2ᵃ). On D2ᵇ the marginal note is completed in red ink which has failed to reproduce. The invisible entry reads: 'it would also fit the late earl of Halifax'.

Mack's introduction to his transcription provides a valuable discussion of the genesis of the poem. Originally addressed to William Cleland, the switch to Arbuthnot appears to have taken place after August 1734 during which month Pope wrote to his friend, 'I determine to address to you one of my Epistles, written by piece-meal many years, & which I have now made haste to put together' (Sherburn III 428). This piece-meal nature and haste are also evident throughout the separately printed folio and the apparently synchronically printed version in *The Works* of 1735 reproduced here for convenience of comparison. In the former, line numeration is accurate to 70, apart from 50 appearing as '52'. Thereafter only lines 95 and 101 are numbered correctly: all others being wrong by a margin ranging from 1 to 10. It is clear that there were extensive revisions and alterations in the press in both versions, for the line numeration in the collected version, whilst not as erratic as in the folio, still leaves a lot to be desired in terms of accuracy. David Foxon notes in his introduction to the Scolar Press facsimile of 1970 that though the *Works* version appears to be at many points an earlier state of the text, nevertheless in subsequent printings of the poem Pope elected to follow a number of variants found there including eleven lines not incorporated in the folio version. His suggestion is that these lines were among the more offensive, principally relating to Lord Hervey, and that Pope did not wish to create more turbulence than was necessary on the first appearance of the poem.

An Essay on Man

Griffith 336, issue Xa
Foxon P852

This reproduction from Bodleian Library G. Pamph 1487/6; followed by pair of leaves from copy of fine paper edition (Griffith 337, Foxon P853) in the possession of Mr H.B. Forster.

4°: π⁴ A-H⁴ I⁴ (±I2) K¹ [$2 signed (F2 signed 'D2')]

41 leaves, pp. [4] *i-iv 1-7* 8-22 *23* 24-37 *38* 39-54 *55* 56-74 (misprinting 54 as '45')

Watermark: fleur de lis surmounting shield with bend, in π only. Similar to, but not identical with, Heawood 84.

Title in red and black. ESSAY on MAN,/ *HENRY St. JOHN, L. BOLINGBROKE.*/ *LONDON:*/ MDCCXXXIV./ in red.

Originally issued anonymously in parts by Pope who affected ignorance of the author in his correspondence (Sherburn III 351), a pose for which he offered conflicting explanations. He wrote to William Duncombe, 20 October 1734, 'I wanted only to hear truth, and was more afraid of my partial friends than enemies' (Sherburn III 438); though in a letter jointly written with Bolingbroke to Swift, 15 September 1734, he claimed, 'The design of concealing myself was good, and had its full effect; I was thought a divine, a philosopher, and what not? and my doctrine had a sanction I could not have given to it' (Sherburn III 433).

Line numeration in Epistle I is correct.

In Epistle II line numbers suggest late addition of couplets between 135 and '140' (*recte* 142) and between '150' and '155' (*recte* 152 and 159). Numeration is corrected as from line 195. Comparison with Mack's facsimile and transcript suggests that in the first instance the additional lines are 139-40:

> The ruling Passion, be it what it will,
> The ruling Passion conquers Reason still.

These lines are not in Mack. Reworkings of the second passage are so extensive as to make it impossible to deduce the addition.

Errors in Epistle III appear to be arithmetical rather than indicators of revision: 129 is misnumbered '130' and the error continues until corrected at line 310 (*en route* 216 appears as '251'); and 315 is misnumbered '320', the true total is 318.

As David Foxon pointed out in 'Two cruces in Pope bibliography' (*TLS*, 24 January 1958, p. 52) Epistle IV was printed from the standing type of the first separately printed folio edition of January 1733/34, though with the insertion of the omitted lines 377 and 378:

> When Statesmen, Heroes, Kings, in dust repose,
> Whose Sons shall blush their Fathers were thy foes.

There is also a substantive revision in the following line, from: 'And shall this Verse . . .' to 'Shall then this Verse. . . .' There are some errors in line numeration. 35 is misnumbered '30', 200 as '205', 204 as '210' and this error continues to line 295 which is misnumbered '300'; this error in turn continues to the end of the Epistle with the exception of line 320 which marked as '352'. The true total is 388: these errors do not suggest revisions in the press.

The annotations are in an unidentified hand.

I2 and K1 are cancels. Foxon, in his introduction to the Scolar Press facsimile of 1969, suggested that K1 might be a cancel for a pair of leaves of which 'K2' contained an 'Index to the Ethic Epistles' which was referred to by Joseph Spence, 'the most exact account of his plan as it stood then will best appear from a leaf which he annexed to about a dozen copies of the poem, printed in that year, and sent as presents to some of his most particular friends. Most of these were afterwards called in again. . . .' (*Anecdotes,* ed. James Osborn, Oxford, [1966], I 132). At the end of this section is reproduced the only known copy of this leaf, apparently conjugate with the original K1, to be found in a fine paper copy owned by Mr H.B. Forster.

Geoffrey Day
University of Cambridge

Acknowledgements

An Essay on Criticism, Df. 5.73, is reproduced by permission of Edinburgh University Library.

The Rape of the Lock, JA 664/9, is reproduced by permission of Edinburgh University Library.

The Dunciad Variorum, 642.K.2(1), is reproduced by permission of the Trustees of the British Library.

An Epistle from Mr. Pope, to Dr. Arbuthnot, Bodleian M.3 19 Art. 17, is reproduced by permission of the Bodleian Library, followed by reproduction of 'Epistle VII to Dr. Arbuthnot' from the Edinburgh University Library copy of *The Works,* 1735, Volume II.

An Essay on Man, G. Pamph 1487/6, is reproduced by permission of the Bodleian Library.

Abbreviations

Foxon   D.F. Foxon *English Verse 1701-1750* Cambridge: Cambridge University Press, 2 vols, 1975.

Griffith   Reginald Harvey Griffith *Alexander Pope A Bibliography* Austin: University of Texas, 2 vols, 1922-27.

Heawood   Edward Heawood *Watermarks mainly of the 17th and 18th centuries* Hilversum: Paper Publications Society, 1950.

Mack   Maynard Mack *The Last and Greatest Art* Newark: University of Delaware Press, 1984.

Sherburn   George Sherburn (ed.) *The Correspondence of Alexander Pope* Oxford: Clarendon Press, 5 vols, 1956.

AN
ESSAY
ON
CRITICISM.

3 — 20

2 June 1712

AN

ESSAY

ON

CRITICISM.

—— *Si quid noviſti rectius iſtis,*
Candidus imperti; ſi non, his utere mecum.
HORAT.

LONDON:

Printed for *W. Lewis* in *Ruſſel-Street, Covent-Garden*; And Sold by
W. Taylor at the *Ship* in *Pater-Noſter-Row, T. Osborn* in *Grays-Inn*
near the Walks, and *J. Graves* in St. *James's-Street.* MDCCXI.

AN

ESSAY

ON

CRITICISM.

IS hard to say, if greater Want of Skill
Appear in *Writing* or in *Judging* ill;
But, of the two, less dang'rous is th' Offence,
To tire our *Patience*, than mis-lead our *Sense*:
Some few in *that*, but Numbers err in *this*,
Ten Censure wrong for one who Writes amiss;
A *Fool* might once *himself* alone expose,
Now *One* in *Verse* makes many more in *Prose*.

'Tis

'Tis with our *Judgments* as our *Watches*, none
Go juſt *alike*, yet each believes his own.
In *Poets* as true *Genius* is but rare,
True *Taſte* as ſeldom is the *Critick*'s Share;
Both muſt alike from Heav'n derive their Light,
Theſe *born* to Judge, as well as thoſe to Write.
† Let ſuch teach others who themſelves excell,
And *cenſure freely* who have *written well*.
Authors are partial to their *Wit*, 'tis true,
But are not *Criticks* to their *Judgment* too?

　　Yet if we look more cloſely, we ſhall find
* Moſt have the *Seeds* of Judgment in their Mind;
Nature affords at leaſt a *glimm'ring Light*;
The *Lines*, tho' touch'd but faintly, are drawn right.
But as the ſlighteſt Sketch, if juſtly trac'd,
Is by ill *Colouring* but the more diſgrac'd,
So by *falſe Learning* is *good Senſe* defac'd;
Some are bewilder'd in the Maze of Schools,
And ſome made *Coxcombs* Nature meant but *Fools*.

---

† —— *De Pictore, Sculptore, Fictore, niſi Artifex judicare non poteſt.* Pliny.
* *Omnes tacito quodam ſenſu, ſine ulla arte, aut ratione, quæ ſint in artibus ac ra-*
tionibus recta ac prava dijudicant. Cic. de Orat. lib. 3.

In fearch of *Wit* thefe lofe their *common Senfe,*

And then turn Criticks in their own Defence.

Thofe hate as *Rivals* all that write; and others

But envy *Wits,* as *Eunuchs* envy *Lovers.*

All *Fools* have ftill an Itching to deride,

And fain *wou'd* be upon the *Laughing Side:*

If *Mævius* Scribble in *Apollo*'s fpight,

There are, who *judge* ftill *worfe* than he can *write.*

　　Some have at firft for *Wits,* then *Poets* paft,

Turn'd *Criticks* next, and prov'd plain *Fools* at laft;

Some neither can for *Wits* nor *Criticks* pafs,

As heavy Mules are neither *Horfe* nor *Afs.*

Thofe half-learn'd Witlings, num'rous in our Ifle,

As half-form'd Infects on the Banks of *Nile;*

Unfinifh'd Things, one knows not what to call,

Their Generation's fo *equivocal*:

To tell 'em, wou'd a *hundred Tongues* require,

Or *one vain Wit's,* that wou'd a hundred tire.

　　But *you* who feek to *give* and *merit* Fame,

And juftly bear a Critick's noble Name,

Be

Be sure *your self* and your own *Reach* to know,
How far your *Genius, Taste,* and *Learning* go;
Launch not beyond your Depth, but be discreet,
And mark *that Point* where Sense and Dulness *meet*.
Nature to all things fix'd the Limits fit,
And wisely curb'd proud Man's pretending Wit:
As on the *Land* while *here* the *Ocean* gains,
In *other Parts* it leaves wide sandy Plains;
Thus in the *Soul* while *Memory* prevails,
The solid Pow'r of *Understanding* fails;
Where Beams of warm *Imagination* play,
The *Memory's* soft Figures melt away.
One *Science* only will one *Genius* fit;
So *vast* is Art, so *narrow* Human Wit:
Not only bounded to *peculiar Arts,*
But ev'n in *those,* confin'd to *single Parts.*
Like Kings we lose the Conquests gain'd before,
By vain Ambition still t'extend them more:
Each might his *sev'ral Province* well command,
Wou'd all but *stoop* to what they *understand.*

First

Firſt follow NATURE, and your Judgment frame

By her juſt Standard, which is ſtill the ſame:

Unerring Nature, ſtill divinely bright,

One *clear, unchang'd,* and *Univerſal* Light,

Life, Force, and Beauty, muſt to all impart,

At once the *Source,* and *End,* and *Teſt* of *Art.*

That *Art* is beſt which moſt reſembles *Her;*

Which ſtill *preſides,* yet never does *Appear;*

In ſome fair Body thus the ſprightly Soul

With Spirits feeds, with Vigour fills the whole,

Each Motion guides, and ev'ry Nerve ſuſtains;

It ſelf unſeen, but in th' *Effects,* remains.

There are whom Heav'n has bleſt with ſtore of WIT,

Yet want as much again to manage it;

For *Wit* and *Judgment* ever are at ſtrife,

Tho' meant each other's Aid, like *Man* and *Wife.*

'Tis more to *guide* than *ſpur* the Muſe's Steed;

Reſtrain his Fury, than provoke his Speed;

The winged Courſer, like a gen'rous Horſe,

Shows moſt true Mettle when you *check* his Courſe.

　　　　　　　　　　　　　　　　Thoſe

Those R U L E S of old *discover'd*, not *devis'd*,
Are *Nature* still, but *Nature Methodiz'd*;
Nature, like *Monarchy*, is but restrain'd
By the same Laws which first *herself* ordain'd.

First learned *Greece* just Precepts did indite,
When to repress, and when indulge our Flight:
High on *Parnassus'* Top her Sons she show'd,
And pointed out those arduous Paths they trod,
Held from afar, aloft, th' Immortal Prize,
And urg'd the rest by equal Steps to rise;
From great *Examples useful Rules* were giv'n;
She drew from *them* what they deriv'd from *Heav'n*,
The gen'rous Critick *fann'd* the *Poet's Fire*,
And taught the World, *with Reason to Admire*.
Then Criticism the Muses Handmaid prov'd,
To dress her Charms, and make her more belov'd;
But following Wits from that Intention stray'd;
Who cou'd not win the Mistress, woo'd the Maid,
Set up themselves, and drove a *sep'rate* Trade:

Against

Againſt the Poets *their own Arms* they turn'd,

Sure to hate moſt the Men from whom they *learn'd.*

So modern *Pothecaries,* taught the Art

By *Doctor's Bills* to play the *Doctor's Part,*

Bold in the Practice of *miſtaken Rules,*

Preſcribe, apply, and call their *Maſters Fools.*

Some on the Leaves of ancient Authors prey,

Nor Time nor Moths e'er ſpoil'd ſo much as they:

Some dryly plain, without Invention's Aid,

Write dull *Receits* how Poems may be made:

Theſe loſt the Senſe, their Learning to diſplay,

And thoſe explain'd the Meaning quite away.

    You then whoſe Judgment the right Courſe wou'd ſteer,

Know well each A N C I E N T's proper *Character,*

His *Fable, Subject, Scope* in ev'ry Page,

Religion, Country, Genius of his *Age* :

Without all theſe at once before your Eyes,

You may *Confound,* but never *Criticize.*

Be *Homer's* Works your *Study,* and *Delight,*

Read them by Day, and meditate by Night,

B

Thence

Thence form your Judgment, thence your Notions bring,
And trace the Mufes *upward* to their *Spring* ;
Still with *It felf compar'd*, his *Text* perufe ;
And let your *Comment* be the *Mantuan Mufe.*

   When firft great *Maro* in his boundlefs Mind
A Work, t'outlaft Immortal *Rome* defign'd,
Perhaps he feem'd *above* the Critick's Law,
And but from *Nature's Fountains* fcorn'd to draw :
But when t'examine ev'ry Part he came,
Nature and *Homer* were, he found, the *fame* :
Convinc'd, amaz'd, he checkt the bold Defign,
And did his Work to Rules as ftrict confine,
As if the *Stagyrite* o'erlook'd each Line.
Learn hence for Ancient *Rules* a juft Efteem ;
To copy *Nature* is to copy *Them.*

   Some Beauties yet, no Precepts can declare,
For there's a *Happinefs* as well as *Care.*
Mufick refembles *Poetry*, in each
Are *namelefs Graces* which no Methods teach,
And which a *Mafter-Hand* alone can reach.

† If, where the *Rules* not far enough extend,

(Since Rules were made but to promote their End)

Some Lucky L I C E N C E answers to the full

Th' Intent propos'd, *that Licence* is a *Rule*.

Thus *Pegasus*, a nearer way to take,

May boldly deviate from the common Track.

Great Wits sometimes may *gloriously offend*,

And *rise* to *Faults* true Criticks *dare not mend* ;

From *vulgar Bounds* with *brave Disorder* part,

And *snatch* a *Grace* beyond the Reach of Art,

Which, without passing thro' the *Judgment*, gains

The *Heart*, and all its End *at once* attains.

In *Prospects*, thus, some *Objects* please our Eyes,

Which *out of* Nature's *common Order* rise,

The shapeless *Rock*, or hanging *Precipice*.

But Care in Poetry must still be had,

It asks *Discretion* ev'n in *running Mad* ;

B 2   And

---

† *Neque tam sancta sunt ista Præcepta, sed hoc quicquid est, Utilitas excogitavit ; Non negabo autem sic utile esse plerunque ; verum si eadem illa nobis aliud suadebit utilitas, hanc, relictis magistrorum autoritatibus, sequemur.* Quintil. l. 2. cap. 13.

And tho' the *Ancients* thus their *Rules* invade,

(As *Kings* diſpenſe with *Laws* Themſelves have made)

Moderns, beware ! Or if you muſt offend

Againſt the *Precept*, ne'er tranſgreſs its *End*,

Let it be *ſeldom*, and *compell'd by Need*,

And have, at leaſt, *Their Precedent* to plead.

The Critick elſe proceeds without Remorſe,

Seizes your Fame, and puts his Laws in force.

I know there are, to whoſe preſumptuous Thoughts

Thoſe *Freer Beauties*, ev'n in *Them*, ſeem Faults :

Some Figures *monſtrous* and *miſ-ſhap'd* appear,

Conſider'd *ſingly*, or beheld too *near*,

Which, but *proportion'd* to their *Light*, or *Place*,

Due Diſtance *reconciles* to Form and Grace.

A prudent Chief not always muſt diſplay

His Powr's in *equal Ranks*, and *fair Array*,

But with th' *Occaſion* and the *Place* comply,

Oft *hide* his Force, nay ſeem ſometimes to *Fly*.

Thoſe are but *Stratagems* which *Errors* ſeem,

Nor is it *Homer Nods*, but *We* that *Dream*.

Still

Still green with Bays each *ancient* Altar ſtands,

Above the reach of *Sacrilegious* Hands,

Secure from *Flames*, from *Envy's* fiercer Rage,

Deſtructive *War*, and all-devouring *Age*.

See, from *each Clime* the Learn'd their Incenſe bring ;

Hear, in *all Tongues* Triumphant *Pæans* ring !

In Praiſe ſo juſt, let ev'ry Voice be join'd,

And fill the *Gen'ral Chorus* of *Mankind* !

Hail *Bards Triumphant* ! born in *happier Days* ;

Immortal Heirs of *Univerſal* Praiſe !

Whoſe Honours with Increaſe of Ages *grow*,

As Streams roll down, *enlarging* as they flow !

Nations *unborn* your mighty Names ſhall ſound,

And Worlds applaud that muſt not yet be *found* !

Oh may ſome Spark of *your* Cœleſtial Fire

The laſt, the meaneſt of your Sons inſpire,

(That with weak Wings, from far, purſues your Flights ;

Glows while he *reads*, but *trembles* as he *writes*)

To teach vain Wits that Science *little known*,

T' admire Superior Senſe, and *doubt* their own !

O F

OF all the Causes which conspire to blind
Man's erring Judgment, and misguide the Mind,
What the weak Head with strongest Byass rules,
Is *Pride*, the *never-failing Vice of Fools*.
Whatever Nature has in *Worth* deny'd,
She gives in large Recruits of *needful Pride*;
For as in *Bodies*, thus in *Souls*, we find
What wants in *Blood* and *Spirits*, swell'd with *Wind*;
Pride, where Wit fails, steps in to our Defence,
And fills up all the *mighty Void* of *Sense*!
If once right Reason drives *that Cloud* away,
Truth breaks upon us with *resistless Day*;
Trust not your self; but your Defects to know,
Make use of ev'ry *Friend* —— and ev'ry *Foe*.

A *little Learning* is a dang'rous Thing;
Drink deep, or taste not the *Pierian* Spring:
There *shallow Draughts* intoxicate the Brain,
And drinking *largely* sobers us again.

Fir'd

Fir'd with the Charms fair *Science* does impart,

In *fearless Youth* we tempt the Heights of Art;

While from the bounded *Level* of our Mind,

Short Views we take, nor see the *Lengths behind*,

But *more advanc'd,* survey with strange Surprize

New, distant Scenes of *endless* Science rise !

So pleas'd at first, the towring *Alps* we try,

Mount o'er the Vales, and seem to tread the Sky;

Th' Eternal Snows appear already past;

And the first *Clouds* and *Mountains* seem the last:

But *those attain'd,* we tremble to survey

The growing Labours of the lengthen'd Way,

Th' *increasing* Prospect *tires* our wandring Eyes,

Hills peep o'er Hills, and *Alps* on *Alps* arise !

† A perfect Judge will *read* each Work of Wit

With the same Spirit that its Author *writ,*

Survey the *Whole,* nor seek slight Faults to find;

Where *Nature moves,* and *Rapture warms* the Mind;

Nor

---

† *Diligenter legendum est, ac pœne ad scribendi sollicitudinem: Nec per partes modo scrutanda sunt omnia, sed perlectus liber utique ex Integro resumendus.* Quin-tilian.

Nor lose, for that malignant dull Delight,

The *gen'rous Pleasure* to be charm'd with Wit.

But in such Lays as neither *ebb,* nor *flow,*

Correctly cold, and *regularly low,*

That shunning Faults, one quiet *Tenour* keep;

We cannot *blame* indeed------but we may *sleep.*

In Wit, as Nature, what affects our Hearts

Is not th' Exactness of peculiar Parts;

'Tis not a *Lip,* or *Eye,* we Beauty call,

But the joint Force and full *Result* of all.

Thus when we view some well-proportion'd Dome,

(The *World*'s just Wonder, and ev'n *thine* O *Rome!*)

No single Parts unequally surprize;

All comes *united* to th' admiring Eyes;

No monstrous Height, or Breadth, or Length appear;

The *Whole* at once is *Bold,* and *Regular.*

Whoever thinks a faultless Piece to see,

Thinks what ne'er was, nor is, nor e'er shall be.

In ev'ry Work regard the *Writer's End,*

Since none can compass more than they *Intend;*

And

And if the *Means* be juſt, the *Conduct* true,
Applauſe, in ſpite of trivial Faults, is due.
As Men of Breeding, oft the Men of Wit,
T' avoid *great Errors*, muſt the *leſs* commit,
Neglect the Rules each *Verbal Critick* lays,
For *not* to know ſome Trifles, is a Praiſe.
Moſt Criticks fond of ſome ſubſervient Art,
Still make the *Whole* depend upon a *Part*,
They talk of *Principles*, but Parts they prize,
And All to one lov'd Folly Sacrifice.

Once on a time, *La Mancha*'s Knight, they ſay,
A certain *Bard* encountring on the Way,
Diſcours'd in Terms as juſt, with Looks as Sage,
As e'er cou'd D———s, of the Laws o' th' Stage;
Concluding all were deſp'rate Sots and Fools,
That durſt depart from *Ariſtotle*'s Rules.
Our Author, happy in a Judge ſo nice,
Produc'd his Play, and beg'd the Knight's Advice,
Made him obſerve the *Subject* and the *Plot*,
The *Manners, Paſſions, Unities*, what not?

C   All

All which, exact to *Rule* were brought about,

Were but a *Combate in the Lifts* left out.

What! Leave the Combate out? Exclaims the Knight;

Yes, or we muft renounce the *Stagyrite.*

Not fo by Heav'n (he anfwers in a Rage)

Knights, Squires, and Steeds, muft enter on the Stage.

The Stage can ne'er fo vaft a Throng contain.

Then build a New, or act it in a Plain.

  Thus Criticks, of lefs *Judgment* than *Caprice,*

Curious, not *Knowing,* not *exact,* but *nice,*

Form *fhort Ideas*; and offend in *Arts*

(As moft in *Manners*) by a *Love to Parts.*

Some to *Conceit* alone their Tafte confine,

And glitt'ring Thoughts ftruck out at ev'ry Line;

Pleas'd with a Work where nothing's juft or fit;

One *glaring Chaos* and *wild Heap* of *Wit*:

Poets like Painters, thus, unskill'd to trace

The *naked Nature* and the *living Grace,*

With *Gold* and *Jewels* cover ev'ry Part,

And hide with *Ornaments* their *Want of Art.*

            † *True*

† *True Wit* is *Nature* to Advantage dreſt,

What oft was *Thought,* but ne'er before *Expreſt,*

Something, whoſe Truth convinc'd at Sight we find,

That gives us back the Image of our Mind :

As Shades more ſweetly recommend the Light,

So modeſt Plainneſs ſets off ſprightly Wit :

For *Works* may have more *Wit* than does 'em good,

As *Bodies* periſh through Exceſs of *Blood.*

Others for *Language* all their Care expreſs,

And value *Books,* as Women *Men,* for *Dreſs :*

Their Praiſe is ſtill——*The Stile is excellent :*

The *Senſe,* they humbly take upon Content.

Words are like *Leaves* ; and where they moſt abound,

Much *Fruit* of *Senſe* beneath is rarely found.

Falſe Eloquence, like the *Priſmatic Glaſs,*

Its gawdy Colours ſpreads on *ev'ry place* ;

The Face of Nature we no more Survey,

All glares *alike,* without *Diſtinction* gay :

C 2   But

---

† *Naturam intueamur, hanc ſequamur* ; *Id facillimè accipiunt animi quod agno-ſcunt.* Quintil. lib. 8. c. 3.

But true *Expreſſion,* like th' unchanging *Sun,*

Clears, and *improves* whate'er it ſhines upon,

It *gilds* all Objects, but it *alters* none.

Expreſſion is the *Dreſs* of *Thought,* and ſtill

Appears more *decent* as more *ſuitable;*

A vile Conceit in pompous Style expreſt,

Is like a Clown in regal Purple dreſt;

For diff'rent *Styles* with diff'rent *Subjects* ſort,

As ſeveral Garbs with Country, Town, and Court.

* Some by *Old Words* to Fame have made Pretence;

Ancients in *Phraſe,* meer Moderns in their *Senſe!*

Such *labour'd Nothings,* in ſo *ſtrange* a Style,

Amaze th' unlearn'd, and make the Learned *Smile.*

Unlucky, as *Fungoſo* in the † Play,

Theſe Sparks with aukward Vanity diſplay

What the Fine Gentlemen wore *Yeſterday!*

And but ſo mimick ancient Wits at beſt,

As Apes our Grandſires in their *Doublets dreſt.*

---

* *Abolita & abrogata retinere, inſolentiæ cujuſdam eſt, & frivolæ in parvis jactantiæ.* Quint. lib. 1. c. 6.

Opus eſt ut Verba a vetuſtate repetita neque crebra ſint, neque manifeſta, quia nil eſt odioſius affectatione, nec utique ab ultimis repetita temporibus. Oratio, cujus ſumma virtus eſt perſpicuitas, quam ſit vitioſa ſi egeat interprete? Ergo ut novorum optima erunt maxime vetera, ita veterum maxime nova. Idem.

† Ben. Johnſon's *Every Man in his Humour.*

In *Words*, as *Fashions*, the same Rule will hold ;

Alike Fantastick, if *too New*, or *Old*;

Be not the *first* by whom the *New* are try'd,

Nor yet the *last* to lay the *Old* aside.

   * But most by *Numbers* judge a Poet's Song,

And *smooth* or *rough*, with such, is *right* or *wrong* ;

In the bright *Muse* tho' thousand *Charms* conspire,

Her *Voice* is all these tuneful Fools admire,

Who haunt *Parnassus* but to please their Ear,

Not mend their Minds; as some to *Church* repair,

Not for the *Doctrine*, but the *Musick* there.

These *Equal Syllables* alone require,

† Tho' oft the Ear the *open Vowels* tire,

While *Expletives* their feeble Aid *do* join,

And ten low Words oft creep in one dull Line,

While they ring round the same *unvary'd Chimes*,

With sure *Returns* of still *expected Rhymes*.

                             Where-

---

* *Quis populi sermo est? quis enim? nisi carmine molli Nunc demum numero fluere, ut per læve severos Effigit junctura ungues: scit tendere versum, Non secus ac si oculo rubricam dirigat uno.* Persius, Sat. 1.

† *Fugiemus crebras vocalium concursiones, quæ vastam atque hiantem orationem reddunt.* Cic. ad Herenn. lib. 4. *Vide etiam* Quintil. lib. 9. *c.* 4.

Where-e'er you find *the cooling Weſtern Breeze,*

In the next Line, it *whiſpers thro' the Trees ;*

If *Chryſtal Streams with pleaſing Murmurs creep,*

The Reader's threaten'd (not in vain) with *Sleep.*

Then, at the *laſt,* and *only* Couplet fraught

With ſome *unmeaning* Thing they call a *Thought,*

A *needleſs Alexandrine* ends the Song,

That like a wounded Snake, drags its ſlow Length along.

Leave ſuch to tune their own dull Rhimes, and know

What's *roundly ſmooth,* or *languiſhingly ſlow ;*

And praiſe the *Eaſie Vigor* of a Line,

Where *Denham's* Strength, and *Waller's* Sweetneſs join.

'Tis not enough no Harſhneſs gives Offence,

The *Sound* muſt ſeem an *Eccho* to the *Senſe.*

Soft is the Strain when *Zephyr* gently blows,

And the *ſmooth Stream* in *ſmoother Numbers* flows ;

But when loud Surges laſh the ſounding Shore,

The *hoarſe, rough Verſe* ſhou'd like the *Torrent* roar.

When *Ajax* ſtrives, ſome Rock's vaſt Weight to throw,

The Line too *labours,* and the Words move *ſlow ;*

Not

Not fo, when fwift *Camilla* fcours the Plain,

Flies o'er th'unbending Corn, and skims along the Main.

Hear how * *Timotheus'* various Lays furprize,

And bid Alternate Paffions fall and rife!

While, at each Change, the Son of *Lybian Jove*

Now *burns* with Glory, and then *melts* with Love;

Now his *fierce Eyes* with *fparkling Fury* glow;

Now *Sighs* fteal out, and *Tears begin to flow*:

Perfians and *Greeks* like *Turns of Nature* found,

And the *World's Victor* ftood fubdu'd by *Sound*!

The Pow'r of Mufick all our Hearts allow;

And what *Timotheus* was, is *Dryden* now.

   Avoid *Extreams*; and fhun the Fault of fuch,

Who ftill are pleas'd *too little*, or *too much*.

At ev'ry Trifle fcorn to take Offence,

That always fhows *Great Pride*, or *Little Senfe*;

Thofe *Heads* as *Stomachs* are not fure the beft

Which naufeate all, and nothing can digeft.

                        Yet

---

*Alexander's *Feaft*, or the Power of *Mufick*; An Ode by Mr. Dryden.

Yet let not each gay *Turn* thy Rapture move,
For Fools *Admire,* but Men of Senſe *Approve;*
As things ſeem *large* which we thro' *Miſts* deſcry,
Dulneſs is ever apt to *Magnify.*

Some the *French* Writers, ſome our *own* deſpiſe;
The *Ancients* only, or the *Moderns* prize:
Thus *Wit,* like *Faith,* by each Man is apply'd
To *one ſmall Sect,* and All are *damn'd beſide.*
Meanly they ſeek the Bleſſing to confine,
And force *that Sun* but on a *Part* to Shine;
Which not alone the *Southern Wit* ſublimes,
But ripens Spirits in cold *Northern Climes;*
Which from the firſt has ſhone on *Ages paſt,*
Enlights the *preſent,* and ſhall warm the *laſt:*
(Tho' *each* may feel *Increaſes* and *Decays,*
And ſee now *clearer* and now *darker Days*)
Regard not then if Wit be *Old* or *New,*
But blame the *Falſe,* and value ſtill the *True.*

Some ne'er advance a Judgment of their own,
But *catch* the *ſpreading Notion* of the Town;

They

They reafon and conclude by *Precedent,*

And own *ftale Nonfenfe* which they ne'er invent.

Some judge of Author's *Names,* not *Works,* and then

Nor praife nor damn the *Writings,* but the *Men.*

Of all this *Servile Herd* the worft is He

That in *proud Dulnefs* joins with *Quality,*

A conftant Critick at the Great-man's Board,

To *fetch and carry* Nonfenfe for my Lord.

What *woful ftuff* this Madrigal wou'd be,

In fome ftarv'd Hackny Sonneteer, or me?

But let a *Lord* once own the *happy Lines,*

How the *Wit brightens*! How the *Style refines*!

Before *his* facred Name flies ev'ry Fault,

And each *exalted* Stanza *teems* with *Thought*!

 The *Vulgar* thus through *Imitation* err;

As oft the *Learn'd* by being *Singular*;

So much they fcorn the Crowd, that if the Throng

By *Chance* go right, they *purpofely* go wrong:

So Schifmatics the *dull Believers* quit,

And are but damn'd for having *too much Wit.*

D

Some

Some praiſe at Morning what they blame at Night;
But always think the *laſt* Opinion *right*.
A Muſe by theſe is like a Miſtreſs us'd,
This hour ſhe's *idoliz'd*, the next *abus'd*,
While their weak Heads, like Towns unfortify'd,
'Twixt Senſe and Nonſenſe daily change their Side.
Ask them the Cauſe; *They're wiſer ſtill*, they ſay;
And ſtill to Morrow's wiſer than to Day.
We think our *Fathers* Fools, ſo *wiſe* we grow;
Our *wiſer Sons*, no doubt, will think *us* ſo.
Once *School-Divines* our zealous Iſle o'erſpread;
Who knew moſt *Sentences* was *deepeſt read*;
Faith, Goſpel, All, ſeem'd made to be *diſputed*,
And none had *Senſe enough to be Confuted.*
Scotiſts and *Thomiſts*, now, in Peace remain,
Amidſt their *kindred Cobwebs* in *Duck-Lane.*
If *Faith* it ſelf has *diff'rent Dreſſes* worn,
What wonder *Modes* in *Wit* ſhou'd take their Turn?
Oft, leaving what is Natural and fit,
The *current Folly* proves our *ready Wit,*

And

And Authors think their Reputation safe,

Which lives as long as *Fools* are pleas'd to *Laugh.*

    Some valuing those of their own *Side,* or *Mind,*

Still make themselves the measure of Mankind;

Fondly we think we honour Merit then,

When we but praise *Our selves* in *Other Men.*

Parties in *Wit* attend on those of *State,*

And publick Faction doubles private Hate.

Pride, Malice, Folly, against *Dryden* rose,

In various Shapes of *Parsons, Criticks, Beaus;*

But *Sense* surviv'd, when *merry Jests* were past;

For rising Merit will *buoy up* at last.

Might he return, and bless once more our Eyes,

New *Bl——s* and new *M——s* must arise;

Nay shou'd great *Homer* lift his awful Head,

Zoilus again would start up from the Dead.

Envy will *Merit* as its *Shade* pursue,

But like a Shadow, proves the *Substance* too ,

For envy'd Wit, like *Sol* Eclips'd, makes known

Th' *opposing Body's* Grossness, not its *own.*

                 When

When firſt that Sun too powerful Beams diſplays,
It draws up Vapours which obſcure its Rays;
But ev'n thoſe Clouds at laſt adorn its Way,
Reflect new Glories, and augment the Day.

Be thou the *firſt* true Merit to befriend;
His Praiſe is loſt, who ſtays till *All* commend;
Short is the Date, alas, of *Modern Rhymes*;
And 'tis but juſt to let 'em live *betimes*.
No longer now that Golden Age appears,
When *Patriarch-Wits* ſurviv'd a *thouſand Years*;
Now Length of *Fame* (our *ſecond* Life) is loſt,
And bare Threeſcore is all ev'n That can boaſt:
Our Sons their Father's *failing Language* ſee,
And ſuch as *Chaucer* is, ſhall *Dryden* be.
So when the faithful *Pencil* has deſign'd
Some *fair Idea* of the Maſter's Mind,
Where a *new World* leaps out at his command,
And ready Nature waits upon his Hand;
When the ripe Colours *ſoften* and *unite*,
And ſweetly *melt* into juſt Shade and Light,

When

When mellowing Time does full Perfection give,

And each Bold Figure juſt begins to *Live*;

The *treach'rous Colours* in few Years decay,

And all the bright Creation fades away!

    Unhappy *Wit*, like moſt miſtaken Things,

Repays not half that *Envy* which it brings:

In *Youth* alone its empty Praiſe we boaſt,

But ſoon the Short-liv'd Vanity is loſt!

Like ſome fair *Flow'r* that in the *Spring* does riſe,

And gaily Blooms, but ev'n in blooming *Dies*.

What is this *Wit* that does our Cares employ?

The *Owner's Wife*, that *other Men* enjoy,

The more his *Trouble* as the more *admir'd*;

Where *wanted*, ſcorn'd, and envy'd where *acquir'd*;

Maintain'd with *Pains*, but forfeited with *Eaſe*;

Sure *ſome* to *vex*, but never *all* to *pleaſe*;

'Tis what the *Vicious fear*, the *Virtuous ſhun*;

By *Fools* 'tis *hated*, and by *Knaves undone*!

    Too much does *Wit* from *Ign'rance* undergo,

Ah let not *Learning* too commence its Foe!

                       Of

Of old, thoſe found *Rewards* who cou'd *excel,*
And ſuch were *Prais'd* who but *endeavour'd well* :
Tho' *Triumphs* were to *Gen'rals* only due,
Crowns were reſerv'd to grace the *Soldiers* too.
Now thoſe that reach *Parnaſſus'* lofty Crown,
Employ their Pains to ſpurn ſome others down ;
And while Self-Love each jealous Writer rules,
Contending Wits become the *Sport of Fools* :
But ſtill the *Worſt* with moſt Regret commend,
And each *Ill Author* is as bad a *Friend.*
To what baſe Ends, and by what abject Ways,
Are Mortals urg'd by *Sacred Luſt of Praiſe* ?
Ah ne'er ſo *dire* a *Thirſt of Glory* boaſt,
Nor in the *Critick* let the *Man* be loſt !
Good-Nature and *Good-Senſe* muſt ever join ;
To Err is *Humane* ; to Forgive, *Divine.*
But if in Noble Minds ſome Dregs remain,
Not yet purg'd off, of Spleen and ſow'r Diſdain,
Diſcharge that Rage on more Provoking Crimes,
Nor fear a Dearth in theſe Flagitious Times.

No

No Pardon vile *Obscenity* should find,

Tho' *Wit* and *Art* conspire to move your Mind;

But *Dulness* with *Obscenity* must prove

As Shameful sure as *Impotence* in *Love.*

In the fat Age of Pleasure, Wealth, and Ease,

Sprung the rank Weed, and thriv'd with large Increase;

When *Love* was all an easie Monarch's Care;

Seldom at *Council,* never in a *War*:

Jilts rul'd the State, and Statesmen *Farces* writ;

Nay *Wits* had *Pensions,* and *young Lords* had *Wit*:

The Fair sate panting at a *Courtier's Play,*

And not a Mask went *un-improv'd* away:

The modest Fan was lifted up no more,

And Virgins *smil'd* at what they *blush'd* before——

The following Licence of a Foreign Reign

Did all the Dregs of bold *Socinus* drain;

Then *first* the *Belgian Morals* were extoll'd;

We their *Religion* had, and they our *Gold*:

Then Unbelieving Priests reform'd the Nation,

And taught more *Pleasant* Methods of Salvation;

Where

Where Heav'ns Free Subjects might their *Rights* difpute,
Left God himfelf fhou'd feem too *Abfolute.*
Pulpits their *Sacred Satire* learn'd to fpare,
And Vice *admir'd* to find a *Flatt'rer there !*
Encourag'd thus, Witt's *Titans* brav'd the Skies,
And the Prefs groan'd with Licenc'd *Blafphemies* ————
Thefe Monfters, Criticks ! with your Darts engage,
Here point your Thunder, and exhauft your Rage !
Yet fhun their Fault, who, *Scandaloufly nice,*
Will needs *miftake* an Author *into Vice ;*
All feems Infected that th'Infected fpy,
As all looks yellow to the Jaundic'd Eye.

Learn then what MORALS Criticks ought to fhow,
For 'tis but *half* a *Judge's Task,* to *Know.*
'Tis not enough, Wit, Art, and Learning join ;
In all you fpeak, let Truth and Candor fhine :
That not alone what to your *Judgment's* due,
All may allow ; but feek your *Friendfhip* too.

Be

Be *silent* always when you *doubt* your Senſe;

Speak when you're *ſure*, yet ſpeak with *Diffidence*;

Some poſitive perſiſting Fops we know,

That, if *once wrong*, will needs be *always ſo*;

But you, with Pleaſure own your Errors paſt,

And make each Day a *Critick* on the laſt.

'Tis not enough your Counſel ſtill be *true*,

Blunt Truths more Miſchief than *nice Falſhoods* do;

Men muſt be *taught* as if you taught them *not*;

And Things *ne'er known* propos'd as Things *forgot*:

Without *Good Breeding*, *Truth* is not approv'd,

That only makes *Superior* Senſe *belov'd*.

Be Niggards of Advice on no Pretence;

For the *worſt Avarice* is that of *Senſe*:

With mean Complacence ne'er betray your Truſt,

Nor be ſo *Civil* as to prove *Unjuſt*;

Fear not the Anger of the Wiſe to raiſe;

Thoſe beſt can *bear Reproof*, who *merit Praiſe*.

E   'Twere

'Twere well, might Criticks ſtill this Freedom take;

But *Appius* reddens at each Word you ſpeak,

And *ſtares, Tremendous!* with a *threatning Eye,*

Like ſome *fierce Tyrant* in *Old Tapeſtry!*

Fear moſt to tax an *Honourable* Fool,

Whoſe Right it is, *uncenſur'd* to be dull;

Such without *Wit* are Poets when they pleaſe,

As without *Learning* they can take *Degrees.*

Leave dang'rous *Truths* to unſucceſsful *Satyrs,*

And *Flattery* to fulſome *Dedicators,*

Whom, when they *Praiſe,* the World believes no more,

Than when they promiſe to give *Scribling* o'er.

'Tis beſt ſometimes your Cenſure to reſtrain,

And *charitably* let dull Fools be *vain:*

Your Silence there is better than your *Spite,*

For who can *rail* ſo long as they can *write?*

Still humming on, their old dull Courſe they keep,

And *laſh'd* ſo long, like *Tops,* are laſh'd *aſleep.*

Falſe

False Steps but help them to renew the Race,

As after *Stumbling*, Jades will *mend* their Pace.

What Crouds of thefe, impenitently bold,

In *Sounds* and jingling *Syllables* grown old,

Still *run on* Poets in a raging Vein,

Ev'n to the Dregs and *Squeezings* of the *Brain*;

Strain out the laft, dull droppings of their Senfe,

And Rhyme with all the *Rage* of *Impotence*!

Such fhamelefs *Bards* we have; and yet 'tis true,

There are as mad, abandon'd *Criticks* too.

* The Bookful Blockhead, ignorantly read,

With *Loads* of *Learned Lumber* in his Head,

With his own Tongue ftill edifies his Ears,

And always *Lift'ning to Himfelf* appears.

All Books he reads, and all he reads affails,

From *Dryden*'s *Fables* down to *D——y*'s *Tales*.

E 2   With

---

* *Nihil pejus eft iis, qui paullum aliquid ultra primas litteras progreffi, falfam fibi fcientiæ perfuafionem induerunt : Nam & cedere præcipiendi peritis indignantur, & velut jure quodam poteftatis, quo ferè hoc hominum genus intumefcit, imperiofi, atque interim fævientes, Stultitiam fuam perdocent.* Quintil. lib. 1. ch. 1.

With *him*, moſt Authors ſteal their Works, or buy;

Garth did not write his own *Diſpenſary*.

Name a new *Play*, and *he's* the Poet's *Friend*,

Nay ſhow'd his Faults——but when wou'd Poets mend?

No Place ſo Sacred from ſuch Fops is barr'd,

Nor is *Paul's Church* more ſafe than *Paul's Church-yard*:

Nay, run to *Altars*; *there* they'll talk you dead;

For *Fools* ruſh in where *Angels* fear to tread.

Diſtruſtful *Senſe* with modeſt Caution ſpeaks;

It ſtill *looks home*, and *ſhort Excurſions* makes;

But *ratling Nonſenſe* in full *Vollies* breaks;

And never ſhock'd, and never turn'd aſide,

Burſts out, reſiſtleſs, with a thundring Tyde!

    But where's the Man, who Counſel *can* beſtow,

Still *pleas'd* to *teach*, and yet not *proud* to *know*?

Unbiaſs'd, or by *Favour* or by *Spite*;

Not *dully prepoſſeſt*, or *blindly right*;

Tho'

Tho' Learn'd, well-bred; and tho' well-bred, sincere;

Modestly bold, and Humanly severe?

Who to a *Friend* his Faults can freely show,

And gladly praise the Merit of a *Foe?*

Blest with a *Taste* exact, yet unconfin'd;

A *Knowledge* both of *Books* and *Humankind*;

Gen'rous *Converse*; a *Soul* exempt from *Pride*;

And *Love to Praise*, with *Reason* on his Side?

Such once were *Criticks*, such the Happy *Few*,

Athens and *Rome* in better Ages knew.

The mighty *Stagyrite* first left the Shore,

Spread all his Sails, and durst the Deeps explore;

He steer'd securely, and discover'd far,

Led by the Light of the *Mæonian Star.*

Not only *Nature* did his Laws obey,

But *Fancy's* boundless Empire own'd his Sway.

Poets, a *Race* long unconfin'd and free,

Still fond and proud of *Savage Liberty,*

Re-

Receiv'd his Rules, and stood convinc'd 'twas fit
Who conquer'd *Nature*, shou'd preside o'er *Wit*.

 Horace still charms with graceful Negligence,
And without Method *talks* us into Sense,
Does like a *Friend* familiarly convey
The *truest Notions* in the *easiest way*.
He, who Supream in Judgment, as in Wit,
Might boldly censure, as he boldly writ,
Yet *judg'd* with *Coolness* tho' he sung with *Fire*;
His *Precepts* teach but what his *Works* inspire.
Our Criticks take a contrary Extream,
They *judge* with *Fury*, but they *write* with *Fle'me*:
Nor suffers *Horace* more in wrong *Translations*
By *Wits*, than *Criticks* in as wrong *Quotations*.

 Fancy and Art in gay *Petronius* please,
The *Scholar's Learning*, and the *Courtier's Ease*.

 In grave *Quintilian's* copious Work we find
The justest *Rules*, and clearest *Method* join'd;

            Thus

Thus *useful Arms* in Magazines we place,

All rang'd in *Order,* and difpos'd with *Grace,*

Nor thus alone the Curious Eye to pleafe,

But to be *found,* when Need requires, with Eafe.

    The *Mufes* fure *Longinus* did infpire,

And bleft *their Critick* with a *Poet's Fire.*

An ardent *Judge,* that Zealous in his Truft,

With *Warmth* gives Sentence, yet is always *Juft;*

Whofe *own Example* ftrengthens all his Laws,

And *Is himfelf* that great *Sublime* he draws.

    Thus long fucceeding Criticks juftly reign'd,

Licence reprefs'd, and *ufeful Laws* ordain'd;

Learning and *Rome* alike in Empire grew,

And *Arts* ftill *follow'd* where her *Eagles flew;*

From the fame Foes, at laft, both felt their Doom,

And the fame Age faw *Learning* fall, and *Rome.*

With *Tyranny,* then *Superftition* join'd,

As that the *Body,* this enflav'd the *Mind;*

                                  All

All was *Believ'd,* but nothing *underſtood,*

And to be *dull* was conſtru'd to be *good* ;

A *ſecond* Deluge Learning thus o'er-run,

And the *Monks* finiſh'd what the *Goths* begun.

    At length, *Eraſmus,* that *great, injur'd* Name,

(The *Glory* of the Prieſthood, and the *Shame* !)

Stemm'd the *wild Torrent* of a *barb'rous Age,*

And drove thoſe *Holy Vandals* off the Stage.

    But ſee ! each *Muſe,* in *Leo's* Golden Days,

Starts from her Trance, and trims her wither'd Bays !

Rome's ancient *Genius,* o'er its *Ruins* ſpread,

Shakes off the *Duſt,* and rears his rev'rend Head !

Then *Sculpture* and her *Siſter-Arts* revive;

Stones leap'd to *Form,* and *Rocks* began to *live;*

With *ſweeter Notes* each *riſing Temple* rung ;

A *Raphael* painted, and a † *Vida* ſung !

                          Im-

---

† M. Hieronymus Vida, *an excellent* Latin *Poet, who writ an Art of Poetry in Verſe.*

Immortal *Vida* ! on whoſe honour'd Brow

The Poet's *Bays* and Critick's *Ivy* grow :

Cremona now ſhall ever boaſt thy Name,.

As next in Place to *Mantua*, next in Fame *!*

But ſoon by Impious Arms from *Latium* chas'd,

Their *ancient Bounds* the baniſh'd Muſes paſt ;

Thence Arts o'er all the *Northern World* advance ;

But *Critic Learning* flouriſh'd moſt in *France.*

The *Rules*, a Nation born to ſerve, obeys,

And *Boileau* ſtill in Right of *Horace* ſways.

But *we*, brave *Britains*, *Foreign Laws* deſpis'd,

And kept *unconquer'd*, and *unciviliz'd*,

Fierce for the *Liberties of Wit*, and bold,

We ſtill defy'd the *Romans*, *as of old.*

Yet *ſome* there were, among the *ſounder Few*

Of thoſe who *leſs preſum'd*, and *better knew*,

F   *Such*

Who durſt aſſert the *juſter Ancient Cauſe,*

And here *reſtor'd* Wit's *Fundamental Laws.*

Such was *Roſcomon*——not more *learn'd* than *good,*

With Manners gen'rous as his Noble Blood;

To him the Wit of *Greece* and *Rome* was known,

And ev'ry Author's *Merit,* but his own.

Such late was *Walſh,* —— the Muſes Judge and Friend,

Who juſtly knew to blame or to commend;

To Failings *mild,* but *zealous* for Deſert;

The *cleareſt Head,* and the *ſincereſt Heart.*

This humble Praiſe, lamented *Shade!* receive,

This Praiſe at leaſt a grateful Muſe may give!

The Muſe, whoſe early Voice you taught to Sing,

Preſcrib'd her Heights, and prun'd her tender Wing,

(Her Guide now loſt) no more attempts to *riſe,*

But in low Numbers ſhort Excurſions tries:

Con-

Content, if hence th' Unlearn'd their Wants may view,

The Learn'd reflect on what before they knew:

Careless of *Censure*, nor too fond of *Fame*,

Still pleas'd to *praise*, yet not afraid to *blame*,

Averse alike to *Flatter*, or *Offend*,

Not *free* from Faults, nor yet too vain to *mend*.

F I N I S.

BOOKS *lately Publish'd, and Sold by* W. Lewis, *in* Ruffel-Street, Covent-Garden.

THE diverting Works of the Countefs *D' Anois*, Author of the Lady's Travels into *Spain*.

The Works of Mr. *Thomas Brown*, in Profe and Verfe, Serious, Comical and Moral, in Three Volumes.

The Works of Mr. *Congreve* in Three Volumes.

Shakefpear's Works in Six Volumes, being all his Plays.

Hudibras Compleat, with Cuts.

Milton's Paradife Loft, with Cuts.

The Hiftorical and Critical Dictionary of Monfieur *Bayle*, in Four Volumes.

A New Voyage to *Ethiopia*. By Mr. *Poncet*, M. D.

The Works of Mr. *Robert Gould*, in Profe and Verfe; containing his Satyrs, Love-Verfes, &c. In Two Volumes.

Nuptial Dialogues and Debates, or an ufeful Profpect of the Felicity and Difcomforts of a Marry'd Life, in Two Volumes.

The Works of the Right Honourable Sir *Charles Sidley*, containing his Speeches in Parliament.

Mirth diverts all Care: Being a Collection of Delightful Songs, &c.

Mars ftript of his Armour.

The Wooden World diffected.

Epicteti Enchiridion made *Englifh*, in a Poetical Paraphrafe, by *Ellis Walker*, M. A.

Secret Memoirs of *Robert Dudley*, Earl of *Leicefter*, Prime Minifter and Favourite to Queen *Elizabeth*.

The Works of *Lucian*, Tranflated into *Englifh* by feveral Hands; to which is prefix'd the Life of *Lucian* by Mr. *Dryden*.

Bibliotheca Anatomica, Medica, Chirurgica, &c. Containing a Defcription of the feveral Parts of the Body. To be Pulifh'd Monthly.

A Help to Hiftory, or a fhort Memorial of the moft Material Matters of Fact, and Prefages, Domeftick and Foreign, which may be ufeful either in Converfation at prefent, or Hiftory for the future.

The Modern World Difrob'd, or both Sexes ftript of their pretended Virtue.

Lud. Du Guernier inv.   *C. Du Bosc sculp.*

THE
RAPE of the *LOCK.*

AN

HEROI-COMICAL

POEM.

In FIVE CANTO's.

Written by **Mr. *POPE.***

——*A tonso est hoc nomen adepta capillo.*
Ovid.

LONDON:
Printed for Bernard Lintott, at the
Cross-Keys in *Fleetstreet.* 1714.

T O

Mrs. *ARABELLA FERMOR*.

M<small>ADAM</small>,

I T will be in vain to deny that I have some Value for this Piece, since I Dedicate it to You. Yet You may bear me Witneſs, it was intended only to divert a few young

A 2   Ladies,

EPISTLE.

Ladies, who have good Senfe and good Humour enough, to laugh not only at their Sex's little unguarded Follies, but at their own. But as it was communicated with the Air of a Secret, it foon found its Way into the World. An imperfect Copy having been offer'd to a Bookfeller, You had the Good-Nature for my Sake to confent to the Publication of one more correct : This I was forc'd to before I had executed half my Defign, for the *Machinery* was entirely wanting to compleat it.

The *Machinery*, Madam, is a Term invented by the Criticks, to fignify that Part which the Deities, Angels, or Dæmons, are made to act in a Poem : For the ancient Poets are in one refpect like

many

many modern Ladies ; Let an Action be never so trivial in it self, they always make it appear of the utmost Importance. These Machines I determin'd to raise on a very new and odd Foundation, the *Rosicrucian* Doctrine of Spirits.

I know how disagreeable it is to make use of hard Words before a Lady; but 'tis so much the Concern of a Poet to have his Works understood, and particularly by your Sex, that You must give me leave to explain two or three difficult Terms.

The *Rosicrucians* are a People I must bring You acquainted with. The best Account I know of them is in a French Book call'd *Le Comte de Gabalis,* which
both

EPISTLE.

both in its Title and Size is so like a *Novel*, that many of the Fair Sex have read it for one by Mistake. According to these Gentlemen, the four Elements are inhabited by Spirits, which they call *Sylphs*, *Gnomes*, *Nymphs*, and *Salamanders*. The *Gnomes*, or Dæmons of Earth, delight in Mischief; but the *Sylphs*, whose Habitation is Air, are the best-condition'd Creatures imaginable. For they say, any Mortals may enjoy the most intimate Familiarities with these gentle Spirits, upon a Condition very easie to all true *Adepts*, an inviolate Preservation of Chastity.

As to the following Canto's, all the Passages of them are as Fabulous, as the Vision at the Beginning, or the Transformation at the End; (except the Loss of your

EPISTLE.

your Hair, which I always name with Reverence.) The Human Perſons are as Fictitious as the Airy ones; and the Character of *Belinda*, as it is now manag'd, reſembles You in nothing but in Beauty.

If this Poem had as many Graces as there are in Your Perſon, or in Your Mind, yet I could never hope it ſhould paſs thro' the World half ſo Uncenſured as You have done. But let its Fortune be what it will, mine is happy enough, to have given me this Occaſion of aſſuring You that I am, with the trueſt Eſteem,

Madam,

> *Your Moſt Obedient*

> *Humble Servant.*

A. POPE,

Lud.Du Guernier inv.   C.Du Bosc sculp.

THE
RAPE *of the* LOCK.

CANTO I.

HAT dire Offence from am'rous
Causes springs,
What mighty Quarrels rise from
trivial Things,
I sing —— This Verse to *C---l,* Muse! is due ;
This, ev'n *Belinda* may vouchsafe to view :
Slight is the Subject, but not so the Praise,
If She inspire, and He approve my Lays.

Say what ſtrange Motive, Goddeſs! cou'd compel
A well-bred *Lord* t'aſſault a gentle *Belle* ?
Oh ſay what ſtranger Cauſe, yet unexplor'd,
Cou'd make a gentle *Belle* rejeẜ a *Lord* ?
And dwells ſuch Rage in ſofteſt Boſoms then ?
And lodge ſuch daring Souls in Little Men?

Sol thro' white Curtains did his Beams diſplay,
And op'd thoſe Eyes which brighter ſhine than they;
Now *Shock* had giv'n himſelf the rowzing Shake,
And Nymphs prepar'd their *Chocolate* to take;
Thrice the wrought Slipper knock'd againſt the
        Ground,
And ſtriking Watches the tenth Hour reſound.
Belinda ſtill her downy Pillow preſt,
Her Guardian *Sylph* prolong'd the balmy Reſt.
'Twas he had ſummon'd to her ſilent Bed
The Morning Dream that hover'd o'er her Head.
A Youth more glitt'ring than a *Birth-night Beau*,
(That ev'n in Slumber caus'd her Cheek to glow)
                                        Seem'd

Seem'd to her Ear his winning Lips to lay,
And thus in Whispers said, or seem'd to say.

    Fairest of Mortals, thou distinguish'd Care
Of thousand bright Inhabitants of Air!
If e'er one Vision touch'd thy infant Thought,
Of all the Nurse and all the Priest have taught,
Of airy Elves by Moonlight Shadows seen,
The silver Token, and the circled Green,
Or Virgins visited by Angel-Pow'rs,
With Golden Crowns and Wreaths of heav'nly [Flow'rs,
Hear and believe! thy own Importance know,
Nor bound thy narrow Views to Things below.
Some secret Truths from Learned Pride conceal'd,
To Maids alone and Children are reveal'd:
What tho' no Credit doubting Wits may give?
The Fair and Innocent shall still believe.
Know then, unnumber'd Spirits round thee fly,
The light *Militia* of the lower Sky;

      B 2   These

These, tho' unseen, are ever on the Wing,
Hang o'er the *Box*, and hover round the *Ring*.
Think what an Equipage thou haft in Air,
And view with fcorn *Two Pages* and a *Chair*.
As now your own, our Beings were of old,
And once inclos'd in Woman's beauteous Mold;
Thence, by a foft Tranfition, we repair
From earthly Vehicles to thefe of Air.
Think not, when Woman's tranfient Breath is fled,
That all her Vanities at once are dead :
Succeeding Vanities fhe ftill regards,
And tho' fhe plays no more, o'erlooks the Cards.
Her Joy in gilded Chariots, when alive,
And Love of *Ombre*, after Death furvive.
For when the Fair in all their Pride expire,
To their firft Elements the Souls retire :
The Sprights of fiery Termagants in Flame
Mount up, and take a *Salamander's* Name.
Soft yielding Minds to Water glide away,
And fip with *Nymphs*, their Elemental Tea.

The

The graver Prude finks downward to a *Gnome*,
In fearch of Mifchief ftill on Earth to roam.
The light Coquettes in *Sylphs* aloft repair,
And fport and flutter in the Fields of Air.

Know farther yet; Whoever fair and chafte
Rejects Mankind, is by fome *Sylph* embrac'd :
For Spirits, freed from mortal Laws, with eafe
Affume what Sexes and what Shapes they pleafe.
What guards the Purity of melting Maids,
In Courtly Balls, and Midnight Mafquerades,
Safe from the treach'rous Friend, and daring Spark,
The Glance by Day, the Whifper in the Dark;
When kind Occafion prompts their warm Defires,
When Mufick foftens, and when Dancing fires ?
'Tis but their *Sylph*, the wife Celeftials know;
Tho' *Honour* is the Word with Men below.

[Face,
Some Nymphs there are, too confcious of their
For Life predeftin'd to the *Gnomes* Embrace.

Who swell their Prospects and exalt their Pride,
When Offers are disdain'd, and Love deny'd.
Then gay Ideas crowd the vacant Brain;
                                          [Train,
While Peers and Dukes, and all their sweeping
And Garters, Stars, and Coronets appear,
And in soft Sounds, *Your Grace* salutes their Ear.
'Tis these that early taint the Female Soul,
Instruct the Eyes of young *Coquettes* to roll,
Teach Infants Cheeks a bidden Blush to know,
And little Hearts to flutter at a *Beau.*

Oft when the World imagine Women stray,
The *Sylphs* thro' mystick Mazes guide their Way,
Thro' all the giddy Circle they pursue,
And old Impertinence expel by new.
What tender Maid but must a Victim fall
To one Man's Treat, but for another's Ball?
When *Florio* speaks, what Virgin could withstand,
If gentle *Damon* did not squeeze her Hand?

With

With varying Vanities, from ev'ry Part,
They shift the moving Toyshop of their Heart;
                               [knots strive,
Where Wigs with Wigs, with Sword-knots Sword-
Beaus banish Beaus, and Coaches Coaches drive.
This erring Mortals Levity may call,
Oh blind to Truth! the *Sylphs* contrive it all.

    Of these am I, who thy Protection claim,
A watchful Sprite, and *Ariel* is my Name.
Late, as I rang'd the Crystal Wilds of Air,
In the clear Mirror of thy ruling *Star*
I saw, alas! some dread Event impend,
E're to the Main this Morning's Sun descend.
But Heav'n reveals not what, or how, or where:
Warn'd by thy *Sylph*, oh Pious Maid beware!
This to disclose is all thy Guardian can.
Beware of all, but most beware of Man!

                               [long,
    He said; when *Shock*, who thought she slept too
Leapt up, and wak'd his Mistress with his Tongue.
        B 4   'Twas

'Twas then *Belinda* ! if Report ſay true,
Thy Eyes firſt open'd on a *Billet-doux* ;
Wounds, Charms, and *Ardors,* were no ſooner read,
But all the Viſion vaniſh'd from thy Head.

And now, unveil'd, the *Toilet* ſtands diſplay'd,
Each Silver Vaſe in myſtic Order laid.
Firſt, rob'd in White, the Nymph intent adores
With Head uncover'd, the *Coſmetic* Pow'rs.
A heav'nly Image in the Glaſs appears,
To that ſhe bends, to that her Eyes ſhe rears;
Th' inferior Prieſteſs, at her Altar's ſide,
Trembling, begins the ſacred Rites of Pride.
Unnumber'd Treaſures ope at once, and here
The various Off'rings of the World appear;
From each ſhe nicely culls with curious Toil,
And decks the Goddeſs with the glitt'ring Spoil.
This Casket *India*'s glowing Gems unlocks,
And all *Arabia* breaths from yonder Box.

The

The Tortoiſe here and Elephant unite,

Transform'd to *Combs*, the ſpeckled and the white.

Here Files of Pins extend their ſhining Rows,

Puffs, Powders, Patches, Bibles, Billet-doux.

Now awful Beauty puts on all its Arms ;

The Fair each moment riſes in her Charms,

Repairs her Smiles, awakens ev'ry Grace,

And calls forth all the Wonders of her Face ;

Sees by Degrees a purer Bluſh ariſe,

And keener Lightnings quicken in her Eyes.

The buſy *Sylphs* ſurround their darling Care ;

Theſe ſet the Head, and thoſe divide the Hair,

Some fold the Sleeve, while others plait the Gown ;

And *Betty*'s prais'd for Labours not her own.

T H E

THE

RAPE *of the* LOCK.

CANTO II.

NOT with more Glories, in th' Etherial Plain,
The Sun firft rifes o'er the purpled Main,
Than iffuing forth, the Rival of his Beams
Lanch'd on the Bofom of the Silver *Thames*.
Fair Nymphs, and well-dreft Youths around her
But ev'ry Eye was fix'd on her alone.   [fhone,
On her white Breaft a fparkling *Crofs* fhe wore,
Which *Jews* might kifs, and Infidels adore.

Her

Canto 2.

I.ud.Du Guernier inv.   C.Du Bosc sculp.

Her lively Looks a fprightly Mind difclofe,
Quick as her Eyes, and as unfix'd as thofe:
Favours to none, to all fhe Smiles extends,
Oft fhe rejects, but never once offends.
Bright as the Sun, her Eyes the Gazers ftrike,
And, like the Sun, they fhine on all alike.
Yet graceful Eafe, and Sweetnefs void of Pride,
Might hide her Faults, if *Belles* had Faults to hide:
If to her fhare fome Female Errors fall,
Look on her Face, and you'll forget 'em all.

This Nymph, to the Deftruction of Mankind,
Nourifh'd two Locks, which graceful hung behind
In equal Curls, and well confpir'd to deck
With fhining Ringlets her fmooth Iv'ry Neck.
Love in thefe Labyrinths his Slaves detains,
And mighty Hearts are held in flender Chains.
With hairy Sprindges we the Birds betray,
Slight Lines of Hair furprize the Finny Prey,

Fair

Fair Treſſes Man's Imperial Race inſnare,
And Beauty draws us with a ſingle Hair.

Th' Adventrous *Baron* the bright Locks admir'd,
He ſaw, he wiſh'd, and to the Prize aſpir'd:
Reſolv'd to win, he meditates the way,
By Force to raviſh, or by Fraud betray;
For when Succeſs a Lover's Toil attends,
Few ask, if Fraud or Force attain'd his Ends.

For this, e're *Phæbus* roſe, he had implor'd
Propitious Heav'n, and ev'ry Pow'r ador'd,
But chiefly *Love*---to *Love* an Altar built,
Of twelve vaſt *French* Romances, neatly gilt.
There lay the Sword-knot *Sylvia*'s Hands had ſown,
With *Flavia*'s Busk that oft had rapp'd his own:
A Fan, a Garter, half a Pair of Gloves;
And all the Trophies of his former Loves.
With tender *Billet-doux* he lights the Pyre,
And breaths three am'rous Sighs to raiſe the Fire.

                                        Then

Then proſtrate falls, and begs with ardent Eyes
Soon to obtain, and long poſſeſs the Prize:
The Pow'rs gave Ear, and granted half his Pray'r,
The reſt, the Winds diſpers'd in empty Air.

But now ſecure the painted Veſſel glides,
The Sun-beams trembling on the floating Tydes,
While melting Muſick ſteals upon the Sky,
And ſoften'd Sounds along the Waters die.
Smooth flow the Waves, the Zephyrs gently play
Belinda ſmil'd, and all the World was gay.
All but the *Sylph*----With careful Thoughts oppreſs
Th' impending Woe ſate heavy on his Breaſt.
He ſummons ſtrait his Denizens of Air;
The lucid Squadrons round the Sails repair:
Soft o'er the Shrouds Aerial Whiſpers breath,
That ſeem'd but *Zephyrs* to the Train beneath.
Some to the Sun their Inſect-Wings unfold,
Waft on the Breeze, or ſink in Clouds of Gold.

Tran-

Tranſparent Forms, too fine for mortal Sight,
Their fluid Bodies half diſſolv'd in Light.
Looſe to the Wind their airy Garments flew,
Thin glitt'ring Textures of the filmy Dew;
Dipt in the richeſt Tincture of the Skies,
Where Light diſports in ever-mingling Dies,
While ev'ry Beam new tranſient Colours flings,
Colours that change whene'er they wave their
Amid the Circle, on the gilded Maſt,   [Wings.
Superior by the Head, was *Ariel* plac'd;
His Purple Pinions opening to the Sun,
He rais'd his Azure Wand, and thus begun.

Ye *Sylphs* and *Sylphids*, to your Chief give Ear,
Fays, Fairies, Genii, Elves, and *Dæmons* hear!
Ye know the Spheres and various Tasks aſſign'd,
By Laws Eternal, to th' Aerial Kind.
Some in the Fields of pureſt *Æther* play,
And bask and whiten in the Blaze of Day.

Some

Some guide the Course of wandring Orbs on high,
Or roll the Planets thro' the boundless Sky.
Some less refin'd, beneath the Moon's pale Light
Hover, and catch the shooting Stars by Night;
Or suck the Mists in grosser Air below,
Or dip their Pinions in the painted Bow,
Or brew fierce Tempests on the wintry Main,
Or on the Glebe distill the kindly Rain.
Others on Earth o'er human Race preside,
Watch all their Ways, and all their Actions guide:
Of these the Chief the Care of Nations own,
And guard with Arms Divine the *British Throne*.

Our humbler Province is to tend the Fair,
Not a less pleasing, tho' less glorious Care.
To save the Powder from too rude a Gale,
Nor let th' imprison'd Essences exhale,
To draw fresh Colours from the vernal Flow'rs,
To steal from Rainbows ere they drop in Show'rs

A

A brighter Wafh; to curl their waving Hairs,
Affift their Blufhes, and infpire their Airs;
Nay oft, in Dreams, Invention we beftow,
To change a *Flounce,* or add a *Furbelo.*

This Day, black Omens threat the brighteft Fair
That e'er deferv'd a watchful Spirit's Care;
Some dire Difafter, or by Force, or Slight,
But what, or where, the Fates have wrapt in Night.
Whether the Nymph fhall break *Diana's* Law,
Or fome frail *China* Jar receive a Flaw,
Or ftain her Honour, or her new Brocade,
Forget her Pray'rs, or mifs a Mafquerade,
Or lofe her Heart, or Necklace, at a Ball;
Or whether Heav'n has doom'd that *Shock* muft fall.
Hafte then ye Spirits ! to your Charge repair;
The flutt'ring Fan be *Zephyretta's* Care;
The Drops to thee, *Brillante,* we confign;
And *Momentilla,* let the Watch be thine;

Do

Do thou, *Crispissa*, tend her fav'rite Lock;
Ariel himself shall be the Guard of *Shock*.

To Fifty chosen *Sylphs*, of special Note,
We trust th' important Charge, the *Petticoat*:
Oft have we known that sev'nfold Fence to fail,
Tho' stiff with Hoops, and arm'd with Ribs of [Whale.,
Form a strong Line about the Silver Bound,
And guard the wide Circumference around.

Whatever Spirit, careless of his Charge,
His Post neglects, or leaves the Fair at large,
Shall feel sharp Vengeance soon o'ertake his Sins,
Be stopt in *Vials*, or transfixt with *Pins*;
Or plung'd in Lakes of bitter *Washes* lie,
Or wedg'd whole Ages in a *Bodkin's* Eye:
Gums and *Pomatums* shall his Flight restrain,
While clog'd he beats his silken Wings in vain;
Or Alom-*Stypticks* with contracting Power
Shrink his thin Essence like a rivell'd Flower.

C   Or

Or as *Ixion* fix'd, the Wretch shall feel
The giddy Motion of the whirling Mill,
Midst Fumes of burning Chocolate shall glow,
And tremble at the Sea that froaths below !

He spoke; the Spirits from the Sails descend;
Some, Orb in Orb, around the Nymph extend,
Some thrid the mazy Ringlets of her Hair,
Some hang upon the Pendants of her Ear;
With beating Hearts the dire Event they wait,
Anxious, and trembling for the Birth of Fate.

T H E

Lud.Du Guernier inv.   *C.Du Bosc sculp.*

THE

RAPE *of the* LOCK.

CANTO III.

C LOSE by thofe Meads for ever crown'd with [Flow'rs,
   Where *Thames* with Pride furveys his rifing [Tow'rs,
There ftands a Structure of Majeftick Frame,
Which from the neighb'ring *Hampton* takes its [Name.
Here *Britain*'s Statefmen oft the Fall foredoom
Of Foreign Tyrants, and of Nymphs at home;
Here Thou, great *Anna*! whom three Realms obey,
Doft fometimes Counfel take---and fometimes *Tea*.

Hither the Heroes and the Nymphs refort,
To tafte awhile the Pleafures of a Court;
In various Talk th' inftructive hours they paft,
Who gave a *Ball,* or paid the *Vifit* laft:
One fpeaks the Glory of the *Britifh Queen,*
And one defcribes a charming *Indian Screen*;
A third interprets Motions, Looks, and Eyes;
At ev'ry Word a Reputation dies.
Snuff, or the *Fan,* fupply each Paufe of Chat,
With finging, laughing, ogling, and all that.

Mean while declining from the Noon of Day,
The Sun obliquely fhoots his burning Ray;
The hungry Judges foon the Sentence fign,
And Wretches hang that Jury-men may Dine;
The Merchant from th' *Exchange* returns in Peace,
And the long Labours of the *Toilette* ceafe ———
Belinda now, whom Thirft of Fame invites,
Burns to encounter two adventrous Knights,

At

At *Ombre* fingly to decide their Doom;
And fwells her Breaft with Conquefts yet to come.
Strait the three Bands prepare in Arms to join,
Each Band the number of the Sacred Nine.
Soon as fhe fpreads her Hand, th' Aerial Guard
Defcend, and fit on each important Card:
Firft *Ariel* perch'd upon a *Matadore*,
Then each, according to the Rank they bore;
For *Sylphs*, yet mindful of their ancient Race,
Are, as when Women, wondrous fond of Place.

Behold, four *Kings* in Majefty rever'd,
With hoary Whiskers and a forky Beard;
And four fair *Queens* whofe hands fuftain a Flow'r,
Th' expreffive Emblem of their fofter Pow'r;
Four *Knaves* in Garbs fuccinct, a trufty Band,
Caps on their heads, and Halberds in their hand;
And Particolour'd Troops, a fhining Train,
Draw forth to Combat on the Velvet Plain.

C 3

The

The skilful Nymph reviews her Force with Care;
Let Spades be Trumps, she said, and Trumps they were.
Now move to War her Sable *Matadores*,
In Show like Leaders of the swarthy *Moors*.
Spadillio first, unconquerable Lord!
Led off two captive Trumps, and swept the Board.
As many more *Manillio* forc'd to yield,
And march'd a Victor from the verdant Field.
Him *Basto* follow'd, but his Fate more hard
Gain'd but one Trump and one *Plebeian* Card.
With his broad Sabre next, a Chief in Years,
The hoary Majesty of *Spades* appears;
Puts forth one manly Leg, to sight reveal'd;
The rest his many-colour'd Robe conceal'd.
The Rebel-*Knave*, that dares his Prince engage,
Proves the just Victim of his Royal Rage.
Ev'n mighty *Pam* that Kings and Queens o'erthrew,
And mow'd down Armies in the Fights of *Lu*,
Sad Chance of War! now, destitute of Aid,
Falls undistinguish'd by the Victor *Spade* !

                                   Thus

Thus far both Armies to *Belinda* yield;
Now to the *Baron* Fate inclines the Field.
His warlike *Amazon* her Hoft invades,
Th' Imperial Confort of the Crown of *Spades*.
The *Club's* black Tyrant firft her Victim dy'd,
Spite of his haughty Mien, and barb'rous Pride:
What boots the Regal Circle on his Head,
His Giant Limbs in State unwieldy fpread?
That long behind he trails his pompous Robe,
And of all Monarchs only grafps the Globe?

The *Baron* now his *Diamonds* pours apace;
Th' embroider'd *King* who fhows but half his Face,
And his refulgent *Queen*, with Pow'rs combin'd,
Of broken Troops an eafie Conqueft find.
Clubs, Diamonds, Hearts, in wild Diforder feen,
With Throngs promifcuous ftrow the level Green.
Thus when difpers'd a routed Army runs,
Of *Afia's* Troops, and *Africk's* Sable Sons,

With like Confusion different Nations fly,
In various Habits and of various Dye,
The pierc'd Battalions dif-united fall,
In Heaps on Heaps; one Fate o'erwhelms them all.

The *Knave* of *Diamonds* now exerts his Arts,
And wins (oh shameful Chance!) the *Queen* of *Hearts*.
At this, the Blood the Virgin's Cheek forsook,
A livid Paleness spreads o'er all her Look ;
She sees, and trembles at th' approaching Ill,
Just in the Jaws of Ruin, and *Codille*.
And now, (as oft in some distemper'd State)
On one nice *Trick* depends the gen'ral Fate,
An *Ace* of Hearts steps forth : The *King* unseen
Lurk'd in her Hand, and mourn'd his captive *Queen*.
He springs to Vengeance with an eager pace,
And falls like Thunder on the prostrate *Ace*.
The Nymph exulting fills with Shouts the Sky,
The Walls, the Woods, and long Canals reply.

Oh

Oh thoughtlefs Mortals! ever blind to Fate,
Too foon dejeḋed, and too foon elate !
Sudden thefe Honours fhall be fnatch'd away,
And curs'd for ever this Viḋorious Day.

                                                [crown'd,
For lo ! the Board with Cups and Spoons is
The Berries crackle, and the Mill turns round.
On fhining Altars of *Japan* they raife
The filver Lamp, and fiery Spirits blaze.
From filver Spouts the grateful Liquors glide,
And *China*'s Earth receives the fmoking Tyde.
At once they gratify their Scent and Tafte,
While frequent Cups prolong the rich Repaft.
Strait hover round the Fair her Airy Band;
Some, as fhe fip'd, the fuming Liquor fann'd,
Some o'er her Lap their careful Plumes difplay'd,
Trembling, and confcious of the rich Brocade.
Coffee, (which makes the Politician wife,
And fee thro.' all things with his half fhut Eyes)

                                            Sent

Sent up in Vapours to the *Baron*'s Brain
New Stratagems, the radiant Lock to gain.
Ah ceaſe raſh Youth! deſiſt e'er 'tis too late,
Fear the juſt Gods, and think of * *Scylla*'s Fate!
Chang'd to a Bird, and ſent to flit in Air,
She dearly pays for *Niſus*' injur'd Hair!

But when to Miſchief Mortals bend their Mind,
How ſoon fit Inſtruments of Ill they find?
Juſt then, *Clariſſa* drew with tempting Grace
A two-edg'd Weapon from her ſhining Caſe;
So Ladies in Romance aſſiſt their Knight,
Preſent the Spear, and arm him for the Fight.
He takes the Gift with rev'rence, and extends
The little Engine on his Finger's Ends,
This juſt behind *Belinda*'s Neck he ſpread,
As o'er the fragrant Steams ſhe bends her Head:
Swift to the Lock a thouſand Sprights repair,
A thouſand Wings, by turns, blow back the Hair,

* *Vide* Ovid. Metam. 8:

And

And thrice they twitch'd the Diamond in her Ear,
Thrice she look'd back, and thrice the Foe drew near.
Juſt in that inſtant, anxious *Ariel* ſought
The cloſe Receſſes of the Virgin's Thought;
As on the Noſegay in her Breaſt reclin'd,
He watch'd th' Ideas riſing in her Mind,
Sudden he view'd, in ſpite of all her Art,
An Earthly Lover lurking at her Heart.
Amaz'd, confus'd, he found his Pow'r expir'd,
Reſign'd to Fate, and with a Sigh retir'd.

The Peer now ſpreads the glitt'ring *Forfex* wide,
T'incloſe the Lock; now joins it, to divide.
Ev'n then, before the fatal Engine clos'd,
A wretched *Sylph* too fondly interpos'd ;
Fate urg'd the Sheers, and cut the *Sylph* in twain,
(*But Airy Subſtance ſoon unites again)
The meeting Points the ſacred Hair diſſever
From the fair Head, for ever and for ever!

See Milton, *lib.* 6.

Then

Then flash'd the living Lightnings from her Eyes,
And Screams of Horror rend th' affrighted Skies.
Not louder Shrieks by Dames to Heav'n are cast,
When Husbands or when Monkeys breath their laft,
Or when rich *China* Veffels, fal'n from high,
In glittring Duft and painted Fragments lie!

Let Wreaths of Triumph now my Temples twine,
(The Victor cry'd) the glorious Prize is mine!
While Fifh in Streams, or Birds delight in Air,
Or in a Coach and Six the *Britifh* Fair,
As long as *Atalantis* fhall be read,
Or the fmall Pillow grace a Lady's Bed,
While *Vifits* fhall be paid on folemn Days,
When numerous Wax-lights in bright Order blaze,
While Nymphs take Treats, or Affignations give,
So long my Honour, Name, and Praife fhall live!

[date,
What Time wou'd fpare, from Steel receives its
And Monuments, like Men, fubmit to Fate!
                                        Steel

Steel did the Labour of the Gods deſtroy,

And ſtrike to Duſt th' Imperial Tow'rs of *Troy;*

Steel cou'd the Works of mortal Pride confound,

And hew Triumphal Arches to the Ground.
                                          [feel
What Wonder then, fair Nymph! thy Hairs ſhou'd

The conqu'ring Force of unreſiſted Steel?

———————————————————

THE

THE

RAPE *of the* LOCK.

CANTO IV.

BUT anxious Cares the pensive Nymph opprest,
    And secret Passions labour'd in her Breast.
Not youthful Kings in Battel seiz'd alive,
Not scornful Virgins who their Charms survive,
Not ardent Lovers robb'd of all their Bliss,
Not ancient Ladies when refus'd a Kiss,
Not Tyrants fierce that unrepenting die,
Not *Cynthia* when her *Manteau*'s pinn'd awry,

E'er

Lud. Du Guernier inv.   C. Du Bofc sculp.

E'er felt such Rage, Resentment and Despair,
As Thou, sad Virgin! for thy ravish'd Hair.

For, that sad moment, when the *Sylphs* withdrew,
And *Ariel* weeping from *Belinda* flew,
Umbriel, a dusky melancholy Spright,
As ever sully'd the fair face of Light,
Down to the Central Earth, his proper Scene,
Repairs to search the gloomy Cave of *Spleen.*

Swift on his sooty Pinions flitts the *Gnome,*
And in a Vapour reach'd the dismal Dome.
No cheerful Breeze this sullen Region knows,
The dreaded *East* is all the Wind that blows.
Here, in a Grotto, sheltred close from Air,
And screen'd in Shades from Day's detested Glare,
She sighs for ever on her pensive Bed,
Pain at her side, and *Languor* at her Head.

Two Handmaids wait the Throne: Alike in Place,
But diff'ring far in Figure and in Face.

Here ftood *Ill-nature* like an *ancient Maid*,
Her wrinkled Form in *Black* and *White* array'd ;
                                    [Noons,
With ftore of Pray'rs, for Mornings, Nights, and
Her Hand is fill'd ; her Bofom with Lampoons.

    There *Affectation* with a fickly Mien
Shows in her Cheek the Rofes of Eighteen,
Practis'd to Lifp, and hang the Head afide,
Faints into Airs, and languifhes with Pride ;
On the rich Quilt finks with becoming Woe,
Wrapt in a Gown, for Sicknefs, and for Show.
The Fair ones feel fuch Maladies as thefe,
When each new Night-Drefs gives a new Difeafe.

    A conftant *Vapour* o'er the Palace flies ;
Strange Phantoms rifing as the Mifts arife ;
Dreadful, as Hermit's Dreams in haunted Shades,
Or bright as Vifions of expiring Maids.
Now glaring Fiends, and Snakes on rolling Spires,
Pale Spectres, gaping Tombs, and Purple Fires :
                            Now

Now Lakes of liquid Gold, *Elyſian* Scenes,
And Cryſtal Domes, and Angels in Machines.

Unnumber'd Throngs on ev'ry ſide are ſeen
Of Bodies chang'd to various Forms by *Spleen*.
Here living *Teapots* ſtand, one Arm held out,
One bent; the Handle this, and that the Spout:
A Pipkin there like *Homer*'s *Tripod* walks;
Here ſighs a Jar, and there a Gooſe-pye talks;
Men prove with Child, as pow'rful Fancy works,
And Maids turn'd Bottels, call aloud for Corks.

Safe paſt the *Gnome* thro' this fantaſtick Band,
A Branch of healing *Spleenwort* in his hand.
Then thus addreſt the Pow'r—Hail wayward
Who rule the Sex to Fifty from Fifteen, [Queen;
Parent of Vapors and of Female Wit,
Who give th' *Hyſteric* or *Poetic* Fit,
On various Tempers act by various ways,
Make ſome take Phyſick, others ſcribble Plays;

D   Who

Who cauſe the Proud their Viſits to delay,
And ſend the Godly in a Pett, to pray.
A Nymph there is, that all thy Pow'r diſdains,
And thouſands more in equal Mirth maintains.
But oh ! if e'er thy *Gnome* could ſpoil a Grace,
Or raiſe a Pimple on a beauteous Face,
Like Citron-Waters Matron's Checks inflame,
Or change Complexions at a loſing Game;
If e'er with airy Horns I planted Heads,
Or rumpled Petticoats, or tumbled Beds,
Or caus'd Suſpicion when no Soul was rude,
Or diſcompos'd the Head-dreſs of a Prude,
Or e'er to coſtive Lap-Dog gave Diſeaſe,
Which not the Tears of brighteſt Eyes could eaſe:
Hear me, and touch *Belinda* with Chagrin;
That ſingle Act gives half the World the Spleen.

    The Goddeſs with a diſcontented Air
Seems to reject him, tho' ſhe grants his Pray'r.

A

A wondrous Bag with both her Hands she binds,
Like that where once *Ulysses* held the Winds;
There she collects the Force of Female Lungs,
Sighs, Sobs, and Passions, and the War of Tongues.
A Vial next she fills with fainting Fears,
Soft Sorrows, melting Griefs, and flowing Tears.
The *Gnome* rejoicing bears her Gift away,
Spreads his black Wings, and slowly mounts to Day.

Sunk in *Thalestris'* Arms the Nymph he found,
Her Eyes dejected and her Hair unbound.
Full o'er their Heads the swelling Bag he rent,
And all the Furies issued at the Vent.
Belinda burns with more than mortal Ire,
And fierce *Thalestris* fans the rising Fire.
O wretched Maid! she spread her hands, and cry'd,
(While *Hampton's* Ecchos, wretched Maid reply'd)
Was it for this you took such constant Care
The *Bodkin*, *Comb*, and *Essence* to prepare;

D 2   For

For this your Locks in Paper-Durance bound,

For this with tort'ring Irons wreath'd around?

For this with Fillets ſtrain'd your tender Head,

And bravely bore the double Loads of Lead?

Gods! ſhall the Raviſher diſplay your Hair,

While the Fops envy, and the Ladies ſtare!

Honour forbid! at whoſe unrival'd Shrine

Eaſe, Pleaſure, Virtue, All, our Sex reſign.

Methinks already I your Tears ſurvey,

Already hear the horrid things they ſay,

Already ſee you a degraded Toaſt,

And all your Honour in a Whiſper loſt !

How ſhall I, then, your helpleſs Fame defend?

'Twill then be Infamy to ſeem your Friend!

And ſhall this Prize, th' ineſtimable Prize,

Expos'd thro' Cryſtal to the gazing Eyes,

And heighten'd by the Diamond's circling Rays,

On that Rapacious Hand for ever blaze?

Sooner ſhall Graſs in *Hide*-Park *Circus* grow,

And Wits take Lodgings in the Sound of *Bow*;

Sooner

Sooner let Earth, Air, Sea, to *Chaos* fall,
Men, Monkies, Lap-dogs, Parrots, perish all!

She faid; then raging to *Sir Plume* repairs,
And bids her *Beau* demand the precious Hairs:
(*Sir Plume*, of *Amber Snuff-box* juftly vain,
And the nice Conduct of a *clouded Cane*)
With earneft Eyes, and round unthinking Face,
He firft the Snuff-box open'd, then the Cafe,
And thus broke out--- " My Lord, why, what the [Devil?
" Z---ds! damn the Lock! 'fore Gad, you muft be [civil!
" Plague on't! 'tis paft a Jeft---nay prithee, Pox!
" Give her the Hair---he fpoke, and rapp'd his Box.

It grieves me much (reply'd the Peer again)
Who fpeaks fo well fhou'd ever fpeak in vain.
But * by this Lock, this facred Lock I fwear.
(Which never more fhall join its parted Hair,

D 3   Which

* *In allufion to* Achilles's *Oath in* Homer. *Il. 1.*

Which never more its Honours ſhall renew,
Clipt from the lovely Head where once it grew)
That while my Noſtrils draw the vital Air,
This Hand, which won it, ſhall for ever wear.
He ſpoke, and ſpeaking in proud Triumph ſpread
The long-contended Honours of her Head.

But *Umbriel*, hateful *Gnome* ! forbears not ſo;
He breaks the Vial whence the Sorrows flow.
Then ſee ! the *Nymph* in beauteous Grief appears,
Her Eyes half languiſhing, half drown'd in Tears;
On her heav'd Boſom hung her drooping Head,
Which, with a Sigh, ſhe rais'd; and thus ſhe ſaid.

For ever curs'd be this deteſted Day,
Which ſnatch'd my beſt, my fav'rite Curl away!
Happy! ah ten times happy, had I been,
If *Hampton-Court* theſe Eyes had never ſeen!
Yet am not I the firſt miſtaken Maid,
By Love of *Courts* to num'rous Ills betray'd.

Oh

Oh had I rather un-admir'd remain'd
In some lone Isle, or distant *Northern* Land;
Where the gilt *Chariot* never mark'd the way,
Where none learn *Ombre*, none e'er taste *Bohea*!
There kept my Charms conceal'd from mortal Eye,
Like Roses that in Desarts bloom and die.
What mov'd my Mind with youthful Lords to rome?
O had I stay'd, and said my Pray'rs at home!
'Twas this, the Morning *Omens* did foretel;
Thrice from my trembling hand the *Patch-box* fell;
The tott'ring *China* shook without a Wind,
Nay, *Poll* sate mute, and *Shock* was most Unkind!
A *Sylph* too warn'd me of the Threats of Fate,
In mystic Visions, now believ'd too late!
See the poor Remnants of this slighted Hair!
My hands shall rend what ev'n thy own did spare.
This, in two sable Ringlets taught to break,
Once gave new Beauties to the snowie Neck.
The Sister-Lock now sits uncouth, alone,
And in its Fellow's Fate foresees its own;

D 4   Un-

Uncurl'd it hangs,   the fatal Sheers demands ;
And tempts once more thy facrilegious Hands.
Oh hadſt thou, Cruel! been content to ſeize
Hairs leſs in ſight,   or any Hairs but theſe!

———————————————

THE

———————————————

Lud. Du Guernier inv.   C. Du Bosc sculp.

THE

RAPE *of the* LOCK.

CANTO V.

SHE said: the pitying Audience melt in Tears,
But *Fate* and *Jove* had ſtopp'd the *Baron*'s Ears.
In vain *Thaleſtris* with Reproach aſſails,
For who can move when fair *Belinda* fails?
Not half ſo fixt the *Trojan* cou'd remain,
While *Anna* begg'd and *Dido* rag'd in vain.
To Arms, to Arms! the bold *Thaleſtris* cries,
And ſwift as Lightning to the Combate flies.

All

All fide in Parties, and begin th' Attack ;
Fans clap, Silks rufsle, and tough Whalebones crack ;
Heroes and Heroins Shouts confus'dly rife,
And bafe, and treble Voices ftrike the Skies.
No common Weapons in their Hands are found,
Like Gods they fight, nor dread a mortal Wound.

* So when bold *Homer* makes the Gods engage,
And heav'nly Breafts with human Paffions rage ;
'Gainft *Pallas, Mars; Latona, Hermes,* Arms ;
And all *Olympus* rings with loud Alarms.
Jove's Thunder roars, Heav'n trembles all around ;
Blue *Neptune* ftorms, the bellowing Deeps refound ;
    [gives way;
Earth fhakes her nodding Tow'rs, the Ground
And the pale Ghofts ftart at the Flafh of Day !

Triumphant *Umbriel* on a Sconce's Height
Clapt his glad Wings, and fate to view the Fight,
Propt on their Bodkin Spears the Sprights furvey
The growing Combat, or affift the Fray.

* Homer. *Il.* 20.

While thro' the Press enrag'd *Thaleſtris* flies,
And ſcatters Deaths around from both her Eyes,
A *Beau* and *Witling* periſh'd in the Throng,
One dy'd in *Metaphor*, and one in *Song*.
O cruel Nymph ! a living Death I bear,
Cry'd *Dapperwit*, and ſunk beſide his Chair.
A mournful Glance Sir *Fopling* upwards caſt,
* *Thoſe Eyes are made ſo killing* —— was his laſt:
Thus on *Meander*'s flow'ry Margin lies
Th' expiring Swan, and as he ſings he dies.

As bold Sir *Plume* had drawn *Clariſſa* down,
Chloe ſtept in, and kill'd him with a Frown ;
She ſmil'd to ſee the doughty Hero ſlain,
But at her Smile, the Beau reviv'd again.

† Now *Jove* ſuſpends his golden Scales in Air,
Weighs the Mens Wits againſt the Lady's Hair ;

The

* *A Song in the Opera of* Camilla.
† *Vid.* Homer *Il.* 22. & Virg. *Æn.* 12.

The doubtful Beam long nods from fide to fide;
At length the Wits mount up, the Hairs fubfide.

See fierce *Belinda* on the *Baron* flies,
With more than ufual Lightning in her Eyes;
Nor fear'd the Chief th' unequal Fight to try,
Who fought no more than on his Foe to die.
But this bold Lord, with manly Strength indu'd,
She with one Finger and a Thumb fubdu'd:
Juft where the Breath of Life his Noftrils drew,
A Charge of *Snuff* the wily Virgin threw;
The *Gnomes* direct, to ev'ry Atome juft,
The pungent Grains of titillating Duft.
Sudden, with ftarting Tears each Eye o'erflows,
And the high Dome re-ecchoes to his Nofe.

Now meet thy Fate, th' incens'd Virago cry'd,
And drew a deadly *Bodkin* from her Side.
(*The fame, his ancient Perfonage to deck,
Her great great Grandfire wore about his Neck

* *In Imitation of the Progrefs of* Agamemnon's *Scepter in* Homer, *Il.* 2.

In three *Seal-Rings*; which after melted down,
Form'd a vaſt *Buckle* for his Widow's Gown:
Her infant Grandame's *Whiſtle* next it grew,
The *Bells* ſhe gingled, and the *Whiſtle* blew;
Then in a *Bodkin* grac'd her Mother's Hairs,
Which long ſhe wore, and now *Belinda* wears.)

Boaſt not my Fall (he cry'd) inſulting Foe!
Thou by ſome other ſhalt be laid as low.
Nor think, to die dejeﬅs my lofty Mind;
All that I dread, is leaving you behind!
Rather than ſo, ah let me ſtill ſurvive,
And burn in *Cupid*'s Flames,——but burn alive.

Reﬅore the Lock! ſhe cries; and all around
Reﬅore the Lock! the vaulted Roofs rebound.
Not fierce *Othello* in ſo loud a Strain
Roar'd for the Handkerchief that caus'd his Pain.
But ſee how oft Ambitious Aims are croſs'd,
And Chiefs contend 'till all the Prize is loﬅ!

The

The Lock, obtain'd with Guilt, and kept with Pain,
In ev'ry place is fought, but fought in vain:
With fuch a Prize no Mortal muft be bleft,
So Heav'n decrees! with Heav'n who can conteft?

Some thought it mounted to the Lunar Sphere,
* Since all things loft on Earth, are treafur'd there.
There Heroe's Wits are kept in pondrous Vafes,
And Beau's in *Snuff-boxes* and *Tweezer-Cafes.*
There broken Vows, and Death-bed Alms are found,
And Lovers Hearts with Ends of Riband bound;
The Courtiers Promifes, and Sick Man's Pray'rs,
The Smiles of Harlots, and the Tears of Heirs,
Cages for Gnats, and Chains to Yoak a Flea;
Dry'd Butterflies, and Tomes of Cafuiftry.

But truft the Mufe——fhe faw it upward rife,
Tho' mark'd by none but quick Poetic Eyes:
(So *Rome*'s great Founder to the Heav'ns withdrew,
To *Proculus* alone confefs'd in view.)

* *Vid.* Ariofto. Canto 34.

A fudden Star, it fhot thro' liquid Air,
And drew behind a radiant *Trail of Hair.*
Not *Berenice's* Locks firft rofe fo bright,
The Skies befpangling with difhevel'd Light.
The *Sylphs* behold it kindling as it flies,
And pleas'd purfue its Progrefs thro' the Skies.

This the *Beau-monde* fhall from the *Mall* furvey,
And hail with Mufick its propitious Ray.
This, the bleft Lover fhall for *Venus* take,
And fend up Vows from *Rofamonda's* Lake.
This *Partridge* foon fhall view in cloudlefs Skies,
When next he looks thro' *Galilæo's* Eyes;
And hence th' Egregious Wizard fhall foredoom
The Fate of *Louis,* and the Fall of *Rome.*

Then ceafe, bright Nymph! to mourn the ravifh'd [Hair
Which adds new Glory to the fhining Sphere!
Not all the Treffes that fair Head can boaft
Shall draw fuch Envy as the Lock you loft.

For,

For, after all the Murders of your Eye,

When, after Millions flain, your felf fhall die ;

When thofe fair Suns fhall fett, as fett they muft,

And all thofe Treffes fhall be laid in Duft;

This Lock, the Mufe fhall confecrate to Fame,

And mid'ft the Stars infcribe *Belinda*'s Name !

F I N I S.

THE

DUNCIAD,

VARIORVM.

WITH THE

PROLEGOMENA of *SCRIBLERUS.*

LONDON.

Printed for A. DOD. 1729.

PIECES contained in this BOOK.

ADVERTISEMENT.

IT will be sufficient to say of this Edition, that the reader has here a much more correct and compleat copy of the DUNCIAD, than has hitherto appeared: I cannot answer but some mistakes may have slipt into it, but a vast number of others will be prevented, by the Names being now not only set at length, but justified by the authorities and reasons given. I make no doubt, the Author's own motive to use real rather than feign'd names, was his care to preserve the Innocent from any false Applications; whereas in the former editions which had no more than the Initial letters, he was made, by Keys printed here, to hurt the inoffensive; and (what was worse) to abuse his friends, by an impression at Dublin.

The Commentary which attends the Poem, was sent me from several hands, and consequently must be unequally written; yet will it have one advantage over most commentaries, that it is not made upon conjectures, or a remote distance of time: and the reader cannot but derive one pleasure from the very Obscurity of the persons it treats of, that it partakes of the nature of a Secret, which most people love to be let into, tho' the Men or the Things be ever so inconsiderable or trivial.

Of the Persons it was judg'd proper to give some account: for since it is only in this monument that they must expect to survive, (and here survive they will, as long as the English tongue shall remain such as it was in the reigns of Queen ANNE and King GEORGE) it seem'd but humanity to bestow a word or two upon each, just to tell what he was, what he writ, when he liv'd, or when he dy'd.

If a word or two more are added upon the chief Offenders; 'tis only as a paper pinn'd upon the breast, to mark the Enormities for which they *suffer'd; left the Correction only fhould be remember'd, and the Crime forgotten.*

In fome Articles, it was thought fufficient barely to tranfcribe from Jacob, Curl, and other writers of their own rank, who were much better acquainted with them than any of the Authors of this Comment can pretend to be. Moft of them had drawn each other's Characters on certain occafions; but the few here inferted, are all that could be faved from the general deftruction of fuch Works.

Of the part of Scriblerus I need fay nothing: his Manner is well enough known, and approv'd by all but thofe who are too much concern'd to be judges.

The Imitations of the Ancients are added, to gratify thofe who either never read, or may have forgotten them; together with fome of the Parodies, and Allufions to the moft excellent of the Moderns. If any man from the frequency of the former, may think the Poem too much a Cento; our Poet will but appear to have done the fame thing in jeft, which Boileau did in earneft; and upon which Vida, Fracaftorius, and many of the moft eminent Latin Poets profeffedly valued themfelves.

A
LETTER
TO THE
PUBLISHER,

Occafioned by the prefent

Edition of the DUNCIAD.

IT is with pleafure I hear that you have procured a
correct Edition of the DUNCIAD, which the many
furreptitious ones have rendered fo neceffary; and
it is yet with more, that I am informed it will be at-
tended with a COMMENTARY: a work fo neceffary, that
I cannot think the Author himfelf would have omit-
ted it, had he approv'd of the firft appearance of this
Poem.

Such Notes as have occurr'd to me I herewith fend you;
you will oblige me by inferting them amongft thofe
which are, or will be, tranfmitted to you by others:
fince not only the Author's friends, but even ftrangers,
appear ingag'd by humanity, to fome care of an orphan

of fo much genius and fpirit, which its parent feems to have abandoned from the very beginning, and fuffered to ftep into the world naked, unguarded, and unattended.

It was upon reading fome of the abufive papers lately publifh'd, that my great regard to a perfon whofe friendfhip I fhall ever efteem as one of the chief honours of my life, and a much greater refpect to Truth than to him or any man living, ingag'd me in Enquiries, of which the inclos'd Notes are the fruit.

I perceiv'd, that moft of thefe authors had been (doubtlefs very wifely) the firft Aggreffors: they had try'd till they were weary, what was to be got by railing at each other; no body was either concern'd, or furpriz'd, if this or that Scribler was prov'd a Dunce: but every one was curious to read what could be faid to prove Mr. POPE one, and was ready to pay fomething for fuch a difcovery: A ftratagem which wou'd they fairly own, might not only reconcile them to me, but fcreen them from the refentment of their lawful fuperiors, whom they daily abufe, only (as I charitably hope) to get that by them, which they cannot get from them.

I found this was not all: ill fuccefs in that had tranfported them to perfonal abufe, either of himfelf, or (what I think he could lefs forgive) of his friends. They had call'd men of virtue and honour Bad Men, long before he had either leifure or inclination to call them

Bad Writers : and some had been such old offenders, that he had quite forgotten their persons as well as their slanders, till they were pleas'd to revive them.

Now what had Mr. POPE done before to incense them ? He had publish'd those works which are in the hands of every body, in which not the least mention is made of any of them : And what has he done since ? He has laugh'd and written the DUNCIAD. What has that said of them ? a very serious truth which the publick had said before, that they were dull : and what it had no sooner said, but they themselves were at great pains to procure or even purchase room in the prints, to testify under their hands to the truth of it.

I should still have been silent, if either I had seen any inclination in my friend to be serious with such accusers, or if they had only attack'd his writings : since whoever publishes, puts himself on his tryal by his country. But when his moral character was attack'd, and in a manner from which neither Truth nor Virtue can secure the most Innocent, in a manner which though it annihilates the credit of the accusation with the just and impartial, yet aggravates very much the guilt of the accuser, (I mean by authors without Names :) Then I thought, since the danger is common to all, the concern ought to be so ; and that it was an act of justice to detect the Authors, not only on this account, but as many of them are the same, who for several years paſt, have made free with the greateſt Names in Church and State, expos'd to the world the private misfortunes of Families, abus'd all even to Women, and whoſe proſtituted papers (for one or other Party, in the unhappy Diviſions of their Country) have inſulted the Fallen, the Friendleſs, the Exil'd, and the Dead.

Beſides this, which I take to be a publick concern, I have already confeſs'd I had a private one. I am one of that number who have long lov'd and eſteem'd Mr. POPE, and had often declared it was not his Capacity or Writings (which we ever thought the leaſt valuable part of his character) but the honeſt, open, and beneficent Man, that we moſt eſteem'd and lov'd in him. Now if what theſe people ſay were believ'd, I muſt appear to all my friends either a fool or a knave, either impos'd on my ſelf, or impoſing on them: So that I am as much intereſted in the confutation of theſe calumnies, as he is himſelf.

I am no Author, and conſequently not to be ſuſpected either of jealouſy or reſentment againſt any of the men, of whom ſcarce one is known to me by ſight; and as for their writings, I have ſought them (on this one occaſion) in vain, in the cloſets and libraries of all my acquaintance. I had ſtill been in the dark, if a Gentleman had not procur'd me (I ſuppoſe from ſome of themſelves, for they are generally much more dangerous friends than enemies) the paſſages I ſend you. I ſolemnly proteſt I have added nothing to the malice or abfurdity of them, which it behoves me to declare, fince the vouchers themfelves will be fo foon and fo irrecoverably loft. You may in fome meafure prevent it, by preferving at leaft their * Titles, and difcovering (as far as you can depend on the truth of your information) the names of the conceal'd authors.

The firft objection I have heard made to the Poem is, that the perfons are too obfcure for Satyre. The perfons themfelves, rather than allow the objection, would forgive the Satyre ; and if one could be tempted to afford it a ferious anfwer, were not all affaffinates, popular infurrections, the infolence of the rabble without doors and of domefticks within, moft wrongfully chaftized, if the Meannefs of offenders indemnified them from punifhment ? On the contrary, obfcurity renders them more dangerous, as lefs thought of : Law can pronounce judgment only on open Facts, Morality alone can pafs cenfure on Intentions of mifchief ; fo that for fecret calumny or the arrow flying in the dark, there is no publick punifhment left, but what a good writer inflicts.

The next objection is, that thefe fort of authors are Poor. That might be pleaded as an excufe at the Old Baily for leffer crimes than defamation, for 'tis the cafe of almoft all who are try'd there ; but fure it can here be none, fince no man will pretend that the robbing another of his reputation fupplies the want of it in himfelf. I queftion not

* Which we have done in a Lift in the *Appendix*, N⸰ 2.

b

but such authors are poor, and heartily wish the objection were removed by any honeft livelihood.   But Poverty here is the accident, not the fubject: he who defcribes malice and villany to be pale and meagre, expreffes not the leaft anger againft palenefs or leannefs, but againft malice and villany.   The apothecary in ROMEO and JULIET is poor, but is he therefore juftified in vending poifon? Not but poverty itfelf becomes a juft fubject of fatyre, when it is the confequence of vice, prodigality, or neglect of one's lawful calling; for then it increafes the publick burden, fills the ftreets and high-ways with Robbers, and the garrets with Clippers, Coiners, and Weekly Journalifts.

But admitting that two or three of thefe, offend lefs in their morals, than in their writings; muft poverty make nonfenfe facred? If fo, the fame of bad authors would be much better taken care of, than that of all the good ones in the world; and not one of a hundred had ever been call'd by his right name.

They miftake the whole matter: It is not charity to encourage them in the way they follow, but to get 'em out of it: For men are not bunglers becaufe they are poor, but they are poor becaufe they are bunglers.

Is it not pleafant enough to hear our authors crying out on the one hand, as if their perfons and characters were too facred for Satyre; and the publick objecting on the other, that they are too mean even for Ridicule? But whether bread or fame be their end, it muft be allow'd, our author by and in this poem, has mercifully given 'em a little of both.

There are two or three, who by their rank and fortune have no benefit from the former objections (fuppofing them good) and thefe I was forry to fee in fuch company. But if without any provocation, two or three gentlemen will fall upon one, in an affair wherein his intereft and reputation are equally embark'd; they cannot certainly, after they had been content to print themfelves his enemies, complain of being put into the number of them?

Others, I'm told, pretend to have been once his Friends; furely they are their enemies who fay fo, fince nothing can be more odious than to treat a friend as they have done: but of this I can't perfuade my felf, when I confider the conftant and eternal averfion of all bad writers to a good one.

Such as claim a merit from being his Admirers, I wou'd gladly ask, if it lays him under any perfonal obligation? at that rate he would be the moft oblig'd humble fervant in the world. I dare fwear, for thefe in particular, he never defir'd them to be his Admirers, nor promis'd in return to be theirs; that had truly been a fign he was of their acquaintance; but wou'd not the malicious world have fufpected fuch an approbation of fome motive worfe than ignorance, in the Author of the ESSAY on CRITICISM? Be it as it will, the reafons of their Admiration and of his Contempt are equally fubfifting; for His Works and Theirs are the very fame that they were.

b 2

One therefore of their accusations I believe may be juft, " That he has a contempt for their writings." And there is another which would probably be fooner allow'd by himfelf, than by any good judge befide, " That his " own have found too much fuccefs with the publick." But as it cannot confift with his modefty to claim this as a juftice, it lies not on him, but entirely on the public, to defend its own judgment.

There remains what in my opinion might feem a better plea for thefe people, than any they have made ufe of. If Obfcurity or Poverty were to exempt a man from fatyr, much more fhould Folly or Dulnefs, which are ftill more involuntary, nay as much fo as perfonal deformity. But even this will not help them: Deformity becomes the object of ridicule when a man fets up for being handfome: and fo muft Dulnefs when he fets up for a Wit. They are not ridicul'd becaufe Ridicule in itfelf is or ought to be a pleafure; but becaufe it is juft, to undeceive or vindicate the honeft and unpretending part of mankind from impofition, becaufe particular intereft ought to yield to general, and a great number who are not naturally Fools ought never to be made fo in complaifance to a few who are. Accordingly we find that in all ages, all vain pretenders, were they ever fo poor or ever fo dull, have been conftantly the topicks of the moft candid Satyrifts, from the Codrus of JUVENAL to the Damon of BOILEAU.

Having mention'd BOILEAU, the greateſt Poet and moſt judicious Critic of his age and country, admirable for his talents, and yet perhaps more admirable for his judgment in the proper application of them ; I cannot help remarking the reſemblance betwixt Him and our Author in Qualities, Fame, and Fortune; in the diſtinctions ſhewn to them by their Superiors, in the general eſteem of their Equals, and in their extended reputation amongſt Foreigners; in the latter of which ours has met with the better fortune, as he has had for his Tranſlators perſons of the moſt eminent rank and abilities in their reſpective Nations.* But the reſemblance holds in nothing more, than in their being equally abus'd by the ignorant pretenders to Poetry of their times; of which not the leaſt memory will remain but in their own writings, and in the notes made upon them. What BOILEAU has done in almoſt all his Poems, our Author has only in this: I dare anſwer for him he will do it in no more ; and on his principle of attacking few but who had ſlander'd him, he could not have done it at all had he been confin'd from cenſuring obſcure and worthleſs perſons, for ſcarce any other were his enemies. However, as the parity is ſo remarkable, I hope

---

* Eſſay on Criticiſm in *French* Verſe by General *Hamilton*. The ſame in Verſe alſo by Monſieur *Roboton*, Counſellor and Privy Secretary to King *George* I.
Rape of the Lock, in *French*, *Paris*, 1728.
——— ——— In *Italian* Verſe, by the Abbe *Conti*, a Noble *Venetian* ; and by the Marqueſs *Ranzoni*, Envoy Extraordinary from *Modena* to King *George* II.
Others of his Works by *Salvini* of *Florence*, &c.
His Eſſays and Diſſertations on *Homer*, in *French*, *Paris* 1728.

it will continue to the laſt ; and if ever he ſhall give us an edition of this Poem himſelf, I may ſee ſome of 'em treated as gently (on their repentance or better merit) as Perault and Quinault were at laſt by BOILEAU.

In one point I muſt be allow'd to think the character of our Engliſh Poet the more amiable. He has not been a follower of fortune or ſucceſs : He has liv'd with the Great without Flattery, been a friend to Men in power without Penſions, from whom as he ask'd, ſo he receiv'd no favour but what was done Him in his friends. As his Satyrs were the more juſt for being delay'd, ſo were his Panegyricks ; beſtow'd only on ſuch perſons as he had familiarly known, only for ſuch virtues as he had long obſerv'd in them, and only at ſuch times as others ceaſe to praiſe if not begin to calumniate them, I mean when out of Power or out of Faſhion.† A Satyr therefore on writers ſo notorious for the contrary, became no man ſo well as himſelf ; as none (it is plain) was ſo little in Their friendſhips, or ſo much in that of thoſe whom they had moſt abus'd, namely the Greateſt and Beſt of All Parties. Let me add a further reaſon, that tho' ingag'd in their friendſhips, he never eſpous'd their animoſities ; and can almoſt ſingly challenge this honour,

---

† As Mr. *Wycherley*, at the time the Town declaim'd againſt his Book of Poems : Mr. *Walſh*, after his death : Sir *William Trumbull*, when he had reſign'd the Office of Secretary of State : Lord *Bolingbroke* at his leaving *England* after the Queen's death : Lord *Oxford* in his laſt decline of Life : Mr. Secretary *Craggs* at the end of the South-Sea Year, and after his death : Others, only in *Epitaphs*.

not to have written a line of any man, which thro' Guilt, thro' Shame, or thro' Fear, thro' variety of Fortune, or change of Interefts, he was ever unwilling to own.

I fhall conclude with remarking what a pleafure it muft be to every reader of humanity, to fee all along, that our Author, in his very laughter, is not indulging his own Ill nature, but only punifhing that of others. To his Poem thofe alone are capable to do Juftice, who to ufe the words of a great Writer, know how hard it is (with regard both to his Subject and his Manner) VETUSTIS DARE NOVITATEM, OBSOLETIS NITOREM, OBSCURIS LUCEM, FASTIDITIS GRATIAM. I am,

Your moft humble Servant,

St. *James's*
Dec. 22,
1728.

WILLIAM CLELAND.

DENNIS, Rem. on Pr. *Arth*.

I Cannot but think it the moſt *reaſonable* thing in the world, to diſtinguiſh Good writers, by diſcouraging the Bad. Nor is it an *ill-natur'd* thing, in relation even to the very *perſons* upon whom the Reflections are made: It is true, it may deprive them, a little the ſooner, of a *ſhort Profit* and a *tranſitory Reputation*: But then it may have a good effect, and oblige them (before it be too late) to decline that for which they are ſo very *unfit*, and to have recourſe to *ſomething* in which they may be more ſucceſsful.

The *Perſons* whom *Boileau* has attack'd in his writings, have been for the moſt part *Authors*, and moſt of thoſe Authors, *Poets*: And the cenſures he hath paſs'd upon them have been *confirm'd by all Europe*. [Character of Mr. *P.* 1716.]

GILDON, Pref. to his *New Rehearſ.*

It is the common cry of the *Poetaſters* of the Town, and their Fautors, that it is an *Ill-natur'd thing* to expoſe the *Pretenders* to Wit and Poetry. The Judges and Magiſtrates may with full as good reaſon be reproach'd with *Ill-nature*, for putting the Laws in execution againſt a Thief or Impoſtor —— The ſame will hold in the Republick of Letters, if the Criticks and Judges will let every *Ignorant Pretender* to Scribling, paſs on the World.

THEOBALD, Lett. to *Miſt*, Jun. 22, 1728.

ATTACKS may be levelled, either againſt *Failures* in *Genius*, or againſt the *Pretenſions* of *writing without one*.

CONCANEN, *Ded.* to the *Auth.* of the *Dunc.*

A *Satyre* upon *Dulneſs*, is a thing, that has been *uſed* and *allowed* in *All Ages*.

Out of thine own Mouth will I judge thee, wicked Scribler!

MARTINUS SCRIBLERUS

HIS

PROLEGOMENA

TO THE

DUNCIAD.

TESTIMONIES

OF

AUTHORS,

Concerning our POET and his WORKS.

MARTINUS SCRIBLERUS Lectori S.

BEFORE we prefent thee with our Exercitations on the moft delectable Poem of the Dunciad (drawn from the many volumes of our *Adverfaria* on modern Authors) we fhall here, according to the laudable ufage of Editors, collect the various judgments of the Learned concerning our Poet: Various indeed, not only of different authors, but of the fame author at different feafons. Nor fhall we gather only the Teftimonials of fuch eminent Wits as would of courfe defcend to pofterity, and confequently be read without our collection; but we fhall likewife with incredible labour feek out for divers others, which but for this our diligence, could never at the diftance of a few months, appear to the eye of the moft curious. Hereby thou may'ft not only receive the delectation of Variety, but alfo arrive at a more certain judgment, by a grave and circumfpect comparifon of the witneffes with each other, or of each with himfelf. Hence alfo thou wilt be enabled to draw reflections, not only of a critical but of a moral nature, by being let into many particulars of the perfon as well as genius, and of the fortune as well as merit, of our Author: In which, if I relate fome things of little concern peradventure to thee, and fome of as little even to him; I entreat thee to confider how minutely all true criticks and commenta-

tors

tors are wont to infift upon fuch, and how material they feem to themfelves if to none other. Forgive me therefore gentle reader, if (following learned example) I ever and anon become tedious; allow me to take the fame pain to find whether my author were good or bad, well or ill-natured, modeft or arrogant; as another, whether his were fair or brown, fhort or tall, or whether he wore a coat or a caffock?

WE purpofed to begin with his Life, Parentage and Education : but as to thefe, even his Cotemporaries do exceedingly differ. One faith, he was educated at home [1]; another that he was bred abroad at St. *Omer*'s by Jefuits [2]; a third, not at St. *Omer*'s, but at *Oxford* [3]; a fourth, that he had no Univerfity education at all [4]. Thofe who allow him to be bred at home, differ as much concerning his Tutor: One faith, he was kept by his father on purpofe [5]; a fecond, that he was an itinerant prieft [6]; a third, that he was a parfon [7]; one calleth him a fecular clergyman of the church of *Rome* [8]; another, a Monk. [9] As little agree they about his Father; whom one fuppofeth, like the father of *Hefiod*, a tradefman or merchant [10]; another a hufband-man, *&c.* [11]   Nor hath an author been wanting to give our Poet fuch a Father, as *Apuleius* hath to *Plato*, *Iamblicus* to *Pythagoras*, and divers to *Homer*; namely a *Dæmon*: For thus Mr. *Gildon*. [12] " Certain it " is, that his Original is not from *Adam* but the devil, and that he " wanteth nothing but horns and tail to be the exact refemblance of " his infernal father." Finding therefore fuch contrariety of opinions, and (whatever be ours of this fort of generation) not being fond to enter into controverfy, we fhall defer writing the life of our Poet, till authors can determine among themfelves what parents or education he had, or whether he had any education or parents at all ?

1 *Giles Jacob*'s Lives of Poets, vol. 2. in his life.   2 *Dennis*'s reflect. on the Effay on Crit. 3 Dunciad diffected, p. 4.   4 Guardian, N°. 40.   5 *Jacob, ib.*   6 Dunc. diff. *ibid.*   7 Farmer *P.* and his fon, *ibid.* verfe 32.   8 Dunc. diff.   9 Characters of the Times, p. 45.   10. Female Dunciad, pag. ult.   11 Dunc. diffect. 12. Whom Mr. *Curl* (Key to the Dunc. 1ft. edit.) declares to be author of the *Character of Mr. Pope* and his writings, in a letter to a friend, printed for *S. Popping.* 1716. where this paffage is to be found, pag. 10.

Proceed

Proceed we to what is more certain, his Works, tho' not less uncertain the judgments concerning them: beginning with his ESSAY ON CRITICISM, of which hear first the most Ancient of criticks,

Mr. JOHN DENNIS.

a " His precepts are false, or trivial, or both: his thoughts are crude,
" and abortive, his expressions absurd, his numbers harsh, and unmu-
" sical, without cadence, or variety, his rhymes trivial, and common—
" instead of majesty, we have something that is very mean; instead
" of gravity, something that is very boyish: and instead of perspicuity,
" and lucid order, we have but too often obscurity and confusion."
And in another place. — " What rare *Numbers* are here? would not
" one swear this youngster had espoused some antiquated muse, who
" had sued out a divorce from some superannuated sinner upon account
" of impotence, and who being poxt by her former spouse, has got
" the gout in her decrepit age, which makes her *hobble so damna-*
" *bly.*" *a.* No less peremptory is the censure of our hypercritical historian.

Mr. OLDMIXON:

" I dare not say any thing of the Essay on Criticism in verse; but if
" any more curious reader has discover'd in it something *new*, which
" is not in *Dryden*'s prefaces, dedications, and his essay on dramatick
" poetry, not to mention the *French* criticks; I should be very glad
" to have the benefit of the discovery." *b.*

He is followed (as in fame, so in judgment) by the modest and simple-minded

Mr. LEONARD WELSTED;

Who, out of great respect to our poet not naming him, doth yet glance at his essay (together with the Duke of *Buckingham*'s, and the criticisms of *Dryden* and of *Horace*, which he more openly taxeth.) *c.* " As to the numerous treatises, essays, arts, *&c.* both

a. Reflections critical and satyrical on a rhapsody call'd, an Essay on Criticism. Printed for **R. Lintot**. *b.* Essay on Criticism in Prose, 8vo 1728. *c.* Preface to his poems, p. 18, 53.

" in

" in verſe and proſe, that have been written by the moderns on this
" ground work, they do but *hackney the ſame thoughts over again,*
" making them ſtill more *trite.* Moſt of their pieces are nothing but
" a pert, inſipid heap of *common place.* *Horace* has even in his Art of
" poetry thrown out ſeveral things which plainly ſhew, he thought an
" art of poetry was of no uſe, even while he was writing one." To
all which great authorities we can only oppoſe that of

Mr. Addison.

" *d.* The Art of Criticiſm (ſaith he) which was publiſhed ſome months
" ſince, is a maſter-piece in its kind. The obſervations follow one ano-
" ther, like thoſe in *Horace's* art of poetry, without that methodical
" regularity, which would have been requiſite in a proſe writer. They
" are ſome of them *uncommon,* but ſuch as the reader muſt aſſent to,
" when he ſees them explain'd with that eaſe and perſpicuity in
" which they are delivered. As for thoſe which are the *moſt known*
" and the moſt *receiv'd,* they are placed in ſo beautiful a light, and
" illuſtrated with ſuch apt alluſions, that they have in them *all the*
" *graces of novelty :* and make the reader, who was before acquainted
" with them, ſtill more convinc'd of their truth, and ſolidity. And
" here give me leave to mention what Monſieur *Boileau* has ſo well
" enlarged upon, in the preface to his works: That wit, and fine
" writing, doth not conſiſt ſo much in advancing things that are
" *new,* as in giving things that are *known* an agreeable turn. It is
" impoſſible for us who live in the latter ages of the world, to
" make obſervations in criticiſm, morality, or any art or ſcience,
" which have not been touch'd upon by others: we have little elſe
" left us, but to repreſent the *common ſenſe* of mankind in more ſtrong,
" more beautiful, or more uncommon lights. If a reader examines
" *Horace's* art of poetry, he will find but few precepts in it, which he
" may not meet with in *Ariſtotle* ; and which were not *commonly known*
" by all the poets of the *Auguſtan* age. His way of expreſſing, and ap-

---

" plying

" plying them, not his *invention* of them, is what we are chiefly
" to admire.

" *Longinus* in his reflections has given us the same kind of Sublime,
" which he observes in the several passages that occasioned them. I
" cannot but take notice that our *English* Author, has, after the same
" manner, exemplify'd several of his Precepts, in the very precepts
" themselves." He then produces some instances of a particular kind
of beauty in the *Numbers*, and concludes with saying, that " there are
" three poems in our tongue of the same nature, and each a master-
" piece in its kind; The Essay on translated verse, The Essay on the
" Art of Poetry; and the Essay on Criticism.

Of WINDSOR FOREST, positive is the judgment of the affir-
mative

Mr. JOHN DENNIS,

" That it is a wretched rhapsody, *impudently* writ in *emulation* of
" the *Cooper's Hill* of Sir *John Denham*. The Author of it is obscure,
" is ambiguous, is affected, is temerarious, is barbarous." *e.* But the
author of the *Dispensary*

Dr. GARTH

In the preface to his poem of *Claremont*, differs from this opinion:
" Those who have seen those two excellent poems of *Cooper's Hill*, and
" *Windsor-Forest*, the one by Sir *John Denham*, and the other by
" Mr. *Pope*, will shew a great deal of candour, if they approve of this."

Of his EPISTLE of ELOISA, we are told, by the obscure Author
of a " poem called *Sawney*, *(f.)* " That because *Prior*'s Henry and
" *Emma* charm'd the finest tastes, our author writ his *Eloise*, in *oppofi-*
" *tion* to it ; but forgot innocence and virtue. If you *take away her*
" *tender thoughts, and her fierce desires*, all the rest is of no value:" In
which, methinks, his judgment resembled that of a *French* taylor on
a Villa and gardens by the *Thames :* " All this is very fine, but *take away*

---

e. Letters to *B. B.* at the end of the remarks on *Pope's Homer*, 1717. *f.* Printed 1728. pag. 12.

" *the*

" *the river*, and it is good for nothing." But very contrary hereunto, was the judgment of

Mr. PRIOR

himself, saying in his *Alma*, *g*.

> O *Abelard!* ill fated youth,
> Thy tale will justify this truth.
> But well I weet, thy cruel wrong
> Adorns a nobler Poet's song:
> *Dan Pope*, for thy misfortune griev'd,
> With kind concern and skill has weav'd
> A silken web; and ne'er shall fade
> Its colours: gently has he laid
> The mantle o'er thy sad distress,
> And *Venus* shall the texture bless, *&c.*

Come we now to his Translation of the ILIAD, celebrated by numerous pens, yet shall it suffice to mention the indefatigable

Sir RICHARD BLACKMORE, Kt.

Who (tho' otherwise a severe censurer of our author) yet stileth this a *laudable translation. h.* That ready writer

Mr. OLDMIXON,

In his forementioned Essay, frequently commends the same. And the painful

Mr. LEWIS THEOBALD

thus extolls it. *i.* "The spirit of *Homer* breathes all through this transla-
" tion. —— I am in doubt, whether I should most admire the *just-*
" *ness to the original*, or the force, and beauty of the *language*, or the
" founding variety of the *numbers?* But when I find all these meet, it
" puts me in mind of what the poet says of one of his heroes: That

---

g. Alma Cant. 2. *h.* in his Essays, vol. 1. printed for *E. Curl*. *i.* Censor, vol. 2. N°. 33.

" he

" he alone rais'd and flung with ease, a weighty stone, that two com-
" mon men could not lift from the ground; just so, one single person
" has performed in this translation, what I once despaired to have seen
" done by the force of several masterly hands." Indeed the same gentle-
man appears to have chang'd his sentiment, in his *Essay* on the *Art of
sinking in reputation*, where he says thus: " In order to sink in reputa-
" tion, let him take it into his head to descend into *Homer* (let the
" world wonder, as it will, how the devil he got there) and pretend
" to do him into *English*, so his version denote his neglect of the man-
" ner how." Strange Variation! We are told in

Mist's Journal, *June* 8.

" That this Translation of the *Iliad*, was not in all respects conform-
" able to the fine taste of his friend, Mr. *Addison*. Insomuch, that he
" employed a younger muse, in an undertaking of this kind, which he
" supervis'd himself." Whether Mr. *Addison* did find it conform-
able to his taste, or not, best appears from his own testimony the year
following its publication, in these words.

Mr. Addison, *Freeholder*.

k. " When I consider my self as a *British* freeholder, I am in a par-
" ticular manner pleased with the labours of those who have improv'd
" our language, with the translation of old *Greek* and *Latin* authors:——
" We have already most of their Historians in our own tongue, and
" what is more for the honour of our language, it has been taught to
" express with elegance the greatest of their Poets in each nation. The
" illiterate among our countrymen may learn to judge from *Dryden*'s
" *Virgil*, of the most perfect Epic performance. And those parts of
" *Homer* which have been publish'd already by Mr. *Pope*, give us rea-
" son to think that the *Iliad* will appear in *English* with as little dis-
" advantage to that immortal poem."
As to the rest, there is a slight mistake, for this younger *Muse* was

elder: Nor was the gentleman (who is a friend of our author) employ'd by Mr. *Addison* to tranflate it *after* him, fince he faith himfelf that he did it *before.* i. Contrariwife, that Mr. *Addison* ingag'd our author in this work, appeareth by declaration thereof in the preface to the *Iliad,* printed fome years before his death, and by his own letters of *Oct.* 26. and *Nov.* 2. 1713. where he declares it his opinion that no other perfon was equal to it.

Next comes his SHAKESPEAR on the ftage. " Let him (quoth one, whom I take to be

Mr. THEOBALD) *Mift, March* 30, 1728.

" publifh fuch an author as he has leaft ftudied, and forget to difcharge " even the dull duty of an editor. In this project let him lend the " bookfeller *his name,* (for a competent fum of money tho') *to pro-* " *mote the credit* of an *exorbitant fubfcription.*" Gentle reader, be pleas'd but to caft thine eye on the PROPOSAL below quoted, and on what follows (fome months after the former affertion) in the fame Journalift of *June* 8. " The bookfeller propos'd the book " by fubfcription, and rais'd fome thoufands of pounds for the fame : " I believe the gentleman did *not fhare in the profits of this extrava-* " *gant Subfcription.*

" After the *Iliad,* he undertook (faith

MIST's JOURNAL, *June* 8.)

" the fequel of that work, the *Odyffey:* and having fecur'd the fuc- " cefs by a numerous fubfcription, he imployed fome *Underlings* to " perform what, *according to his propofals,* fhould come from his *own* " *hands.*" To which heavy charge we can in truth oppofe nothing but the words of

Mr. POPE's PROPOSALS for the ODYSSEY,

(printed by *J. Watts, Jan.* 10, 1724.) " I take this occafion to de-

i. *Vid.* Pref. to Mr. *Tickel's* Tranflation of the firft Book of the Iliad, 4*to,*

" clare

" clare that the SUBSCRIPTION for SHAKESPEAR *belongs wholly to*
" Mr. *Tonson:* And that the future Benefit of THIS PROPOSAL
" is not folely for my own ufe, but for that *of Two of my friends,*
" who have *affifted me in this work.*" But thefe very gentlemen are
extolled above our Poet himfelf, by another of *Mift's* Journals, *March*
30, 1728, faying, " that he would not advife Mr. *Pope* to try the
." experiment again, of getting a great part of a book done by *Affift-*
" *ants,* leaft thofe *extraneous parts* fhould unhappily afcend to the *fub-*
" *lime,* and retard the declenfion of the whole." Behold! thefe Un-
derlings are become good writers!

If any fay, that before the faid propofals were printed, the Sub-
fcription was begun without declaration of fuch Affiftance; verily thofe
who fet it on foot, or (as their term is) fecur'd it, to wit the right
Honourable the LORD VISCOUNT HARCOURT, were he living
would teftify, and the right Honourable the LORD BATHURST
now living doth teftify, that the fame is a Falfhood.

Sorry I am, that perfons profeffing to be learned, or of whatever
rank of Authors, fhould either falfely tax, or be falfely taxed. Yet let
us, who are only reporters, be impartial in our citations and proceed.

MIST'S JOURNAL, *June* 8.

" Mr. *Addifon* rais'd this Author from obfcurity, obtain'd him the
" acquaintance and friendfhip of the *whole body* of our *nobility,* and
" transferr'd his powerful interefts with thofe great men to this rifing
" Bard, who frequently levied by that means unufual contributions
" on the publick.—No fooner was his body lifelefs, but this author, re-
" viving his refentment, libell'd the memory of his departed friend, and
" what was ftill more heinous, made the fcandal publick." Grievous
the accufation! unknown the accufer! the perfon accufed no witnefs in
his own caufe, the perfon in whofe regard accus'd, dead! But if there
be living any one nobleman whofe friendfhip, yea any one gentleman
whofe fubfcription Mr. *Addifon* procur'd to our author; let him ftand

forth, that truth may appear! *Amicus Plato, amicus Socrates, sed magis amica veritas.* But in verity the whole story of the libel is a *Lye*; Witnefs thofe perfons of integrity, who feveral years before Mr. *Addifon*'s deceafe, did fee and approve of the faid verfes, in no wife a libel but a friendly rebuke, fent privately in our author's own hand to Mr. *Addifon* himfelf, and never made publick till by *Curl* their own bookfeller in his mifcellanies, 12*mo.* 1727. One name alone which I am authorized here to declare, will fufficiently evince this truth, that of the Right Honourable the EARL of BURLINGTON.

Next is he taxed of a crime, (with *fome authors* I doubt, more heinous than any in *morality*) to wit plagiarifm, from the inventive and quaint-conceited

JAMES MOORE SMITH, Gent.

1. " Upon reading the third volume of *Pope*'s Mifcellanies, I found " five lines which I thought excellent, and happening to praife them, " a gentleman produced a modern comedy (the *Rival Modes*) pub- " lifhed laft year, where were the fame verfes to a tittle, (fpeaking of " women.)

> See how the world its pretty flaves rewards!
> A youth of frolicks, an old age of cards:
> Fair to no purpofe; artful to no end;
> Young without lovers; old without a friend;
> A fop their paffion, but their prize a fot;
> Alive, ridiculous; and dead, forgot.

" Thefe gentlemen are undoubtedly the firft plagiaries that pre- " tended to make a reputation by ftealing from a man's works in his " own life-time, and out of a publick print." Let us join to this what is written by the author of the *Rival Modes,* the faid Mr. *James Moore Smith,* in a letter to our author himfelf, (who had informed him, a month before that play was acted, *Jan.* 27, 1726-7. that thefe verfes which he had before given him leave to infert in it, would

---

1. Daily Journal, *March* 18, 1728.

be

be known for his, some copies being got abroad) " He desires never-
" theless, that since the Lines had been read in his Comedy to se-
" veral, Mr. *P.* would not deprive it of them, *&c.*" Surely if we add
the testimonies of the Lord BOLINGBROKE, of the Lady to whom
the said verses were originally addrest, of *Hugh Bethel,* Esq; and
others who knew them as our author's long before the said gentle-
man composed his play; It is hoped, the ingenuous that affect not
error, will rectify their opinion by the suffrage of so honourable
personages.

And yet followeth another charge, insinuating no less than his
enmity both to church and state, which could come from no other
Informer than the said

Mr. JAMES MOORE SMITH.

m. " The *Memoirs of a Parish clark* was a very dull and unjust
" abuse of an excellent person who wrote in defence of our *Religion*
" and *Constitution*; and who has been dead many years." Verily
this also seemeth most untrue; it being known to divers that these
memoirs were written at the seat of the Lord *Harcourt* in *Oxford-
shire* before that excellent person (Bish. *Burnet's*) death, and many
years before the appearance of that History of which they are pre-
tended to be an abuse. Most true it is, that Mr. *Moore* had such a
design, and was himself the man who prest Dr. *Arburthnot* and
Mr. *Pope* to assist him therein: and that he borrow'd those memoirs
of our author when that history came forth, with intention to turn
them to such abuse. But being able to obtain from our author but
one single Hint, and either changing his mind or having more mind
than ability, he contented himself to keep the said memoirs and read
them as his own to all his acquaintance. A noble person there is, into
whose company Mr. *Pope* once chanced to introduce him, who well
remembreth the conversation of Mr. *Moore* to have turned upon the
" contempt he had for the work of that reverend prelate, and how

m. Daily Journal, *April* 3, 1728.

" full

" full he was of a defign he declared *himfelf* to have, of expofing it."
This noble perfon is the EARL of PETERBOROUGH.

Here in truth fhould we crave pardon of all the forefaid right ho-
nourable and worthy perfonages, for having mention'd them in the
fame page with fuch weekly riff-raff railers and rhymers; but that
we had their own ever-honour'd commands for the fame, and that
they are introduc'd not as witneffes in the controverfy, but as wit-
neffes that cannot be controverted; not to difpute, but to decide.

Certain it is, that dividing our writers into two claffes, of fuch who
were acquaintance, and of fuch who were ftrangers to our author;
the former are thofe who fpeak well, and the other thofe who fpeak
evil of him. Of the firft clafs, the moft noble

JOHN Duke of BUCKINGHAM

fums up his perfonal character in thefe lines,

> *n.* And yet fo wond'rous, fo fublime a thing
> As the great Iliad, fcarce fhould make me fing,
> Unlefs I juftly could at once commend
> A *good companion*, and as *firm a friend*;
> One *moral*, or a meer *well-natur'd deed*,
> Can all defert in fciences exceed.

So alfo is he decypher'd by the honourable

SIMON HARCOURT.

> *o.* Say, wond'rous youth, what column wilt thou chufe?
> What laurel'd arch, for thy triumphant Mufe?
> Tho' each great Ancient court thee to his fhrine,
> Tho' ev'ry laurel thro' the dome be thine,
> Go to the *good and juft*, an awful train!
> *Thy foul's delight* ———

Recorded in like manner for his virtuous difpofition, and gentle

---

n. Verfes to Mr. *P.* on his tranflation of *Homer.*   *o.* Poem prefixt to his works.

bearing

bearing, by the ingenious

Mr. WALTER HART,

in this Apoſtrophe.

> *p.* O! ever worthy, ever crown'd with praiſe!
> Bleſt in thy *life*, and bleſt in all thy *lays.*
> Add, that the Siſters ev'ry thought refine,
> And ev'n thy *life* be *faultleſs* as thy line.
> Yet envy ſtill with fiercer rage purſues,
> Obſcures the *virtue*, and defames the Muſe:
> A ſoul like thine, in pain, in grief reſign'd,
> Views with vain ſcorn the malice of mankind.

The witty and moral Satyriſt

Dr. EDWARD YOUNG,

wiſhing ſome check to the corruptions and evil manners of the times,
calls out upon our poet, to undertake a taſk ſo worthy of his virtue.

> *q.* Why ſlumbers *Pope*, who leads the Muſes' train,
> Nor hears that *Virtue*, which he *loves*, complain?

To the ſame tune alſo ſingeth that learned Clerk of *Suffolk*

Mr. WILLIAM BROOME,

> *r.* Thus, nobly riſing in fair *virtue's cauſe*,
> From thy own *life* tranſcribe th' *unerring laws.*

And divers more, with which we will not tire the reader.

Let us rather recreate thee by turning to the other ſide, and ſhewing his character drawn by thoſe with whom he never convers'd, and
whoſe countenances he could not know, tho' turned againſt him: Firſt
again commencing with the high-voiced, and never-enough-quoted

JOHN DENNIS;

Who in his reflections on the Eſſay on Criticiſm thus deſcribeth him.

---

p. In his poems, printed for *B. Lintott*.   *q.* Univerſal Paſſion Satyr 1.   *r.* In his
poems, and at the end of the Odyſſey.

" A little

" A little affected hypocrite, who has nothing in his mouth but
" candour, truth, friendſhip, good nature, humanity, and magnani-
" mity. H is ſo great a lover of falſhood, that whenever he has a
" mind o calumniate his cotemporaries, he upbraids them with
" ſome defect which is juſt *contrary to ſome good quality*, for which all
" their *friends and their acquaintance* commend them. He ſeems to
" have a particular pique to *People of Quality*, and authors of that
" rank——He muſt derive his religion from St. *Omer's.*"——But in the
character of Mr. *P.* and his writings, (printed by *S. Popping* 1716,) he
ſaith, " tho' he is a Profeſſor of the worſt religion, yet he *laughs at*
" *it*; but that, " neverthleſs, he is a *virulent Papiſt*; and yet a *Pil-*
" *lar* for the *Church of England.*"   Of both which opinions

Mr. THEOBALD

ſeems alſo to be; declaring in *Miſt*'s Journal of *June* 22, 1728:
" That if he is not ſhrewdly abus'd, he hath made it his practice to
" cackle to *both parties* in their own ſentiments." But, as to his *Pique*
againſt *people of quality*, the ſame Journaliſt doth not agree, but ſaith
(May 8, 1728.) he had by ſome means or other the *acquaintance*
and *friendſhip* of the *whole body of our nobility.*"

However contradictory this may appear, Mr. *Dennis* and *Gildon* in
the character laſt cited, make it all plain, by aſſuring us: " That he
" is a creature that reconciles all contradictions: he is a beaſt, and a
" man: a Whig, and a Tory, a writer (at one and the ſame time) of
" Guardians and Examiners; an aſſertor of liberty, and of the diſpen-
" ſing power of kings; a jeſuitical profeſſor of truth, a baſe and a
" foul pretender to candour." So that, upon the whole account, we
muſt conclude him either to have been a great hypocrite, or a very
honeſt man; a terrible impoſer upon both parties, or very moderate to
either?

Be it, as to the judicious reader ſhall ſeem good. Sure it is, he
is little favour'd of certain authors; whoſe wrath is perillous: For one
declares he ought to have a *price ſet on his head* and to be hunted down

as

as a *wild beaſt*: Another expreſly, that it will be well if he *eſcape with his life*: r One deſires he wou'd *cut his own throat* or *hang him-ſelf*: s Paſquin ſeem'd rather inclined it ſhou'd be done by the govern-ment, repreſenting him ingag'd in grievous deſigns with a Lord of Parliament, then under proſecution: t. Mr. *Dennis* himſelf hath writ-ten to a *Miniſter*, that he is one of the moſt *dangerous perſons in this kingdom*: u. A third gives information of *Treaſon* diſcover'd in his poem: x. Mr. *Curl* boldly ſupplies an imperfect verſe with *Kings* and *Princeſſes*; y. and another yet bolder, publiſhes at length the Two moſt SACRED NAMES in this Nation as members of the Dunciad! z.

This is prodigious! yet is it no leſs ſtrange, that in the midſt of theſe invectives his enemies have (I know not how) born teſtimony to ſome merit in him:

Mr. THEOBALD,

in cenſuring his *Shakeſpear* declares, " he has ſo great an *eſteem* for " Mr. *Pope*, and ſo high an *opinion* of his *genius*, and *excellencies*; " That notwithſtanding he profeſſes a *veneration almoſt riſing to Idola-* " *try* for the writings of this inimitable poet, he would be very loth " even to do *him* juſtice, at the expence of that *other gentleman's* cha-" racter. a.

Mr. CHARLES GILDON,

After having violently attack'd him in many pieces, at laſt came to wiſh from his heart, " That Mr. *Pope* wou'd be prevailed upon to " give us *Ovid*'s Epiſtles by his hand: for it is certain we ſee the ori-" ginal of *Sapho* to *Phaon* with much more life and likeneſs in his

r. *Theobald*, Letter in Miſt's Journal, *June* 22, 1728. r. *Smedley*, Pref. to Gullive-riana, p. 16. s. Gulliveriana, pag. 332. t. Anno 1723. u. This preſent year.
x. Pag. 6, 7. of the Preface to a Book intiuled, a Collection of all the Letters, Eſſays, Verſes, and Advertiſements, occaſion'd by *Pope* and *Swift*'s Miſcellanies, printed for *A. Moore*, 8vo. 1728. y. Key to the Dunc. 3d edit. p. 18. z. A Liſt of perſons, &c. at the end of the foremen-tion'd Collection of all the Letters, Eſſays, &c. a. Introduction to his *Shakeſpear* reſtor'd, *in quarto*, pag. 3.

D   verſion,

" verſion, than in that of Sir *Car Scrope*. And this (he adds) is the
" more to be wiſh'd, becauſe in the *Engliſh* tongue we have ſcarce
" any thing truly and naturally written upon Love [b]." He alſo, in
taxing Sir *Richard Blackmore* for his Heterodox opinions of *Homer*,
challengeth him to anſwer what Mr. *Pope* hath ſaid in his preface to
that Poet. One who takes the name of

H. STANHOPE,

the maker of certain verſes to *Duncan Campbell*, [c] in that poem
which is wholly a ſatyr on Mr. *Pope*, confeſſeth,

> 'Tis true, if fineſt notes alone cou'd ſhow
> ('Tun'd juſtly high, or regularly low)
> That we ſhould fame to theſe meer vocals give;
> *Pope*, more than we can offer, ſhou'd receive:
> For when ſome gliding river is his theme,
> His lines run ſmoother than the ſmootheſt ſtream, &c.

Mr. THOMAS COOKE,

After much blemiſhing our author's *Homer*, cryeth out,

> But in his other works what beauties ſhine?
> While ſweeteſt Muſic dwells in ev'ry line.
> Theſe he admir'd, on theſe he ſtamp'd his praiſe,
> And bade them live to brighten future days. [d]

MIST's JOURNAL, *June* 8, 1728.

Altho' he ſays, " the ſmooth Numbers of the Dunciad are all that
" recommend it, nor has it any other merit," Yet in that ſame paper
hath theſe words: " The author is allowed to be a perfect maſter
" of an eaſy, and elegant verſification: *In all his works*, we find the
" moſt *happy turns*, and *natural ſimiles*, wonderfully ſhort and thick
" ſown." The Eſſay on the Dunciad alſo owns, pag. 25. it is very full
of *beautiful Images.*

---

[b]. Commentary on the Duke of *Buckingham's* Eſſay, 8°. 1721, pag. 97, 98.   [c]. Printed under the Title of the Progreſs of Dulneſs, 12°. 1728.   [d]. Battle of Poets, *fol.* pag. 15.

.Mr.

Mr. GILDON and DENNIS

in the moſt furious of all their works, (the forecited Character, p. 5.) do jointly confeſs "That ſome men, *of good underſtanding*, value him " for his rhymes:" And pag. 17. " That he has got, like Mr. *Bayes* " in the Rehearſal, (that is like Mr. *Dryden)* a notable knack of rhym- " ing and writing ſmooth verſe."

To the *Succeſs* of all his pieces, they do unanimouſly give teſtimo- ny: But it is ſufficient, *inſtar omnium*, to behold this laſt great Critick ſorely lamenting it, even from the Eſſay on Criticiſm to this Day of the Dunciad! " A moſt notorious inſtance! (quoth he) of the " depravity of genius and taſte, the *Approbation* this Eſſay meets " with! *e.* — I can ſafely affirm, that I never attack'd any of theſe " writings, unleſs they had *Succeſs*, infinitely beyond their merit. *f.* — " This, tho' an empty, has been a *popular* ſcribler: The Epidemic " madneſs of the times has given him *reputation*" *g.* — If after the cruel treatment ſo many extraordinary men *(Spenſer*, Lord *Bacon, Ben. Johnſon, Milton, Butler, Otway*, and others) have received from this " country, for theſe laſt hundred years; I ſhou'd ſhift the ſcene, and " ſhew all that penury chang'd at once to riot and profuſeneſs: " and *h.* more ſquander'd away upon *one objeEt* than wou'd have ſa- " tisfy'd the greater part of thoſe extraordinary men: The reader to " whom this one creature ſhould be unknown, wou'd fancy him a " prodigy of art and nature, would believe that all the great qualities " of theſe perſons were centred in him alone—— But if I ſhould " venture to aſſure him, that the PEOPLE of ENGLAND had made " *ſuch* a choice—The reader would either believe me a *malicious enemy*,

---

e. Dennis Pref. to the Reflect. on the Eſſay on Crit.   *f.* Pref. to his Rem. on *Homer.*   *g.* Ibid. *(h.)* What this vaſt ſum was, Mr. DENNIS himſelf in another place informs us (pref. to his Remarks on the Rape of the Lock, p. 15.) to wit, *a hundred a year.* Whereby we ſee how great he ſuppoſed the moderation of thoſe extraordinary men; even greater than that of his friend Mr. *Giles Jacob*, who ſaid of himſelf

One hundred pounds a year, I think wou'd do For me, if ſingle—— Or if marry'd, two.

" and

" and *flanderer*; or that the reign of the laſt (Queen *Ann's*) *Mini-*
" *ſtry*, was deſign'd by fate to encourage *Fools*. *i.*

However, leſt we imagine our Author's Succeſs was conſtant and
univerſal, they acquaint us of certain works in a leſs degree of repute,
whereof (altho' own'd by others) yet do they aſſure us he is the
writer. Of this ſort Mr. DENNIS aſcribes to him *k.* *Two Farces*, whoſe
names he does not tell, but aſſures us *there is not one jeſt in them*; and
an Imitation of *Horace*, whoſe title he does not mention, but aſſures
us, *it is much more execrable than all his works*. *l.*   The DAILY
JOURNAL, *May* 11, 1728. aſſures us, " he is below *Tom Durfey* in
" the *Drama*, becauſe (as that writer thinks) *the Marriage Hater*
" *match'd* and the *Boarding School* are better than the *What d'ye call*
" *it*; Which is not Mr. *P*'s but Mr. *Gay*'s. Mr. GILDON aſ-
ſures us, in his *New Rehearſal* printed 1714, pag. 48, " that he was
" writing a *Play* of the Lady *Jane Gray*; But it afterwards prov'd
to be Mr. *Rowe*'s. The ſame Mr. *Gildon* and *Dennis* aſſure us, " he
" wrote a pamphlet called Dr. *Andrew Tripe*; *m.* which prov'd
to be one Dr. *Wagſtaff*'s. Mr. THEOBALD aſſures us, in *Miſt*
" of the 27th of *April*, " That the treatiſe of the *Profund* is very
" dull, and that Mr. *Pope* is the author of it :" The writer of *Gul-*
liveriana is of another opinion, and ſays " the whole or great-
" eſt part of the merit of this treatiſe muſt and can only be aſ-
" cribed to *Gulliver*. *n.* [Here gentle reader cannot I but ſmile at the
ſtrange blindneſs and poſitiveneſs of men, knowing the ſaid treatiſe to
appertain to none other but to me, *Martinus Scriblerus*.}

Laſtly we are aſſured, in *Miſt* of *June* 8. " That his own *Plays* and
" *Farces* wou'd better have adorn'd the Dunciad, than thoſe of Mr.
" *Theobald*: for he had neither genius for Tragedy, or Comedy :"
Which whether true or not, is not eaſy to judge; in as much as he
hath attempted neither.

i. Rem. on Hom. pag. 8, 9.   *k.* Rem. on Hom. p. 8.   *l.* Charact. of Mr. *P.* p. 7.
m. Ibid. p. 6.   *n. Gulliveriana*, pag. 336.

But

But from all that hath been said, the difcerning reader will collect, that it little avail'd our author to have any Candour, fince when he declar'd he did not write for others, it was not credited: As little to have any Modefty, fince when he declin'd writing in any way himfelf, the prefumption of others was imputed to him. If he *fingly* enterpris'd one great work, he was tax'd of Boldnefs and Madnefs to a prodigy: *o.* if he took *affiftants* in another, it was complain'd of and reprefented as a great injury to the public. *p.* The loftieft Heroicks, the loweft ballads, treatifes againft the ftate or church, fatyr on lords, and ladies, raillery on wits and authors, fquabbles with bookfellers, or even full and true accounts of monfters, poyfons, and murders: of any hereof was there nothing fo good, nothing fo bad, which hath not at one or other feafon been to him afcribed. If it bore no author's name, then lay he concealed; if it did, he father'd it on that author to be yet better concealed. If it refembled any of his ftyles then was it evident; if it did not, then difguis'd he it on fet purpofe. Yea, even direct oppofitions in religion, principles, and politicks, have equally been fuppofed in him inherent. Surely a moft rare, and fingular character! of which let the reader make what he can.

Doubtlefs moft Commentators wou'd hence take occafion to turn all to their author's advantage; and from the teftimony of his very enemies wou'd affirm, That his Capacity was boundlefs, as well as his Imagination; That he was a perfect mafter of all Styles, and all Arguments; And that there was in thofe times no other writer, in any kind, of any degree of excellence fave he himfelf. But as this is not our own fentiment, we fhall determine on nothing; but leave thee, gentle reader! to fteer thy judgment equally between various opinions, and to chufe whether thou wilt believe the Teftimonies of thofe who knew him, or of thofe who knew him not?

---

o. *Burnet* Homerides, pag. 1. of his Tranflation of the *Iliad*.
p. The *London,* and *Mift*'s Journals, on his Undertaking of the *Odyffey*.

MARTINUS

MARTINUS SCRIBLERUS,

OF THE

POEM.

THIS Poem, as it celebrateth the moſt grave and antient of things, Chaos, Night and Dulneſs, ſo is it of the moſt grave and antient kind. *Homer*, (ſaith *Ariſtotle*) was the firſt who gave the *Form*, and (ſaith *Horace*) who adapted the *Meaſure*, to heroic poeſy. But even before this, may be rationally preſumed from what the antients have left written, was a piece by *Homer* compoſed, of like nature and matter with this of our Poet. For of Epic ſort it appeareth to have been, yet of matter ſurely not unpleaſant, witneſs what is reported of it by the learned Arcbiſhop *Euſtathius*, in Odyſſ. κ. And accordingly *Ariſtotle* in his poetic, chap. 4. doth further ſet forth, that as the Iliad and Odyſſey gave example to Tragedy, ſo did this poem to Comedy its firſt Idæa.

From theſe authors alſo it ſhou'd ſeem, that the Hero or chief perſonage of it was no leſs *obſcure*, and his *underſtanding* and *ſentiments* no leſs quaint and ſtrange (if indeed not more ſo) than any of the actors in our poem. MARGITES was the name of this perſonage, whom Antiquity recordeth to have been *Dunce the Firſt*; and ſurely from what we hear of him, not unworthy to be the root of ſo ſpreading a tree, and ſo numerous a poſterity. The poem therefore celebrating him, was properly and abſolutely a *Dunciad*; which tho' now unhappily loſt, yet is its nature ſufficiently known by the infallible tokens aforeſaid. And thus it doth appear, that the firſt Dunciad was the firſt

Epic

Epic poem, written by *Homer* himself, and anterior even to the Iliad or Odyssey.

Now forasmuch as our Poet had translated those two famous works of *Homer* which are yet left; he did conceive it in some sort his duty to imitate that also which was lost: And was therefore induced to bestow on it the same Form which *Homer*'s is reported to have had, namely that of Epic poem, with a title also framed after the antient *Greek* manner, to wit, that of *Dunciad*.

Wonderful it is, that so few of the moderns have been stimulated to attempt some Dunciad! Since in the opinion of the multitude, it might cost less pain and oil, than an imitation of the greater Epic. But possible it is also that on due reflection, the maker might find it easier to paint a *Charlemagne*, a *Brute* or a *Godfry*, with just pomp and dignity heroic, than a *Margites*, a *Codrus*, a *Flecknoe*, or a *Tibbald*.

We shall next declare the occasion and the cause which moved our Poet to this particular work. He lived in those days, when (after providence had permitted the Invention of Printing as a scourge for the Sins of the learned) Paper also became so cheap, and printers so numerous, that a deluge of authors cover'd the land: Whereby not only the peace of the honest unwriting subject was daily molested, but unmerciful demands were made of his applause, yea of his money, by such as would neither earn the one, or deserve the other: At the same time, the Liberty of the Press was so unlimited, that it grew dangerous to refuse them either: For they would forthwith publish slanders unpunish'd, the authors being anonymous; nay the immediate publishers thereof lay sculking under the wings of an Act of Parliament, assuredly intended for better purposes.

Now our author living in those times, did conceive it an endeavour well worthy an honest satyrist, to dissuade the dull and punish the malicious, *the only way that was left*. In that public-spirited view he laid the plan of this Poem, as the greatest service he was capable

(without

(without much hurt or being flain) to render his dear country. Firſt, taking things from their original, he confidereth the Caufes creative of fuch authors, namely *Dulneſs* and *Poverty*; the one born with them, the other contracted, by neglect of their proper talent thro' felf conceit of greater abilities. This truth he wrapp'd in an *Allegory* (as the conſtitution of Epic poefy requires) and feigns, that one of thefe Goddeſſes had taken up her abode with the other, and that they jointly infpir'd all fuch writers and fuch works. He proceedeth to fhew the *qualities* they beſtow on thefe authors, and the *effects* they produce: Then the *materials* or *ſtock* with which they furnifh them, and (above all) that *ſelf-opinion* which caufeth it to feem to themfelves vaſtly greater than it is, and is the prime motive of their fetting up in this fad and forry merchandize. The great power of thefe Goddeſſes acting in alliance (whereof as the one is the mother of induſtry, fo is the other of plodding) was to be exemplify'd in fome *one*, *great* and *remarkable action*. And none cou'd be more fo than that which our poet hath chofen, the introduction of the loweſt diverfions of the rabble in *Smithfield* to be the entertainment of the court and town; or in other words, the Action of the Dunciad is the Removal of the Imperial feat of Dulneſs from the City to the polite world; as that of the Æneid is the Removal of the empire of *Troy* to *Latium*. But as *Homer*, finging only the *Wrath* of *Achilles*, yet includes in his poem the whole hiſtory of the *Trojan* war, in like manner our author hath drawn into this fingle action the whole hiſtory of Dulneſs and her children. To this end fhe is reprefented at the very opening of the poem, taking a view of her forces, which are diſtinguifh'd into thefe three kinds, Party writers, dull poets, and wild criticks.

A *Perſon* muſt be fix'd upon to fupport this action, who (to agree with the faid defign) muſt be fuch an one as is capable of being all three. This *phantom* in the poet's mind, muſt have a *name:* He feeks for one who hath been concerned in the *Journals*, written

bad

bad *Plays* or *Poems*, and publifhed low *Criticifms:* He finds his name to be *Tibbald*, and he becomes of courfe the Hero of the poem.

The *Fable* being thus according to beft example one and entire, as contain'd in the propofition; the *Machinary* is a continued chain of Allegories, fetting forth the whole power, miniftry, and empire of Dulnefs, extended thro' her fubordinate inftruments, in all her various operations.

This is branched into *Epifodes*, each of which hath its Moral apart, tho' all conducive to the main end. The crowd affembled in the fecond book demonftrates the defign to be more extenfive than to bad poets only, and that we may expect other Epifodes, of the Patrons, Encouragers, or Paymafters of fuch authors, as occafion fhall bring them forth. And the third book, if well confider'd, feemeth to embrace the whole world. Each of the Games relateth to fome or other vile clafs of writers. The firft concerneth the Plagiary, to whom he giveth the name of *More*; the fecond the libellous Novellift, whom he ftyleth *Eliza*; the third the flattering Dedicator; the fourth the bawling Critick or noify Poet; the fifth the dark and dirty Party-writer; and fo of the reft, affigning to each fome *proper name* or other, fuch as he cou'd find.

As for the *Characters*, the publick hath already acknowledged how juftly they are drawn: The manners are fo depicted, and the fentiments fo peculiar to thofe to whom applied, that furely to transfer them to any other, or wifer, perfonages, wou'd be exceeding difficult. And certain it is, that every perfon concerned, being confulted apart, will readily own the refemblance of every portrait, his own excepted.

The Defcriptions are fingular; the Comparifons vety quaint; the Narration various, yet of one colour. The purity and chaftity of Diction is fo preferved, that in the places moft fufpicious not the *words* but only the *images* have been cenfured, and yet are thofe images no other than have been fanctified by antient and claffical authority (tho' as was the manner of thofe good times, not fo curioufly wrapped

E   up)

up) yea and commented upon by moft grave doctors, and approved criticks.

As it beareth the name of Epic, it is thereby fubjected to fuch fevere indifpenfable rules as are laid on all Neotericks, a ftrict imitation of the antient; infomuch that any deviation accompanied with whatever poetic beauties, hath always been cenfured by the found critick. How exact that Imitation hath been in this piece, appeareth not only by its general ftructure, but by particular allufions infinite, many whereof have efcaped both the commentator and poet himfelf; yea divers by his exceeding diligence are fo alter'd and interwoven with the reft, that feveral have already been, and more will be, by the ignorant abufed, as altogether and originally his own.

In a word, the whole poem proveth itfelf to be the work of our Author when his faculties were in full vigour and perfection: at that exact time of life when years have ripened the judgment, without diminifhing the imagination; which by good criticks is held to be punctually at *forty*. For, at that feafon it was that *Virgil* finifhed his *Georgics*; and Sir *Richard Blackmore* at the like age compofing his *Arthurs*, declared the fame to be the very *Acme* and pitch of life for Epic poefy: tho' fince he hath altered it to *fixty*, * the year in which he publifhed his *Alfred*. True it is, that the talents for Criticifm, namely fmartnefs, quick cenfure, vivacity of remark, certainty of affeveration, indeed all but acerbity, feem rather the gifts of Youth than of riper age: But it is far otherwife in *Poetry*; witnefs the works of Mr. *Rymer* and Mr. *Dennis*, who beginning with criticifm, became afterwards fuch Poets as no age hath parallel'd. With good reafon therefore did our author chufe to write his *Effay* on that fubject at twenty, and referve for his maturer years, this great and wonderful work of the *Dunciad*.

---

* See his Effay on Heroic poetry.

DUN-

DUNCIADOS PERIOCHA:

O R,

ARGUMENTS to the BOOKS.

BOOK the FIRST.

THE Propofition of the fubject. The Invocation, and the Infcription. Then the Original of the great empire of *Dulnefs*, and caufe of the continuance thereof. The beloved feat of the Goddefs is defcribed, with her chief attendants and officers, her functions, operations, and effects. Then the poem hafts into the midft of things, prefenting her on the evening of a Lord Mayor's day, revolving the long fucceffion of her fons, and the glories paft, and to come. She fixes her eye on *Tibbald* to be the inftrument of that great event which is the fubject of the poem. He is defcribed penfive in his ftudy, giving up the caufe, and apprehending the period of her empire from the old age of the prefent monarch *Settle*. Wherefore debating whether to betake himfelf to law or politicks, he raifes an altar of proper books, and (making firft his folemn prayer and declaration) purpofes thereon to facrifice all his unfuccefsful writings. As the pyle is kindled, the Goddefs beholding the flame from her feat, flies in perfon and puts it out, by cafting upon it the poem of *Thule*. She forthwith reveals her felf to him, tranfports him to her Temple, unfolds all her arts, and initiates him into her myfteries; then announcing the death of *Settle* that night, anoints, and proclaims him Succeffor.

BOOK the SECOND.

THE King being proclaimed, the folemnity is graced with pub-
lick Games and fports of various kinds; (not inftituted by the
Hero, as by *Æneas* in *Virgil*, but for greater honour by the Goddefs in
perfon; in like manner as the games *Pythia, Ifthmia, &c.* were anciently
faid to be by the Gods, and as *Thetis* herfelf appearing according to
Homer Odyff. 24. propofed the prizes in honour of her fon *Achilles*.
Hither flock the Poets and Criticks, attended (as is but juft) with their
Patrons and Book-fellers. The Goddefs is firft pleafed for her difport
to propofe games to the latter, and fetteth up the phantom of a poet
which the bookfellers contend to overtake. The races defcribed, with
their divers accidents: Next, the game for a Poetefs: Afterwards the
exercifes for the *Poets*, of Tickling, Vociferating, Diving: the firft holds
forth the arts and practices of Dedicators, the fecond of Difputants and
fuftian poets, the third of profund, dark, and dirty authors. Laftly,
for the *Criticks*, the Goddefs propofes (with great propriety) an ex-
ercife not of their parts but their patience; in hearing the works of
two voluminous authors, one in verfe and the other in profe, delibe-
rately read, without fleeping: The various effects of which, with the
feveral degrees and manners of their operation, are here moft lively
fet forth: Till the whole number, not of criticks only, but of fpecta-
tors, actors, and all prefent fall faft afleep, which naturally and ne-
ceffarily ends the games.

BOOK the THIRD.

AFTER the other perfons are difpofed in their proper places of
reft, the Goddefs tranfports the King to her Temple, and
there lays him to flumber with his head on her lap; a pofition of mar-
vellous virtue, which caufes all the vifions of wild enthufiafts, pro-
jectors,

jectors, politicians, inamorato's, castle-builders, chymists and poets. He is immediately carry'd on the wings of fancy to the *Elizian* shade, where on the banks of *Lethe* the souls of the dull are dip'd by *Bavius*, before their entrance into this world. There he is met by the ghost of *Settle*, and by him made acquainted with the wonders of the place, and with those which he is himself destin'd to perform. He takes him to a *Mount of Vision*, from whence he shews him the past triumphs of the empire of Dulness, then the present, and lastly the future. How small a part of the world was ever conquered by *Science*, how soon those conquests were stop'd, and those very nations again reduced to her dominion. Then distinguishing the Island of *Great Britain*, shews by what aids, and by what persons, it shall be forthwith brought to her empire. These he causes to pass in review before his eyes, describing each by his proper figure, character, and qualifications. On a sudden the Scene shifts, and a vast number of miracles and prodigies appear, utterly surprizing and unknown to the King himself, till they are explained to be the wonders of his own reign now commencing. On this subject *Settle* breaks into a congratulation, yet not unmix'd with concern, that his own times were but the types of these; He prophecies how first the nation shall be overrun with farces, opera's, shows; and the throne of Dulness advanced over both the Theatres: Then how her sons shall preside in the seats of arts and sciences, till in conclusion all shall return to their original Chaos: A scene, of which the present Action of the Dunciad is but a Type or Foretaste, giving a Glimpse or *Pisgah-sight* of the promis'd Fulness of her Glory; the Accomplishment whereof will, in all probability, hereafter be the Theme of many other and greater Dunciads.

THE

THE

DUNCIAD,

IN

THREE BOOKS,

WITH

Notes Variorum.

NEMO ME IMPVNE LACESSIT

THE DUNCIAD.

BOOK the FIRST.

BOOKS and the Man I sing, the first who brings
The Smithfield Muses to the Ear of Kings.

F   We

Say great Patricians! (since your selves inspire

These wond'rous works; so Jove and Fate require)

5 Say from what cause, in vain decry'd and curst,

Still Dunce second reigns like Dunce the first?

In eldest time, e'er mortals writ or read,

Ee'r Pallas issued from the Thund'rers head,

Dulness o'er all possess'd her antient right,

10 Daughter of Chaos and eternal Night:

Fate in their dotage this fair idiot gave,

Gross as her sire, and as her mother grave,

REMARKS.

We remit this Ignorant to the first lines of the *Æneid*; assuring him, that *Virgil* there speaketh not of himself, but of *Æneas*.

Arma virumq; cano, Trojæ qui primus ab oris,
Italiam fato profugus, Latinaq; venit
Litora: multum ille & terris jactatus et alto, &c.

I cite the whole three verses, that I may by the way offer a *Conjectural Emendation*, purely my own, upon each: First, *oris* should be read *axis*, it being as we see *Æn.* 2, 513, from the *altar* of *Jupiter Hercæus* that *Æneas* fled as soon as he saw *Priam* slain. In the second line I would read *flatu* for *fato*, since it is most clear it was by *Winds* that he arrived at the *Shore* of *Italy*; *Jactatus* in the third, is surely as improper apply'd to *terris*, as proper to *alto*: To say a man is *tost on land*, is much at one with saying he *walks at sea. Risum teneatis amici?* Correct it, as I doubt not it ought to be, *Vexatus.*
                                                    SCRIBLERUS.

VERSE 2. *The* Smithfield-*Muses.*] *Smithfield* is the place where Bartholomew Fair was kept, whose Shews, Machines, and Dramatical Entertainments, formerly agreeable only to the Taste of the Rabble, were, by the Hero of this Poem and others of equal Genius, brought to the Theatres of Covent-Garden, Lincolns-inn-Fields, and the Hay-Market, to be the reigning Pleasures of the Court and Town. This happened in the Year 1725, and continued to the Year 1728. See Book 3. Verse 191, &c.

VERSE 10. *Daughter of* Chaos, *&c.* The beauty of this whole Allegory being purely of the Poetical kind, we think it not our proper business as a Scholiast, to meddle with it; but leave it (as we shall in general all such) to the Reader: remarking only, that *Chaos* (according to *Hesiod*, Θεογονία) was the Progenitor of all the Gods.
                                                    SCRIBL.

IMITATIONS.

VERSE 3. *Say great* Patricians *(since your selves inspire*
These wond'rous Works.}---Ovid. Met 1.
— *Dü cæptis (nam vos mutastis & illas)*
VERSE 6. Alluding to a verse of Mr. *Dryden's*

not in *Mac Flecno* (as it is said ignorantly in the Key to the *Dunciad*, pag. 1.) but in his verses to Mr. *Congreve.*

And Tom *the Second reigns like* Tom *the First.*

Laborious, heavy, bufy, bold, and blind,

She rul'd, in native Anarchy, the mind.

15	Still her old empire to confirm, fhe tries,

For born a Goddefs, Dulnefs never dies.

O thou! whatever Title pleafe thine ear,

Dean, Drapier, Bickerftaff, or Gulliver!

Whether thou chufe Cervantes' ferious air,

20	Or laugh and fhake in Rab'lais eafy Chair,

Or praife the Court, or magnify Mankind,

Or thy griev'd Country's copper chains unbind ;

From thy Bæotia tho' Her Pow'r retires,

Grieve not at ought our fifter realms acquire :

25	Here pleas'd behold her mighty wings out-fpread,

To hatch a new Saturnian age of Lead.

Where wave the tatter'd enfigns of Rag-Fair,

A yawning ruin hangs and nods in air ;

REMARKS.

VERSE 23. *From thy* Bæotia.] *Bæotia* of old lay under the Raillery of the neighbouring Wits, as *Ireland* does now; tho' each of thofe nations produced one of the greateft Wits, and greateft Generals, of their age.

VERSE 26. *A new* Saturnian *Age of Lead.*] The ancient Golden Age is by Poets ftiled *Saturnian*; but in the Chymical language, *Saturn* is Lead.

VERSE 27. *Where wave the tatter'd Enfigns of* Rag-fair.] *Rag-fair* is a place near the *Tower of London,* where old cloaths and frippery are fold.

VERSE 28. 31. &c. *A yawning ruin hangs and nods in air.*——

Here in one Bed two fhiv'ring Sifters *lie,*
The Cave of Poverty *and* Poetry.

Hear upon this place the forecited Critick on the *Dunciad.* " Thefe lines (faith he) have no " Conftruction, or are Nonfenfe. The two " fhivering Sifters muft be the fifter Caves of Po- " verty and Poetry, or the Bed and Cave of Pover- " ty and Poetry muft be the fame, (queftionlefs) " and the two Sifters the Lord knows who ? O the Conftruction of Grammatical Heads! *Virgil* writeth thus: *Æn.* 1.

Fronte

Keen, hollow winds howl thro' the bleak recess,

30   Emblem of Music caus'd by Emptiness:

Here in one bed two shiv'ring sisters lye,

The cave of Poverty and Poetry.

This, the Great Mother dearer held than all

The clubs of Quidnunc's, or her own Guild-hall.

35   Here stood her Opium, here she nurs'd her Owls,

And destin'd here th' imperial seat of Fools.

Hence springs each weekly Muse, the living boast

Of Curl's chaste press, and Lintot's rubric's post,

Hence hymning Tyburn's elegiac lay,

40   Hence the soft sing-song on Cecilia's day,

REMARKS.

Fronte sub adversa scopulis pendentibus antrum:
Intus aquæ dulces, vivoq; sedilia saxo;
Nympharum domus.——

May we not say in like manner, " The " Nymphs must be the Waters and the Stones, " or the Waters and the Stones must be the " houses of the Nymphs ? *Insulse!* The second line, *Intus aquai, &c.* is in a parenthesis (as are the two lines of our Author, *Keen hollow Winds, &c.*) and it is the *Antrum*, and the *yawning Ruin*, in the line before that parenthesis, which are the *Domus*, and the *Cave*.

Let me again, I beseech thee Reader, present thee with another *Conjectural Emendation* on *Virgil's Scopulis pendentibus* : He is here describing a place, whither the weary Mariners of *Æneas* repaired to dress their Dinner.—— *Fessi——frugesq; receptas Et torrere parant flammis:* What has *Scopulis pendentibus* here to do ? Indeed the *aquæ dulces* and *sedilia* are something; *sweet Waters* to drink, and *Seats* to rest on. The other is surely an error of the Copyists. Restore it, without the least scruple, *Populis prandentibus.*

But for this and a thousand more, expect our Edition of *Virgil*; a Specimen whereof see in the Appendix.

                 SCRIBLERUS

VERSE 33. *The* Great Mother.] *Magna mater,* here applyed to *Dulness.* The *Quidnunc's* was a name given to the ancient Members of certain political Clubs, who were constantly enquiring, *Quid nunc?* what news ?

VERSE 38. Curl's *chaste press, and* Lintot's *rubric post.*] Two Booksellers, of whom see Book 2. The former was fined by the Court of King's-Bench for publishing obscene books.

IMITATIONS.

VERSE 33. *This the* Great Mother. *&c.*].*Æn.*1. *Urbs antiqua fuit——* *Quam Juno fertur terris magis omnibus unam*

Posthabita coluisse Samo; hic illius arma, *Hic currus fuit: hoc regnum Dea gentibus esse* *(Siqua fata sinant) jam tum tenditq; fovetq;.*

Sepulchral lyes our holy walls to grace,

And New-year Odes, and all the Grubftreet race.

'Twas here in clouded majefty fhe fhone;

Four guardian Virtues, round, fupport her Throne;

45 Fierce champion Fortitude, that knows no fears

Of hiffes, blows, or want, or lofs of ears:

Calm Temperance, whofe bleffings thofe partake

Who hunger, and who thirft, for fcribling fake:

REMARKS.

VERSE 39. *Hence hymning* Tyburn's *elegiac lay.*] It is an ancient Englifh cuftom for the Malefactors to fing a Pfalm at their Execution at *Tyburn*; and no lefs cuftomary to print Elegies on their deaths, at the fame time, or before.

VERSE 40 and 42, Allude to the annual Songs compofed to Mufick on St. *Cecilia's* Feaft, and thofe made by the Poet-Laureat for the time being to be fung at Court, on every New-Years-Day, the words of which are happily drown'd in the voices and Inftruments.

VERSE 41. Is a juft Satyr on the Flatteries and Falfehoods admitted to be infcribed on the walls of Churches in Epitaphs.

I muft not here omit a Reflection, which will occur perpetually through this Poem, and cannot but greatly endear the Author to every attentive Obferver of it: I mean that *Candour* and *Humanity* which every where appears in him, to thofe unhappy Objects of the Ridicule of all mankind, the bad Poets. He here imputes all fcandalous rhimes, fcurrilous weekly papers, lying news, bafe flatteries, wretched elegies, fongs, and verfes (even from thofe fung at Court, to ballads in the ftreets) not fo much to Malice or Servility as to Dulnefs; and not fo much

to Dulnefs, as to Neceffity; And thus at the very commencement of his Satyr, makes an Apology for all that are to be fatyrized.

VERSE 48. *Who hunger, and who thirft.*] " This is an infamous Burlefque on a Text in " Scripture, which fhews the Author's delight " is Prophanefs," (faid *Curl* upon this place.) But 'tis very familiar with *Shakefpeare* to allude to Paffages of Scripture. Out of a great number I'll felect a few, in which he both alludes to, and quotes the very Texts from holy Writ. In *All's well that ends well*, *I am no great Nebucadnezzar, I have not much Skill in Grafs.* Ibid. *They are for the flowry Way that leads to the broad Gate, and the great Fire.* Mat. 7. 13. *Much ado about nothing: All, all, and moreover God faw him when he was hid in the Garden,* Gen. 3. 8. (in a very jocofe Scene.) In *Love's Labour loft,* he talks of *Sampfon's* carrying the Gates on his Back; in the Merry Wives of Windfor of *Goliah* and the Weavers Beam; and in Henry 4. *Falftaff's* Soldiers are compared to *Lazarus* and the *Prodigal Son,* &c. The firft part of this Note is Mr. C U R L's: *The reft is Mr.* T H E O B A L D's. Shakefpear Reftor'd *Appendix,* p. 144.

IMITATIONS.

VERSE 39. *Hence hymning Tyburn--- Hence, &c.*]
—Genus unde Latinum
Albanig; patres, atg; alta mœnia Romæ. Virg.
VERSE 43. *In clouded Majefty fhe fhone.*]

Milton, lib. 4. —— *The Moon*
Rifing in clouded Majefty ——
VERSE 46. *That knows no fears Of hiffes, blows, or want, or lofs of ears.*] Horat.
Quem neq; pauperies, neq; mors, neq; vincula terrent.

Prudence, whose glass presents th' approaching jayl :

50 Poetic Justice, with her lifted scale ;

Where in nice balance, truth with gold she weighs,

And solid pudding against empty praise.

     Here she beholds the Chaos dark and deep,

Where nameless somethings in their causes sleep,

55 'Till genial Jacob, or a warm Third-day

Call forth each mass, a poem or a play.

How Hints, like spawn, scarce quick in embryo lie,

How new-born Nonsense first is taught to cry,

Maggots half-form'd, in rhyme exactly meet,

60 And learn to crawl upon poetic feet.

Here one poor Word a hundred clenches makes,

And ductile dulness new meanders takes ;

REMARKS.

VERSE 61. *Here one poor* Word *a hundred* clenches *makes.*] It may not be amiss to give an instance or two of these Operations of *Dulness* out of the Authors celebrated in the Poem. A great Critick formerly held these Clenches in such abhorrence, that he declared, " He that would Pun, would pick a Pocket." Yet Mr. *Dennis*'s works afford us notable Examples in this kind. " *Alexander* Pope hath sent " abroad into the world as many *Bulls* as his " Namesake Pope *Alexander*."— " Let us take " the initial and final letters of his Surname, " viz, A. P——E, and they give you the " Idea of an *Ape.* ---— *Pope* comes from " the Latin word *Popa*, which signifies a little " Wart; or from *Poppysma*, because he was con- " tinually *popping* out squibs of wit, or ra- " ther *Po-pysmata*, or *Po-pisms.* DENNIS. *Daily-Journal* June 11. 1728.

IMITATIONS.

VERSE 53. *Here she beholds the* Chaos *dark and deep, Where nameless* somethings, &c.] That is to say, unformed things, which are either made into Poems or Plays, as the Booksellers or the Players bid most. These lines allude to the following in *Garth's Dispensary*, Cant. 6.

Within the chambers of the Globe they spy
The beds where sleeping Vegetables lie,
'Till the glad summons of a genial ray
Unbinds the Globe, and calls them out to day.
VERSE 62. *And ductile dulness.*] A Parody on another in *Garth. Cant.* 1
How ductile matter new meanders takes.

There motley Images her fancy strike,

Figures ill-pair'd, and Similes unlike.

65   She sees a Mob of Metaphors advance,

Pleas'd with the Madness of the mazy dance:

How Tragedy and Comedy embrace;

How Farce and Epic get a jumbled race;

How Time himself stands still at her command,

70   Realms shift their place, and Ocean turns to land.

Here gay Description Ægypt glads with showers;

Or gives to Zembla fruits, to Barca flowers;

Glitt'ring with ice here hoary hills are seen,

There painted vallies of eternal green,

75   On cold December fragrant chaplets blow,

And heavy harvests nod beneath the snow.

All these and more, the cloud-compelling Queen

Beholds thro' fogs that magnify the scene:

She, tinsel'd o'er in robes of varying hues,

80   With self-applause her wild creation views,

REMARKS.

VERSE 68. *How* Farce *and* Epic — *How* Time *himself,* &c.] Allude to the Transgressions of the *Unities,* in the Plays of such Poets. For the Miracles wrought upon *Time* and *Place,* and the mixture of Tragedy, Comedy, Farce and Epic, *See* Pluto *and* Proserpine, Penelope, &c. *as yet extant.*

VERSE 71. *Ægypt glads with Showers.*] In the lower *Ægypt* Rain is of no use, the over-flowing of the *Nyle* being sufficient to impregnate the soil. — These six verses represent the inconsistencies in the description of Poets, who heap together all glittering and gawdy Images, tho' incompatible in one season, or in one scene.— *See the* Guardian N° 40. *printed in the* Appendix, *Parag.* 7. *See also* Eusden's *whole Works (if to be found.)*

IMITATIONS.

VERSE 77. *The Cloud-compelling Queen.*] From *Homer's* Epithet of *Jupiter,* νεφεληγερετα Ζεus.

Sees momentary monsters rise and fall,

And with her own fools colours gilds them all.

'Twas on the day, when Thorold, rich and grave,

Like Cimon triumph'd, both on land and wave :

85   (Pomps without guilt, of bloodless swords and maces,

Glad chains, warm furs, broad banners, and broad faces)

Now Night descending, the proud scene was o'er,

But liv'd, in Settle's numbers, one day more.

Now May'rs and Shrieves all hush'd and satiate lay,

90   Yet eat in dreams the custard of the day ;

While pensive Poets painful vigils keep,

Sleepless themselves to give their readers sleep.

Much to the mindful Queen the feast recalls,

What City-Swans, once sung within the walls ;

95   Much she revolves their arts, their ancient praise,

And sure succession down from Heywood's days.

REMARKS.

VERSE 83. *'Twas on the Day when* Thorold *rich and grave.*] Sir *George Thorold* Lord Mayor of *London*, in the Year 1720. The Procession of a Lord Mayor is made partly by land, and partly by water.——*Cimon* the famous *Athenian* General obtained a Victory by sea, and another by land, on the same day, over the *Persians* and *Barbarians*.

VERSE 86. *Glad Chains.*] The Ignorance of these Moderns! This was altered in one Edition to *Gold Chains*, shewing more regard to the metal of which the chains of Aldermen are made, than to the beauty of the Latinism and Grecism, nay of figurative speech itself.——

Lætas segetes, glad, for making glad, &c.   SCR.

VERSE 88. *But liv'd in* Settle's *Numbers one day more.*] A beautiful manner of speaking, usual with the Poets in praise of Poetry, in which kind nothing is finer than those lines of Mr. *Addison*.

Sometimes misguided by the tuneful throng,
I look for streams immortaliz'd in song,
That lost in silence and oblivion lye,
Dumb are their fountains, and their channels dry;
Yet run for ever, by the Muses skill,
And in the smooth description murmur still.

VERSE 96. *John Heywood.*] Whose Enterludes were printed in the time of *Henry* the eighth.

She saw with joy the line immortal run,

Each sire imprest and glaring in his son;

So watchful Bruin forms with plastic care

100 Each growing lump, and brings it to a Bear.

She saw old Pryn in restless Daniel shine,

And Eusden eke out Blackmore's endless line;

She saw slow Philips creep like Tate's poor page,

And all the Mighty Mad in Dennis rage.

REMARKS.

VERSE 88. *But liv'd in* Settle's *Numbers one day more.*] *Settle* was alive at this time, and Poet to the City of *London.* His office was to compose yearly panegyricks upon the Lord Mayors, and Verses to be spoken in the Pageants: But that part of the shows being by the frugality of some Lord Mayors at length abolished, the employment of City Poet ceas'd; so that upon *Settle's* demise, there was no successor to that place. This important point of time our Poet has chosen, as the Crisis of the Kingdom of *Dulness,* who thereupon decrees to remove her imperial seat from the City, and over-spread the other parts of the Town: To which great Enterprize all things being now ripe, she calls the Hero of this Poem.

Mr. *Settle* was once a writer in some vogue, particularly with his Party; for he was the author or publisher of many noted Pamphlets in the time of King *Charles* the second. He answered all *Dryden's* political Poems; and being cry'd up on one side, succeeded not a little in his Tragedy of the Empress of Morroco (the first that was ever printed with Cuts.) " Upon this he grew " insolent, the Wits writ against his Play, he re- " plied, and the Town judged he had the better. " In short *Settle* was then thought a formidable " Rival to Mr. *Dryden*; and not only the Town, " but the University of *Cambridge,* was divided " which to prefer; and in both places the younger " sort inclined to *Elkanah.* DENNIS. *Pref. to Rem. on* Hom.

For the latter part of his History, see the third Book, verse 238.

VERSE 101. *Old* Prynn *in restless* Daniel.]

William Prynn and *Daniel de Foe* were writers of Verses, as well as of Politicks; as appears by the Poem of the latter *De jure Divino,* and others, and by these lines in *Cowley's* Miscellanies of the former.

—— *One lately did not fear*
(Without the Muses leave) to plant Verse here.
But it produc'd such base, rough, crabbed, hedge-
Rhymes, as e'en set the bearers ears on edge:
Written by William Prynn Esqui-re, *the*
Year of our Lord, six hundred thirty three.
Brave Jersey *Muse! and he's for his high stile*
Call'd to this day the Homer *of the Isle.*

Both these Authors had a resemblance in their fates as well as writings, having been a-like sentenc'd to the Pillory.

Of *Eusden* and *Blackmore.* See Book 2. *v.* 254. and 300. And *Philips.* See Book 3. *v.* 274.

VERSE 104. *And all the mighty Mad.*] This is by no means to be understood literally, as if Mr. D. were really mad; Not that we are ignorant of the *Narrative* of Dr. *R. Norris,* but it deserveth no more regard than the *Pop upon P.* and the like idle. Trash, written by *James Moor,* or other young and light Persons, who themselves better deserve to be blooded, scarified, or whipped, for such their ungracious merriment with their Elders. No- - it is spoken of that *Excellent* and *Divine Madness,* so often mentioned by *Plato,* that poetical rage and enthusiasm, with which no doubt Mr. *D.* hath, in his time, been highly possessed; and of those *extraordinary hints* and *motions* whereof he himself so feelingly treats in the Preface to Pr. *Arth.* [See Notes on Book 2. verse 256.]   SCRIBL.

G

105   In each she marks her image full exprest,

But chief, in Tibbald's monster-breeding breast;

REMARKS.

VERSE 104. *And all the mighty Mad in Dennis rage.*] This Verse in the surreptitious Editions stood thus, *And furious D-- foam, &c.* which, in that printed in *Ireland*, was unaccountably filled up with the great name of *Dryden*. Mr. Theobald *in the* Censor, Vol. 2. N⁰ 33. also calls him by the Name of *Furius*. " The modern *Furius* is to be look'd on as more " the object of Pity, than of that which he daily " provokes, laughter and contempt. Did we real- " ly know how much this *poor Man (I wish* " *that reflection on* Poverty *had been spar'd)* suf- " fers by being contradicted, or which is the " same thing in effect, by hearing another prai- " sed; we should in compassion sometimes at- " tend to him with a silent nod, and let him " go away with the triumphs of his ill-nature. " --- *Poor* Furius *(again)* when any of his co- " temporaries are spoken well of, quitting the " ground of the present dispute, steps back a " thousand years to call in the succour of the An- " cients. His very *Panegyrick* is *spiteful*, and " he uses it for the same reason as some Ladies " do their commendations of a dead Beauty, " who never would have had their good word, " but that a living one happened to be mention- " ed in their company. His applause is not the " tribute of his *Heart*, but the sacrifice of his " *Revenge*", *&c.* Indeed his pieces against our Poet are somewhat of an angry character, and as they are now scarce extant, a taste of his stile may be satisfactory to the curious. " A young " squab, short Gentleman, whose outward form " though it should be that of downright Mon- " key, would not differ so much from human " shape, as his unthinking immaterial part does " from human understanding. ------ He is as " stupid and as venemous as a hunchbacked " Toad A Book through which folly and ig- " norance, those bretheren so lame and impo- " tent, do ridiculously look very big, and very " dull, and strut, and hobble cheek by jowl, with " their arms on kimbo, being led, and support- " ed, and bully-backed by that blind Hector, Im- " pudence. *Reflect. on the* Essay on Crit. *Page* 26. 29. 30.

It would be unjust not to add his Reasons for this Fury, they are so strong and so coercive. " I regard him (saith he) as an *Enemy*, not so much " to me, as to my King, to my Country, to my " Religion, and to that Liberty which has been " the sole felicity of my life. A vagary of for- " tune, who is sometimes pleased to be frolick- " some, and the epidemick *Madness of the times*, " have given him *Reputation*, and Reputation (as " *Hobbs* says) is *Power*, and *that has made him* " *dangerous*. Therefore I look on it as my duty " to *King George*, whose faithful subject I am, " to my *Country*, of which I have appeared a " constant lover; to the *Laws*, under whose " protection I have so long lived; and to the *Li-* " *berty* of my *Country*, more dear than life to me. " of which I have now for forty years been a " constant asserter, *&c.* I look upon it as my " duty, I say, to do—*you shall see what*— " to pull the Lions skin from this little " *Ass*, which popular errors has thrown " round him; and to show, that this Author " who has been lately so much in vogue, has nei- " ther sense in his thoughts, nor english in his " expressions. DENNIS, *Rem. on* Hom. *Pref.* *p.* 2. *and p.* 91. *&c.)*

Besides these publick-spirited reasons, Mr. *D.* had a *private one*; which by his manner of expressing it in page 92, appears to have been equally strong. He was even in bodily fear of his Life, from the machinations of the said Mr. *P.* " The story (says he) is too long to be told, " but who would be acquainted with it, may " hear it from Mr. *Curl* my Bookseller.—How- " ever, what my reason has suggested to me, " that I have with a just *confidence* said, in de- " fiance of his two clandestine weapons, his *Slan-* " *der* and his *Poyson*". Which last words of his Book plainly discover, Mr. *D* his suspicion was that of being *poysoned*, in like manner as Mr. *Curl* had been before him. Of which fact see *A full and true account of a horrid and barbarous revenge by Poyson on the body of* Edmund Curl; printed in 1716, the year antecedent to that wherein these Remarks of Mr. *Dennis* were published. But what puts it beyond all que- stion, is a passage in a very warm treatise in which

Sees Gods with Dæmons in ſtrange league ingage,

And earth, and heav'n, and hell her battles wage.

She ey'd the Bard, where ſupperleſs he ſate,

110 And pin'd, unconſcious of his riſing fate;

REMARKS,

Mr. *D.* was alſo concerned, price two pence, called, *A true character of Mr.* Pope *and his writings, printed for S. Popping,* 1716. in the tenth page whereof he is ſaid " to have inſulted peo- " ple on thoſe calamities and diſeaſes, which he " himſelf gave them by adminiſtring *Poyſon* to " them"; and is called (*p.* 4.) *a lurking way- laying coward, and a ſtabber in the dark.* Which (with many other things moſt lively ſet forth in that piece) muſt have render'd him a terror, not to Mr. *Dennis* only, but to all Chriſtian People.

For the reſt, Mr. *John Dennis* was the Son of a Sadler in *London,* born in 1657. He paid court to Mr. *Dryden*; and having obtained ſome correſpondence with Mr. *Wycherly* and Mr. *Con- greve,* he immediately obliged the publick with their Letters. He made himſelf known to the Government by many admirable Schemes and Projects; which the Miniſtry, for reaſons beſt known to themſelves, conſtantly kept private. For his character as a writer, it is given us as follows. " Mr. *Dennis* is *excellent* at pinda- " rick writings, *perfectly regular* in all his per- " formances, and a perſon of *ſound Learning.* " That he is maſter of a great deal of *Penetration* " and *Judgment,* his criticiſms (particularly on " Prince *Arthur*) do ſufficiently demonſtrate." From the ſame account it alſo appears, that he writ Plays " more to get *Reputation* than *Money.*" DENNIS *of himſelf.* See *Jacob's* Lives of Dram. Poets, page 68. 69. *compared with* page 286.

VERSE 106. *But chief in* Tibbald] *Lewis Tibbald* (as pronounced) or *Theobald* (as written) was bred an Attorney, and Son to an Attorney (ſays Mr. *Jacob*) of *Sittenburn* in *Kent.* He was Author of many forgotten Plays, Poems, and other pieces, and of ſeveral anonymous Letters in praiſe of them in *Miſt's* Journal. He was con- cerned in a Paper call'd the *Cenſor,* and a tranſ- lation of *Ovid,* as we find from Mr. *Dennis's* Remarks on *Pope's* Homer, p. 9. 10. " There is " a notorious Ideot, one hight *Whachum,* who " from an under-ſpur-leather to the Law, is be-

" come an under-ſtrapper to the Play-houſe, who " has lately burleſqu'd the Metamorphoſes of " *Ovid* by a vile Tranſlation, &c. This Fellow " is concerned in an impertinent Paper called the " *Cenſor*". But notwithſtanding this ſevere cha- racter, another Critick ſays of him " That he " has given us ſome Pieces which met with appro- " bation; and that *the Cave of Poverty* is an ex- " cellent Poem." *Giles Jacob's Lives of the Poets,* vol. 2. p. 211. He had once a mind to tranſlate the *Odyſſey,* the firſt Book whereof was printed in 1717 by *B. Lintott,* and probably may yet be ſeen at his Shop. What is ſtill in memory, is a piece now about a year old, it had the ar- rogant Title of *Shakeſpear Reſtored:* Of this he was ſo proud himſelf, as to ſay in one of *Miſt's Journals, June* 8. " That to expoſe any Er- " rors in it was impracticable." And in an- other, *April* 27. " That whatever care for " the future might be taken either by Mr. " *P.* or any other aſſiſtants, he would ſtill give " above 500 Emendations that *ſhall* eſcape them " *all.*" During the ſpace of two years, while Mr. *Pope* was preparing his Edition of *Shakeſpear,* and publiſhed Advertiſements, requeſting all lovers of the Author to contribute to a more perfect one; this Reſtorer (who had then ſome correſpondence with him, and was ſolliciting favours by Letters) did wholly conceal his deſign, 'till after its pub- lication. Probably that proceeding elevated him to the Dignity he holds in this Poem, which he ſeems to deſerve no other way better than his brethren; unleſs we impute it to the ſhare he had in the Journals, cited among the *Teſtimonies of Authors* prefixed to this work.

VERSE 108. Tibbald's *monſter-breeding breaſt ,Sees Gods with Dæmons,* &c.] This alludes to the extravagancies of the Farces of that au- thor. See book 3. verſ. 109, &c.

VERSE 109. ——*Supper-leſs he ſate.*] It is amazing how the ſenſe of this line hath been miſtaken by all the former Commentators, who moſt idly ſuppoſe it to imply, that the Hero

Studious he sate, with all his books around,

Sinking from thought to thought, a vast profound!

Plung'd for his sense, but found no bottom there;

Then writ, and flounder'd on, in mere despair.

115 He roll'd his eyes that witness'd huge dismay,

Where yet unpawn'd, much learned lumber lay,

Volumes, whose size the space exactly fill'd;

Or which fond authors were so good to gild;

Or where, by sculpture made for ever known,

120 The page admires new beauties, not its own.

Here swells the shelf with Ogilby the great:

There, stamp'd with arms, Newcastle shines compleat,

REMARKS.

of the Poem wanted a supper. In truth a great absurdity! Not that we are ignorant that the Hero of *Homer's Odyssey* is frequently in that circumstance, and therefore it can no way derogate from the grandeur of Epic Poem to represent such Hero under a Calamity, to which the greatest not only of Criticks and Poets, but of Kings and Warriors, have been subject. But much more refin'd, I will venture to say, is the meaning of our author: It was to give us obliquely a curious precept, or what *Bossu* calls a *disguised sentence*, that " Temperance is " the life of Study." The language of Poesy brings all into Action; and to represent a Critic encompast with books, but without a supper, is a picture which lively expresseth how much the true Critic prefers the diet of the mind to that of the body, one of which he always castigates and often totally neglects, for the greater improvement of the other.   SCRIBLERUS.

VERSE 115. *He roll'd his eyes that witness'd huge dismay.*] Milt. l. 1.—— *Round he throws his eyes That witness'd huge affliction and dismay.* The progress of a bad Poet in his thoughts being (like the progress of the Devil in *Milton*) thro' a Chaos, might probably suggest this imitation.

VERSE 120.——*Admires new beauties not its own.* Virg. Geo. 2.

Miraturq; frondes novas, & non sua poma.

VERSE id. &c.] This library is divided into two parts; the one (his polite learning) consists of these books which seem'd to be the models of his poetry, and are preferr'd for one of these three reasons (usual with collectors of Libraries) that they fitted the shelves, or were gilded for shew, or adorned with pictures: The other class our author calls solid Learning; old bodies of Philosophy, old Commentators, old English Printers, or old English Translations; all very voluminous, and fit to erect Altars to Dulness.

VERSE 121. ——Ogilby *the great.*] *John Ogilby* was one, who from a late initiation into literature, made such a progress as might well stile him the *Prodigy* of his time! sending into the world so many *large Volumes!* His translations of *Homer* and *Virgil*, *done to the life,* and with *such excellent Sculptures!* and (what added great grace to his works) he printed them all on *special good Paper,* and in a *very good Letter.* WINSTANLY, *Lives of Poets.*

VERSE 122. *There, stamp'd with arms,* Newcastle *shines compleat.*] The *Dutchess of New-*

Here all his suff'ring brotherhood retire,

And 'scape the martyrdom of jakes and fire ;

125 A Gothic Vatican! of Greece and Rome

Well-purg'd, and worthy Withers, Quarles, and Blome.

    But high above, more solid Learning shone,

The Classicks of an Age that heard of none ;

There Caxton slept, with Wynkin at his side,

130 One clasp'd in wood, and one in strong cow-hide.

There sav'd by spice, like mummies, many a year,

Old Bodies of Philosophy appear.

De Lyra here a dreadful front extends,

And there, the groaning shelves Philemon bends.

REMARKS.

castle was one who busied herself in the ravishing delights of Poetry; leaving to posterity in print three *ample Volumes* of her studious endeavours. WINSTANLY, *ibid.* *Langbaine* reckons up eight Folio's of her Grace's; which were usually adorn'd with gilded Covers, and had her Coat of Arms upon them.

VERSE 126. —— *Worthy* Withers, Quarles, *and* Blome.] It was printed in the surreptitious Editions, *W——ly, W——s*, who were Persons eminent for good life ; the one writ the Life of Christ in verse ; the other some valuable pieces in the lyrick kind on pious subjects. The line is here restor'd according to its Original.

George Withers was a great pretender to poetical zeal against the vices of the times, and abused the greatest Personages in power, which brought upon him *frequent correction.* The *Marshalsea* and *Newgate* were no strangers to him. WINSTANLY. *Quarles* was as dull a writer, but an honester man. *Blome's* books are remarkable for their cuts.

VERSE 129. *Caxton.*] A Printer in the time of *Edw.* 4. *Rich.* 3. and *Henry* 7. *Wynkin de Word,* his successor in that of *Henry* 7 and 8. The former translated into prose *Virgil's Æneis* as a History; of which he speaks in his Proeme in a very singular manner, as of a book hardly known. *Vid. Append. Tibbald* quotes a rare passage from him in *Mist's Journal* of *March* 16, 1728. concerning a *straunge and mervayllouse beaste called Sagittarye,* which he would have *Shakespear* to mean rather than *Teucer,* the Archer celebrated by *Homer.*

VERSE 133. *Nich. de Lyra,* or *Harpsfeld,* a very voluminous Commentator, whose works in five vast Folio's were printed in 1472.

VERSE 134. *Philemon Holland,* Dr. in Physick. He translated *so many books,* that a man would think he had done *nothing else,* insomuch that he might be call'd *Translator General of his age.* The books alone of his turning into English, are sufficient to make a *Country Gentleman* a *compleat Library.* WINSTANLY.

135   Of these twelve volumes, twelve of amplest size,

Redeem'd from tapers and defrauded pyes,

Inspir'd he seizes: These an altar raise:

An hecatomb of pure, unsully'd lays

That altar crowns: A folio Common-place

140 Founds the whole pyle, of all his works the base;

Quarto's, Octavo's, shape the less'ning pyre,

And last, a little Ajax tips the spire.

Then he. Great Tamer of all human art!

First in my care, and nearest at my heart:

145 Dulness! whose good old cause I yet defend,

With whom my Muse began, with whom shall end!

O thou, of business the directing soul,

To human heads like byass to the bowl,

Which as more pond'rous makes their aim more true,

150 Obliquely wadling to the mark in view.

O ever gracious to perplex'd mankind!

Who spread a healing mist before the mind,

And, left we err by Wit's wild, dancing light,

Secure us kindly in our native night.

155 Ah! still o'er Britain stretch that peaceful wand,

Which lulls th' Helvetian and Batavian land.

REMARKS.

VERSE 142. *A little Ajax.*] In *duodecimo*, translated from *Sophocles* by *Tibbald*.

VERSE 146. *With whom my Muse began, with whom shall end.*] Virg. Ecl. 8. *A te principium,*
tibi desinet—from *Theoc.*
'Ἐκ Διὸς ἀρχώμεθα, κỳ εἰς Δία λήγετε, Μᾶσαι.
So *Horace,*
Prima dicte mihi, summa dicende camœna.

Where rebel to thy throne if Science rife,

She does but fhew her coward face and dies:

There, thy good Scholiafts with unweary'd pains

160 Make Horace flat, and humble Maro's ftrains;

Here ftudious I unlucky moderns fave,

Nor fleeps one error in its father's grave,

Old puns reftore, loft blunders nicely feek,.

And crucify poor Shakefpear once a week.

165 For thee I dim thefe eyes, and ftuff this head,

With all fuch reading as was never read;.

For thee fupplying, in the worft of days,

Notes to dull books, and prologues to dull plays;

For thee explain a thing till all men doubt it,

170 And write about it, Goddefs, and about it;

So fpins the filkworm fmall its flender ftore,

And làbours, 'till it clouds itfelf all o'er.

REMARKS.

VERSE 162. *Nor fleeps one error—Old puns reftore, loft blunders, &c.*] As where he laboured to prove *Shakefpear* guilty of terrible *Anacronifms*, or low *Conundrums*, which Time had cover'd; and converfant in fuch authors as *Caxton* and *Wynkin*, rather than in *Homer* or *Chaucer.* Nay fo far had he loft his reverence to this incomparable author, as to fay in print, *He deferved to be whipt.* An infolence which nothing fure can parallel! but that of *Dennis,* who can be proved to have declared before Company, that *Shakefpear was a Rafcal. O tempora! O mores!* SCRIBLERUS.

VERSE 164. *And crucify poor Shakefpear once a week.*] For fome time, once a week or fort-night, he printed in *Mifl's Journal* a fingle remark or poor conjecture on fome *word* or *pointing* of *Shakefpear.*

VERSE 166. *With all fuch reading as was never read.*] Such as *Caxton* above-mentioned, The three deftructions of *Troy* by *Wynkin,* and other like clafficks.

VERSE 168. *Notes to dull books, and prologues to dull plays.*] As to *Cook's Hefiod,* where fometimes a note, and fometimes even *half* a note, are carefully owned by him: And to *Moore's Comedy* of the *Rival Modes,* and other authors of the fame rank: Thefe were people who writ about the year 1726.

Not that my quill to Critiques was confin'd,

My Verſe gave ampler leſſons to mankind;

175　So graveſt precepts may ſucceſsleſs prove,

But ſad examples never fail to move.

As forc'd from wind-guns, lead itſelf can fly,

And pond'rous ſlugs cut ſwiftly thro' the ſky;

As clocks to weight their nimble motion owe,

180　The wheels above urg'd by the load below;

Me, Emptineſs and Dulneſs could inſpire,

And were my Elaſticity and Fire.

Had heav'n decreed ſuch works a longer date,

Heav'n had decreed to ſpare the Grubſtreet-ſtate.

185　But ſee great Settle to the duſt deſcend,

And all thy cauſe and empire at an end!

Cou'd Troy be ſav'd by any ſingle hand,

His gray-gooſe-weapon muſt have made her ſtand.

But what can I? my Flaccus caſt aſide,

190　Take up th' Attorney's (once my better) Guide?

REMARKS.

VERSE 189. *My Flaccus.*] A familiar manner of ſpeaking uſed by modern Criticks of a favourite Author. Mr. *T.* might as juſtly ſpeak thus of *Horace,* as a French wit did of *Tully* ſeeing his works in a library, *Ah! mon cher Ciceron! Je le connois bien: ce'ſt le mem quem Marc Tulle.*

VERSE 190. *Take up th'* Attorney's Guide.] In alluſion to his firſt profeſſion of an Attorney.

IMITATIONS.

VERSE 183. *Had heav'n decreed ſuch works a longer date, &c.*] Virg. Æn. 2.
Me ſi cælicolæ voluiſſent ducere vitam
Has mihi ſervaſſent ſedes. —

VERSE 187. *Could* Troy *be ſaved.* ——His gray-gooſe-weapon.] *Virg.* ibid.
——*Si Pergama dextra*
Defendi poſſent, etiam hac defenſa fuiſſent.

Or rob the Roman geese of all their glories,

And save the state by cackling to the Tories?

Yes, to my Country I my pen consign,

Yes, from this moment, mighty Mist! am thine,

195 And rival, Curtius! of thy fame and zeal,

O'er head and ears plunge for the publick weal.

Adieu my children! better thus expire

Un-stall'd, unsold; thus glorious mount in fire

Fair without spot; than greas'd by grocer's hands,

200 Or shipp'd with Ward to ape and monkey lands,

Or wafting ginger, round the streets to go,

And visit alehouse where ye first did grow.

REMARKS.

VERSE 191. *Or rob the* Roman *geese, &c.*] Relates to the well-known story of the geese that saved the Capitol, of which *Virgil, Æn.* 8. *Atq; hic auratis volitans argenteus anser Porticibus, Gallos in limine adesse canebat.* A passage I have always suspected. Who sees not the Antithesis of *auratis* and *argenteus* to be unworthy the Virgilian Majesty? and what absurdity to say, a Goose *sings?* *canebat?* *Virgil* gives a contrary character of the voice of this silly Bird, in *Ecl.* 9. —*argutos* interstrepere *anser olores.* Read it therefore *adesse strepebat.* And why *auratis porticibus?* Does not the very verse preceding this inform us, *Romuleo recens horrebat regio culmo.* is this *Thatch* in one line, and *Gold* in another, consistent? I scruple not (*repugnantibus omnibus manuscriptis*) to correct it, *auritis. Horace* uses the same epithet in the same sense,

— Auritas *fidibus canoris*

Ducere quercus.

And to say, that *Walls have Ears,* is common even to a proverb.   SCRIBL.

VERSE 194. *Mighty* Mist!] *Nathaniel Mist* was publisher of a famous Tory Paper (see notes on l. 3.) in which this Author was sometimes permitted to have a part.

VERSE 197. *Adieu my Children!*] This is a tender and passionate Apostrophe to his own Works which he is going to sacrifice, agreeable to the nature of man in great affliction, and reflecting like a parent, on the many miserable fates to which they would otherwise be subject.

—— *Felix Priameïa virgo!*

Jussa mori: quæ sortitus non pertulit ullos,

Nec victoris heri tetigit captiva cubile!

Nos patriâ incensâ, diversa per æquora vectæ, &c.

Virg. Æn. 3.

VERSE 200. *Or shipp'd with* Ward *to Ape and monkey land.*] *Edward Ward,* a very voluminous Poet in Hudibrastick Verse, but best known by the *London Spy,* in Prose. He has of late Years kept a publick house in the City (but in a genteel way) and with his wit, humour, and good liquor (Ale) afforded his guests a pleasurable entertainment, especially those of the High-Church party. JACOB *Lives of Poets* vol. 2. p. 225. Great numbers of his works are yearly sold into the Plantations.

H

With that, he lifted thrice the sparkling brand,

And thrice he dropt it from his quiv'ring hand:

205 Then lights the structure, with averted eyes;

The rowling smokes involve the sacrifice.

The opening clouds disclose each work by turns,

Now flames old Memnon, now Rodrigo burns,

In one quick flash see Proserpine expire,

210 And last, his own cold Æschylus took fire.

Then gush'd the tears, as from the Trojan's eyes

When the last blaze sent Ilion to the skies.

REMARKS.

VERSE 208. *Now flames old* Memnon, *now* Rodrigo *burns, In one quick flash see* Proserpine *expire.*]—Memnon, a Hero in the Persian Princess, very apt to take fire, as appears by these lines with with which he begins the Play.

By heav'n it fires my frozen blood with rage,
And makes it scald my aged Trunk——
Rodrigo, the chief personage of the Perfidious Brother, a play written between *T.* and a Watchmaker. The *Rape of Proserpine*, one of the Farces of this Author, in which *Ceres* sets fire to a Corn-field, which endangered the burning of the Play-house.

VERSE 210. *And last, his own cold* Æschylus took fire.] He had been (to use an expression of our Poet) *about* Æschylus for ten years, and had received Subscriptions for the same, but then went *about* other Books. The character of this tragic Poet is Fire and Boldness in a high degree; but our Author supposes it to be very much cooled by the translation; Upon sight of a specimen of it, was made this Epigram,

Alas! poor Æschylus! unlucky Dog!
Whom once a *Lobster* kill'd, and now a *Log.*
But this is a grievous error, for Æschylus was not slain by the fall of a Lobster on his head, but of a Tortoise, *teste* Val. Max. l. 9. cap. 12.
SCRIBL.

IMITATIONS.

VERSE 200. *And visit Alehouse,*] Waller on the Navy,
Those towers of Oak o'er fertile plains may go,
And visit Mountains where they once did grow.
VERSE 203.   *He lifted thrice the sparkling brand, And thrice he dropt it.*] Ovid of Althea on the like occasion, burning her Offspring,

Met. 8. *Tum conata quater flammis imponere torrem,*
Capta quater tenuit.——
VERSE 208, *Now flames old* Memnon, *&c.*] Virg. Æn. 2.
——*Jam Deiphobi dedit ampla ruinam*
Vulcano superante, domus; jam proximus ardet
Ucalegon.

Rowz'd by the light, old Dulneſs heav'd the head,

Then ſnatch'd a ſheet of Thulè from her bed;

215 Sudden ſhe flies, and whelms it o'er the pyre:

Down ſink the flames, and with a hiſs expire.

Her ample preſence fills up all the place;

A veil of fogs dilates her awful face;

Great in her charms! as when on Shrieves and May'rs

220 She looks, and breathes her ſelf into their airs.

She bids him wait her to the ſacred Dome;

Well-pleas'd he enter'd, and confeſs'd his Home:

So ſpirits ending their terreſtrial race,

Aſcend, and recognize their native place:

225 Raptur'd, he gazes round the dear retreat,

And in ſweet numbers celebrates the ſeat.

REMARKS.

VERSE 214. *Thule.*] An unfiniſhed Poem of that name, of which one ſheet was printed fifteen Years ago; by *A. Ph.* a Northern Author. It is an uſual method of putting out a fire, to caſt wet ſheets upon it. Some Criticks have been of opinion, that this ſheet was of the nature of the *Aſbeſtos*, which cannot be conſumed by fire; but I rather think it only an allegorical alluſion to the coldneſs and heavineſs of the writing.

VERSE 221. — *The ſacred* Dome.] The *Cave of Poverty* above-mentioned; where he no ſooner enters, but he Reconnoitres the place of his original; as *Plato* ſays the Spirits ſhall do, at their entrance into the celeſtial Regions. His Dialogue of the Immortality of the Soul was tranſlated by *T.* in the familiar modern ſtile of *Prithee Phædo,* and *For God's ſake Socrates:* printed for *B. Lintot,* 1713.

VERSE 226. *And in ſweet numbers celebrates the ſeat.*] He writ a Poem call'd the *Cave of Poverty,* which concludes with a very extraordinary Wiſh, " That ſome great Genius, or man of diſtin- " guiſhed merit may be *ſtarved,* in order to ce- " lebrate her power, and deſcribe her Cave. It was printed in octavo, 1715.

IMITATIONS.

VERSE 219. *Great in her charms! as when on Shrieves and May'rs*
She looks, and breathes herſelf into their airs.]

Alma parens confeſſa Deam; qualiſq; videri
Cælicolis & quanta ſolet—— Virg. Æ. 2.
- Et lætos oculis afflarat honores.—— Id. Æn. 1.

H 2

Here to her Chosen all her works she shows;

Prose swell'd to verse, Verse loitring into prose;

How random Thoughts now meaning chance to find,

230 Now leave all memory of sense behind:

How Prologues into Prefaces decay,

And these to Notes are fritter'd quite away.

How Index-learning turns no student pale,

Yet holds the Eel of science by the Tail.

235 How, with less reading than makes felons 'scape,

Less human genius than God gives an ape,

Small thanks to France and none to Rome or Greece,

A past, vamp'd, future, old, reviv'd, new piece,

'Twixt Plautus, Fletcher, Congreve, and Corneille,

240 Can make a Cibber, Johnson, or Ozell.

The Goddess then, o'er his anointed head,

With mystic words, the sacred Opium shed;

REMARKS.

VERSE 240. *Can make a* Cibber.] Mr. *Colly Cibber*, an Author and Actor; of a good share of wit, and *uncommon vivacity*, which are much improved by the *conversation* he enjoys, which is of the *best*. JACOB *Lives of* Dram. Poets. p. 38. Besides 2 Volumes of Plays in 4º, he has made up and translated several others. Mr. *Jacob* omitted to remark, that he is particularly admirable in Tragedy.

VERSE 244. —— *Johnson*.] *Charles Johnson*, famous for writing a Play every season, and for being at *Button's* every day. He had probably thriven better in his Vocation had he been a small matter leaner. He may justly be called a Martyr to obesity, and to have fallen a victim to the rotundity of his parts. CHA. of the TIMES, printed by CURL, pag. 19. Some of his Plays are, Love in a Forest (*Shakespear's* As you like it)

Wife's Relief (*Shirley's* Gamester) The Victim (*Racine's* Iphigenia) The Sultaness (*Racine's* Bajazet (the prologue to which abused Dr. *Arburthnot*, Mr. *Pope*, and Mr. *Gay*.) The *Cobler* of *Preston*, his own.

VERSE 240. —— *And Ozell*.] Mr. *John Ozell*, if we credit Mr. *Jacob*, did go to School in "*Leicestershire*, where *somebody* left him some-"*thing* to live on, when he shall retire from "business. He was designed to be sent to *Cam-*"*bridge* in order for Priesthood; but he chose "rather to be placed in an *Office of accounts* in "the City, being qualified for the same by his "skill in *Arithmetick*, and writing the neces-"sary *hands*. He has oblig'd the world with "many translations of French Plays. JACOB *Lives of* Dram. Poets, p. 198.

And lo! her Bird (a monster of a fowl!

Something betwixt a H*** and Owl)

245 Perch'd on his crown.   All hail! and hail again,

My Son! the promis'd land expects thy reign.

Know, Settle, cloy'd with custard and with praise,

Is gather'd to the Dull of antient days,

Safe, where no criticks damn, no duns molest,

250 Where Gildon, Banks, and high-born Howard rest.

I see a King! who leads my chosen sons

To lands, that flow with clenches and with puns:

'Till each fam'd Theatre my empire own,

'Till Albion, as Hibernia, bless my throne!

255 I see! I see!— Then rapt, she spoke no more.

God save King Tibbald!   Grubstreet alleys roar.

So when Jove's block descended from on high,

(As sings thy great fore-father, Ogilby,)

REMARKS.

VERSE 244. A H—r.] A strange Bird from *Switzerland.*

VERSE 250 *Where* Gildon, Banks, *and high-born* Howard *rest.*] *Charles Gildon,* a writer of criticisms and libels of the last age: He publish-ed *Blount's* blasphemous books against the Divinity of Christ, the Oracles of reason, &c. He sig-nalized himself as a Critic, having written some very bad plays; abused Mr. *P.* very scandalously in an anonymous Pamphlet of the Life of Mr. *Wy-cherly* printed by *Curl,* in another called the New Rehearsal printed in 1714, in a third entit-led the compleat Art of English Poetry, in 2 Vo-lumes, and others.

VERSE 250. —*Banks.*] Was author of the play of the Earl of Essex, Ann Boleyn, &c. He fol-lowed the law as a sollicitor, like *Tibbald.*

VERSE 250. —*Hon.* Edward Howard, Au-thor of the British Princes, and a great number of wonderful pieces, celebrated by the late Earls of *Dorset* and *Rochester,* Duke of *Buckingham,* Mr. *Waller,* &c.

VERSE 258. *As sings thy great fore-father* Ogilby.] See his *Æsop* Fab. where this excel-lent hemystic is to be found. Our author shows here and elsewhere, a prodigious Tenderness for a *bad writer.* We see he selects the only good passage perhaps in all that ever *Ogilby* writ; which shows how candid and patient a reader he must have been. What can be more kind and af-fectionate than these words in the preface to his Poems, 4°. 1717. where he labours to call up all our humanity and forgiveness toward them, by the most moderate representation of their

Loud thunder to its bottom shook the bog,

260 And the hoarse nation croak'd, God save King Log!

REMARKS.

eafe that has ever been given by any Author? " Much may be faid to extenuate the fault of " bad Poets: What we call a *Genius* is hard to " be diftinguifhed, by a man himfelf, from a " prevalent inclination: And if it be never fo " great, he can at firft difcover it no other way, " than by that ftrong propenfity, which renders " him the more liable to be miftaken. He has " no other method but to make the experiment " by writing, and fo appealing to the judgment " of others: And if he happens to write ill " (which is certainly no fin in itfelf) he is im-" mediately made the Object of Ridicule! I " wifh we had the humanity to reflect, that even " the worft Authors might endeavour to pleafe " us, and in that endeavour, deferve fomething " at our hands. We have no caufe to quarrel " with them, but for their obftinacy in per-" fifting, and even that may admit of alle-" viating circumftances: For their particular " friends may be either ignorant, or unfincere; " and the reft of the world too well-bred, to " fhock them with a truth, which generally their " Bookfellers are the firft that inform them of.

End of the First Book.

THE

THE

DUNCIAD.

BOOK the SECOND.

HIGH on a gorgeous feat, that far outſhone
    Henley's gilt Tub, or Fleckno's Iriſh Throne,

REMARKS on BOOK the SECOND.

TWO things there are, upon which the very Baſis of all verbal Criticiſm is founded and ſupported: The firſt, that the Author could never fail to uſe the very beſt word, on every occaſion: The ſecond, that the Critick cannot chuſe but know, which it is? This being granted, whenever any doth not fully content us, we take upon us to conclude, firſt that the author could never have us'd it, And ſecondly, that he muſt have uſed That very one which we conjecture in its ſtead.

We cannot therefore enough admire the learned Scriblerus, for his alteration of the Text in the two laſt verſes of the preceding book, which in all the former editions ſtood thus

Hoarſe Thunder to its bottom ſhook the bog,

And the loud nation croak'd, God ſave K. Log!
He has with great judgment tranſpoſed theſe two epithets, putting *hoarſe* to the Nation, and *loud* to the Thunder: And this being evidently the true reading, he vouchſafed not ſo much as to

mention the former; For which aſſertion of the juſt right of a Critick, he merits the acknowledgement of all ſound Commentators.

VERSE 2. Henley's *gilt Tub.*] The pulpit of a Diſſenter is uſually called a Tub; but that of Mr. Orator *Henley* was covered with velvet, and adorned with gold. He had alſo a fair altar, and over it this extraordinary inſcription, *The Primitive Euchariſt.* See the hiſtory of this perſon, book 3. verſe 167.

VERSE 2. Or Fleckno's *Iriſh Throne.*] *Richard Flecknoe* was an Iriſh Prieſt, but had laid aſide (as himſelf expreſſed it) the Mechanick part of Prieſthood. He printed ſome Plays, Poems, Letters and Travels. I doubt not our Author took occaſion to mention him in reſpect to the Poem of Mr. *Dryden,* to which this bears ſome reſemblance; tho' of a character more different from it than that of the *Æneid* from the *Iliad,* or the *Lutrin* of *Boileau* from the *Defaite des Bouts rimées* of *Sarazin.*

IMITATIONS.

VERSE 1. *High on a gorgeous feat.*] Parody of Milton, lib. 2.

  High on a throne of royal ſtate, that far

  Outſhone the wealth of Ormus and of Ind,

  Or where the gorgeous Eaſt with richeſt hand

  Show'rs on her Kings barbaric pearl and gold,

  Satan exalted ſate,———

Or that, where on her Curlls the Public pours

All-bounteous, fragrant grains, and golden show'rs;

5 Great Tibbald fate: The proud Parnaffian fneer,

The confcious fimper, and the jealous leer,

Mix on his look. All eyes direct their rays

On him, and crowds grow foolish as they gaze.

Not with more glee, by hands Pontific crown'd,

10 With fcarlet hats, wide waving, circled round,

Rome in her Capitol faw Querno fit,

Thron'd on fev'n hills, the Antichrift of Wit.

To grace this honour'd day, the Queen proclaims

By herald hawkers, high, heroic Games.

15 She fummons all her fons: An endlefs band

Pours forth, and leaves unpeopled half the land;

A motley mixture! in long wigs, in bags,

In filks, in crapes, in garters, and in rags;

From drawing rooms, from colleges, from garrets,

20 On horfe, on foot, in hacks, and gilded chariots,

REMARKS.

VERSE 3. *Or that, where on her* Curls *the Public pours.*] Edm. *Curl* ftood in the Pillory at *Charing-Crofs*, in *March*, 1727-8.

VERSE 11. Rome *in her Capitol faw* Querno *fit.*] *Camillo Querno* was of *Apulia*, who hearing the great encouragement which *Leo* the tenth gave to Poets, travelled to *Rome* with a Harp in his hand, and fung to it twenty thoufand verfes of a Poem called *Alexias*. He was introduced as a Buffoon to *Leo*, and promoted to the honour of the Laurel; a jeft, which the Court of *Rome* and the Pope himfelf entred into fo far, as to hold a folemn Feftival on his Coronation, at which it is recorded; the Poet himfelf was fo tranfported, as to weep for joy. He was ever after a conftant frequenter of the Pope's Table, drank abundantly, and poured forth verfes without number. PAULUS JOVIUS, *Elog. Vir. doct. ch.* 82. Some idea of his Poetry is given us by *Fam. Strada* in his Prolufions.

All who true dunces in her caufe appear'd,
And all who knew thofe dunces to reward.
Amid that Area wide fhe took her ftand,
Where the tall May-pole once o'erlook'd the Strand;
25 But now, fo ANNE and Piety ordain,
A Church collects the faints of Drury-lane.
With Authors, Stationers obey'd the call,
The field of glory is a field for all;
Glory, and gain, th' induftrious tribe provoke;
30 And gentle Dulnefs ever loves a joke:
A Poet's form fhe plac'd before their eyes,
And bad the nimbleft racer feize the prize;
No meagre, mufe-rid mope, aduft and thin,
In a dun night-gown of his own loofe fkin,
35 But fuch a bulk as no twelve bards could raife,
Twelve ftarveling bards of thefe degen'rate days.
All as a partridge plump, full-fed, and fair,
She form'd this image of well-bodied air,
With pert flat eyes fhe window'd well its head,
40 A brain of feathers, and a heart of lead,

IMITATIONS.

VERSE 31. *A Poet's Form fhe plac'd before their eyes.*] This is what *Juno* does to deceive *Turnus*, Æn. 10.
Tum dea nube cava, tenuem fine viribus umbram,
In faciem Æneæ (vifu mirabile monftrum)
Dardaniis ornat telis, clypeumque jubafque
Divini affimilat capitis——Dat inania verba,
Dat fine mente fonum——
The Reader will obferve how exactly fome of thefe verfes fuit with their allegorical application here to a Plagiary. There feems to me a great propriety in this Epifode, where fuch an one is imag'd by a phantom that deludes the grafp of the expecting Bookfeller.
VERSE 35. *But fuch a bulk as no twelve bards.*] *Virg.* 12.
Vix illud letti bis fex——
Qualia nunc hominum producit corpora tellus.

I

And empty words she gave, and founding strain,
But senseless, lifeless! Idol void and vain!
Never was dash'd out, at one lucky hit,
A Fool, so just a copy of a Wit;
45 So like, that criticks said and courtiers swore,
A wit it was, and call'd the phantom, More.

REMARKS.

VERSE 43. *Never was dash'd out, at one lucky hit.*] Our author here seems willing to give some account of the possibility of *Dulness* making a *Wit*, (which could be done no other way than by *chance.*) The fiction is the more reconcil'd to probability by the known story of *Apelles*, who being at a loss to express the foam of *Alexander's* horse, dash'd his pencil in despair at the picture, and happen'd to do it by that fortunate stroke.

VERSE 46. *And call'd the phantom, More.*] CURL in his Key to the *Dunciad*, affirm'd this to be *James Moore Smyth*, Esq; and it is probable (considering what is said of him in the Testimonies) that some might fancy our author obliged to represent this gentleman as a Plagiary, or to pass for one himself. His case indeed was like that of a man I have heard of, who as he was sitting in company, perceived his next neighbour had stollen his handkerchief. "Sir (said the Thief, finding himself detected) "do not "expose me, I did it for mere want: be so "good but to take it privately out of my pocket "again, and say nothing." The honest man did so, but the other cry'd out, "See Gentle- "men! what a Thief we have among us! look, "he is stealing my handkerchief."

Some time before, he had borrowed of Dr. *Arbuthnot* a paper call'd an Historico-physical account of the *South-Sea*; and of Mr. *Pope* the Memoirs of a Parish Clark, which for two years he kept, and read to the Rev. Dr. *Young*, — *Bilkers*, Esq; and many others, as his own. Being apply'd to for them, he pretended they were lost; but there happening to be another copy of the latter, it came out in *Swift* and *Pope's* Miscellanies. Upon this, it seems he was so far mistaken as to confess his proceeding by an endeavour to hide it: unguardedly printing (in the *Daily Journal* of *Apr.* 3. 1728.) "That

"the contempt which he and others had for "these pieces (which only himself had shown, and handed about as his own) "occasion'd their being lost, "and for that cause only, not return'd." A fact, of which as none but he could be conscious, none but he could be the publisher of it.

This young Gentleman's whole misfortune was too inordinate a passion to be thought a Wit. Here is a very strong instance, attested by Mr. *Savage* son of the late Earl *Rivers*; who having shown some verses of his in manuscript to Mr. *Moore*, wherein Mr. *Pope* was call'd *first of the tuneful train*, Mr. *Moore* the next morning sent to Mr. *Savage* to desire him to give those verses another turn, to wit, "That *Pope* might "now be *the first*, because *Moore* had left "him unrival'd in turning his style to Co- "medy." This was during the rehearsal of the *Rival Modes*, his first and only work; the Town condemn'd it in the action, but he printed it in 1726-7 with this modest Motto,

Hic cæstus, artemque repono.

The smaller pieces which we have heard attributed to this author, are, An Epigram on the Bridge at *Blenheim*, by Dr. *Evans*; *Cosmelia*, by Mr. *Pit*, Mr. *Jones*, &c. The Mock-marriage of a mad Divine, with a Cl — for a Parson, by Dr. *W*. The Saw-pit, a Simile, by a *Friend*. Certain Physical works on Sir *James Baker*; and some unown'd Letters, Advertisements and Epigrams against our author in the *Daily Journal*.

Notwithstanding what is here collected of the Person imagin'd by *Curl* to be meant in this place, we cannot be of that opinion; since our Poet had certainly no need of vindicating half a dozen verses to himself which every reader had done for him; since the name itself is not spell'd *Moore* but *More*; and lastly, since the learned *Scriblerus* has so well prov'd the contrary.

All gaze with ardour: some, a Poet's name,

Others, a sword-knot and lac'd suit inflame.

But lofty Lintot in the circle rose;

50 " This prize is mine; who tempt it, are my foes:

" With me began this genius, and shall end.

He spoke, and who with Lintot shall contend?

Fear held them mute. Alone untaught to fear,

Stood dauntless Curl, " Behold that rival here!

REMARKS.

VERSE 46. *The Phantom,* More.] It appears from hence that this is not the name of a real person, but fictitious; *More* from μωϱΘ. *ftultus,* μωεια, *ftultitia,* to represent the folly of a Plagiary. Thus *Erafmus: Admonuit me* Mori *cognomen tibi, quod tam ad* Moriæ *vocabulum accedit quam es ipfe a re alienus.* Dedication of *Moriæ Encomion* to Sir *Tho. More;* the Farewell of which may be our Author's to his Plagiary. *Vale* More! & *Moriam tuam gnaviter defende. Adieu* More, and *be fure ftrongly to defend thy own folly.*
                                        SCRIBLERUS.

VERSE 49. *But lofty* Lintot.] We enter here upon the episode of the Bookfellers: persons, whose names being more known and famous in the learned world than those of the authors in this Poem, do therefore need lefs explanation. The action of Mr. *Lintot* here imitates that of *Dares* in *Virgil,* rifing juft in this manner to lay hold on a *Bull.* This eminent Bookfeller printed the *Rival Modes* above-mentioned.

VERSE 54. *Stood dauntlefs* Curl, *&c.*] We come now to a character of much refpect, that of Mr. *Edmond Curl.* As a plain repetition of great actions is the beft praife of them, we fhall only fay of this eminent man, that he carried the Trade many lengths beyond what it ever before had arrived at, and that he was the envy and admiration of all his profeffion. He poffeft himfelf of a command over all authors whatever; he caus'd them to write what he pleas'd; they could not call their very names their own. He was not only famous among thefe; he was taken notice of by the *State,* the *Church,* and

the *Law,* and received particular marks of diftinction from each.

It will be own'd that he is here introduc'd with all poffible dignity: he fpeaks like the intrepid *Diomed;* he runs like the fwift-footed *Achilles;* if he falls, 'tis like the beloved *Nifus;* and (what *Homer* makes to be the chief of all praifes) he is *favour'd of the Gods:* He fays but three words, and his prayer is heard; a Goddefs conveys it to the feat of *Jupiter.* Tho' he lofes the prize, he gains the victory; the great Mother her felf comforts him, fhe infpires him with expedients, fhe honours him with an immortal prefent (fuch as *Achilles* receives from *Thetis* and *Æneas* from *Venus*) at once inftructive and prophetical: After this, he is unrival'd and triumphant.

The tribute our author here pays him, is a grateful return for feveral unmerited obligations: Many weighty animadverfions on the Publick affairs, and many excellent and diverting pieces on Private perfons, has he given to his name. If ever he ow'd two verfes to any other, he ow'd Mr. *Curl* fome thoufands. He was every day extending his fame, and inlarging his writings: witnefs innumerable inftances! but it fhall fuffice only to mention the *Court-Poems,* which he meant to publifh as the work of the true writer, a Lady of quality; but being firft threaten'd, and afterwards punifh'd, for it by Mr. *Pope,* he generoufly transferr'd it from *her* to *him,* and has now printed it twelve years in his name. The fingle time that ever he fpoke to *C.* was on that affair, and to that

55 " The race by vigor, not by vaunts is won;

    So take the hindmost Hell.——He said, and run.

    Swift as a bard the bailiff leaves behind,

    He left huge Lintot, and out-stript the wind.

    As when a dab-chick waddles thro' the copse,

60 On feet and wings, and flies, and wades, and hops;

    So lab'ring on, with shoulders, hands, and head,

    Wide as a windmill all his figure spread,

    With legs expanded Bernard urg'd the race,

    And seem'd to emulate great Jacob's pace.

65 Full in the middle way there stood a lake,

    Which Curl's Corinna chanc'd that morn to make,

REMARKS.

happy incident he owes all the favours since received from him. So true is the saying of Dr. *Sydenham*, that " any one shall be, at some time " or other, the better or the worse, for ha- " ving but *seen* or *spoken* to a good, or a bad " man."

VERSE 66.] *Curl's Corinna.*] This name it seems was taken by one Mrs. *T——*, who procured some private Letters of Mr. *Pope's*, while almost a boy, to Mr. *Cromwell*, and sold them without the consent of either of those gentlemen to *Curl*, who printed them in 12?

1727. He has discover'd her to be the publisher in his *Key*, p. 11. But our Poet had no thought of reflecting on her in this passage; on the contrary, he has been inform'd she is a decent woman and in misfortunes. We only take this opportunity of mentioning the manner in which those Letters got abroad, which the author was asham'd of as very trivial things, full not only of levities, but of wrong judgments of men and books, and only excusable from the youth and inexperience of the writer.

IMITATIONS.

VERSE 54, &c.] Something like this is in *Homer*, *Il*. 10. *ver*. 220. of *Diomed*. Two different manners of the same author in his Similes, are also imitated in the two following; the first of the Bailiff, is short, unadorn'd, and (as the Critics well know) from *familiar life*; the second of the Water-fowl more extended, picturesque, and from *rural life*. The 55th verse is likewise a literal translation of one in *Homer*.

VERSE 56. *So take the hindmost Hell.*] Horace de Art.

Occupet extremum scabies; mihi turpe relinqui est.

VERSE 60. *On feet, and wings, and flies, and wades, and hops;*

So lab'ring on, with shoulders, hands, and head.] Milton, lib. 2.

—— *So eagerly the fiend*
O'er bog, o'er steep, thro' strait, rough, dense, or rare,
With head, hands, wings, or feet, pursues his way,
And swims, or sinks, or wades, or creeps, or flies.

(Such was her wont, at early dawn to drop

Her evening cates before his neighbour's fhop,)

Here fortun'd Curl to flide; loud fhout the band,

70 And Bernard! Bernard! rings thro' all the Strand.

Obfcene with filth the Mifcreant lies bewray'd,

Fal'n in the plafh his wickednefs had lay'd;

Then firft (if Poets aught of truth declare)

The caitiff Vaticide conceiv'd a prayer.

75 　Here Jove! whofe name my bards and I adore,

As much at leaft as any God's, or more;

And him and his if more devotion warms,

Down with the Bible, up with the Pope's Arms.

REMARKS.

VERSE 71. *Obfcene with filth*, &c.] Tho' this incident may feem too low and bafe for the dignity of an Epic Poem, the learned very well know it to be but a copy of *Homer* and *Virgil*; the very words Ον,θΟ and *Fimus* are ufed by them, tho' our Poet (in compliance to modern nicety) has remarkably enrich'd and colour'd his language, as well as rais'd the verfi-fication, in thefe two Epifodes. Mr. *Dryden* in *Mac-Fleckno* has not fcrupled to mention the *Morning Toaft* at which the fifhes bite in the *Thames*, *Piffing Ally*, *Reliques of the Bum*, *Whip-ftich*, *Kifs my* ——, &c. but our author is more grave, and (as a fine writer fays of *Virgil* in his *Georgics*) *toffes about his* Dung *with an air of Majefty*. If we confider that the Exer-cifes of his *Authors* could with juftice be no higher than *Tickling*, *Chatt'ring*, *Braying*, or *Diving*, it was no eafy matter to invent fuch Games as were proportion'd to the meaner de-gree of *Bookfellers*. In *Homer* and *Virgil*, *Ajax* and *Nifus*, the perfons drawn in this plight are *Heroes*; whereas here they are fuch, with whom it had been great impropriety to have join'd any but vile ideas; befides the natural connection there is, between Libellers and common Nufances. Ne-verthelefs I have often heard our author own, that this part of his Poem was (as it frequently happens) what coft him moft trouble, and pleas'd him leaft: but that he hoped 'twas ex-cufable, fince levell'd at fuch as underftand no delicate fatire: Thus the politeft men are fometimes obliged to *fwear*, when they hap-pen to have to do with Porters and Oyfter-wenches.

VERSE 78. *Down with the* Bible, *up with the* Pope's Arms.] The Bible, *Curl's* fign, the Crofs-keys, *Lintot's*.

IMITATIONS.

VERSE 69. *Here fortun'd Curl to flide.*] *Virg. Æn.* 5. of *Nifus*.
　Labitur infelix, cæfis ut forte juvencis
　Fufus humum viridefq; fuper madefecerat herbas—
　Concidit, immundoque fimo, facroque cruore.

VERSE 70. *And* Bernard, Bernard.] *Virg. Ecl.* 6.
　—*Ut littus, Hyla, Hyla, omne fonaret.*

A place there is, betwixt earth, air and seas,
80 Where from Ambrosia, Jove retires for ease.
There in his seat two spacious Vents appear,
On this he sits, to that he leans his ear,
And hears the various Vows of fond mankind,
Some beg an eastern, some a western wind:
85 All vain petitions, mounting to the sky,
With reams abundant this abode supply;
Amus'd he reads, and then returns the bills
Sign'd with that Ichor which from Gods distills.

In office here fair Cloacina stands,
90 And ministers to Jove with purest hands;
Forth from the heap she pick'd her Vot'ry's pray'r,
And plac'd it next him, a distinction rare!
Oft, as he fish'd her nether realms for wit,
The Goddess favour'd him, and favours yet.
95 Renew'd by ordure's sympathetic force.
As oil'd with magic juices for the course,
Vig'rous he rises; from th'effluvia strong
Imbibes new life, and scours and stinks along,
Re-passes Lintot, vindicates the race,
100 Nor heeds the brown dishonours of his face.

IMITATIONS.

VERSE 79. See *Lucian's Icaro-Menippus*; where this Fiction is more extended.

VERSE id. *A place there is, betwixt earth, air and seas.*] Ovid Met. 12.

Orbe locus medio est, inter terrasq; fretamq;
Cælestesq; plagas ――

VERSE 88. Alludes to *Homer, Iliad* 5.

――'ρέε δ' Αμβροϊον αίμα Θεοϊο,
'Ιχώρ, οἷᴑ πέρϊε ρέει μακαρεσσι Θεοϊσιν

A stream of nectarous humour issuing flow'd,
Sanguin, such as celestial Spirits may bleed.
Milton.

VERSE 89. *Cloacina.*] The *Roman* Goddess of the Common-shores.

VERSE 93. *Oft as he fish'd,* &c.] See the Preface to *Swift* and *Pope's* Miscellanies.

VERSE 96. *As oil'd with magic juices.*] Alluding to the opinion that there are Ointments us'd by Witches to enable them to fly in the air, &c.

And now the Victor stretch'd his eager hand
Where the tall Nothing stood, or seem'd to stand;
A shapeless shade! it melted from his sight,
Like forms in clouds, or visions of the night!
105 To seize his papers, Curl, was next thy care;
His papers light, fly diverse, tost in air:
Songs, sonnets, epigrams the winds uplift,
And whisk 'em back to Evans, Young, and Swift.
Th' embroider'd Suit, at least, he deem'd his prey;
110 That suit, an unpaid Taylor snatch'd away!
No rag, no scrap, of all the beau, or wit,
That once so flutter'd, and that once so writ.
Heav'n rings with laughter: Of the laughter vain,
Dulness, good Queen, repeats the jest again.

REMARKS.

Verse iii. *An unpaid Taylor.*] This line has been loudly complain'd of (in *Mist, June 8. Dedic. to Sawney,* and others) as a most inhuman satire on the *Poverty of Poets:* but it is thought our author would be acquitted by a Jury of *Taylors.* To me this instance seems unluckily chosen; if it be a satire on any body, it must be on a bad PAYMASTER, since the person they have here apply'd it to was a man of Fortune. Not but Poets may well be jealous of so great a prerogative as *Non-payment:* which Mr. *Dennis* so far asserts as boldly to pronounce, that " if *Homer* himself was not in debt, it was " because no body would trust him." (*Pref. to Rem. on the Rape of the Lock, p.* 15.)

IMITATIONS.

Verse 100. *Nor heeds the brown dishonours of his face.*] *Virg. Æn.* 5.
—— *faciem ostentabat, & udo*
Turpia membra fimo ——
Verse 103. *A shapeless shade, &c.*] *Virg. Æn.* 6.
———— *Effugit imago*
Par levibus ventis, volucrique simillima somno.

Verse 106. *His papers light, fly diverse, tost in air.*] *Virg.* 6. of the Sybils leaves,
Carmina turbata volent rapidis Ludibria Ventis.
The persons mentioned in the next line are some of those, whose Writings, Epigrams or Jests, he had own'd.

115 Three wicked imps of her own Grubstreet Choir

She deck'd like Congreve, Addison, and Prior;

Mears, Warner, Wilkins run: Delusive thought!

Breval, Besaleel, Bond, the Varlets caught.

Curl stretches after Gay, but Gay is gone,

120 He grasps an empty Joseph for a John!

So Proteus, hunted in a nobler shape,

Became when seiz'd, a Puppy, or an Ape.

   To him the Goddess. Son! thy grief lay down,

And turn this whole illusion on the town.

125 As the sage dame, experienc'd in her trade,

By names of Toasts retails each batter'd jade,

(Whence hapless Monsieur much complains at Paris

Of wrongs from Duchesses and Lady Mary's)

REMARKS.

VERSE 116. *Like* Congreve, Addison, *and* Prior.] These Authors being such whose names will reach posterity, we shall not give any account of them, but proceed to those of whom it is necessary. —— *Besaleel Morris* was author of some Satyrs on the Translators of *Homer* (Mr. *Tickel* and our author) with many other things printed in News-papers.——*Bond* writ a Satyr against Mr. *P.*——Capt. *Breval* was author of *The Confederates*, an ingenious dramatic performance, to expose Mr. *P.* Mr. *Gay*, Dr. *Arb.* and some Ladies of quality. CURL, *Key*, p. 11.

VERSE 117. *Mears, Warner, Wilkins.*] Booksellers and Printers of much anonymous stuff.

VERSE 118. *Breval, Besaleel, Bond.*] I foresee it will be objected from this line, that we were in an error in our assertion on verse 46. of this Book, that *More* was a fictitious name, since these persons are equally represented by the Poet as phantoms. So at first sight it may seem: but be not deceived, Reader! these also are not real persons. 'Tis true *Curl* declares *Breval* a Captain, author of a Libel call'd *The Confederates:* But the same *Curl* first said it was written by *Joseph Gay:* Is his second assertion to be credited any more than his first? He likewise affirms *Bond* to be one who writ a Satire on our Poet; but where is such a Satire to be found? where was such a Writer ever heard of? As for *Besaleel*, it carries Forgery in the very name, nor is it, as the others are, a surname. Thou may'st depend on it no such authors ever lived: All phantoms! SCRIBLERUS.

VERSE 120. *Joseph Gay*, a fictitious name put by *Curl* before several pamphlets, which made them pass with many for Mr. *Gay's.*

VERSE 124. *And turn this whole illusion on the town.*] It was a common practice of this Bookseller, to publish vile pieces of obscure hands under the names of eminent authors.

Be thine, my ftationer! this magic gift;
130 Cook fhall be Prior, and Concanen, Swift;
So fhall each hoftile name become our own,
And we too boaft our Garth and Addifon.

With that fhe gave him (piteous of his cafe,
Yet fmiling at his ruful length of face)

REMARKS.

VERSE 130. Cook *fhall be* Prior.] The man here fpecify'd was the fon of a *Muggletonian*, who kept a Publick-houfe at *Braintree* in *Effex*. He writ a thing call'd *The Battle of Poets*, of which *Philips* and *Welfted* were the heroes, and wherein our author was attack'd in his moral character, in relation to his *Homer* and *Shakefpear*: He writ moreover a Farce of *Penelope*, in the preface of which alfo he was fquinted at: and fome malevolent things in the *Britifh*, *London* and *Daily Journals*. His chief work was a tranflation of *Hefiod*, to which *Theobald* writ notes, and half-notes, as hath already been faid.

VERSE ibid. *And* Concanen, Swift.] *Matthew Concanen*, an *Irifhman*, an anonymous flanderer, and publifher of other men's flanders, particularly on Dr. *Swift* to whom he had obligations, and from whom he had received both in a collection of Poems for his benefit and otherwife, no fmall affiftance; To which *Smedley* (one of his brethren in enmity to *Swift*) alludes in his *Metam.* of *Scriblerus*, p. 7. accufing him of having " boafted of what he had not written, " but others had revis'd and done for him." He was alfo author of feveral fcurrilities in the *Britifh* and *London Journals*; and of a pamphlet call'd a *Supplement* to the *Profund*, wherein he deals very unfairly with our Poet, not only frequently blaming Mr. *Broome*'s verfes as his, (for which he might indeed feem in fome degree accountable, having corrected what that gentleman did) but thofe of the Duke of *Buckingham*, and

others. To this rare piece, fome-body humoroufly caus'd him to take for his motto, *De profundis clamavi.*

VERSE 132. *And we too boaft our* Garth *and* Addifon.] Nothing is more remarkable than our author's love of praifing good writers. He has celebrated Sir *Ifaac Newton*, Mr. *Dryden*, Mr. *Congreve*, Mr. *Wycherley*, Dr. *Garth*, Mr. *Walfh*, Duke of *Buckingham*, Mr. *Addifon*, Lord *Lanfdown*; in a word, almoft every man of his time that deferv'd it. It was very difficult to have that pleafure in a poem on This fubject, yet he found means to infert their panegyrick, and here has made even Dulnefs out of her own mouth pronounce it. It muft have been particularly agreeable to him to celebrate Dr. *Garth*; both as his conftant friend thro' life, and as he was his predeceffor in this kind of Satire. The *Difpenfary* attack'd the whole Body of Apothecaries, a much more ufeful one undoubtedly than that of the bad Poets (if in truth this can be call'd a Body, of which no two members ever agreed) It alfo did what *Tibbald* fays is unpardonable, drew in *parts of private character*, and introduced *perfons independent of his Subject*. Much more would *Boileau* have incurr'd his cenfure, who left all fubjects whatever on all occafions, to fall upon the bad Poets; which it is to be fear'd wou'd have been more immediately His concern.

VERSE 134. *Ruful length of face.*] " The " decrepid perfon or figure of a man are no re-

IMITATIONS.

VERSE 133. —— *piteous of his cafe,*
Yet fmiling at his ruful length of face.]
Virg. Æn. 5.

—— *Rifit pater optimus illi.*
Me liceat cafum miferare infontis amici ——
Sic fatus, Gætuli tergum immane leonis, &c.

K

135 A shaggy Tap'stry, worthy to be spread
On Codrus' old, or Dunton's modern bed;
Instructive work! whose wry-mouth'd portraiture
Display'd the fates her confessors endure.

REMARKS.

" flections upon his *Genius:* An honest mind " will love and esteem a *man of worth,* tho' he " be deform'd or poor. Yet the author of the " Dunciad hath libell'd a person for his *ruful* " *length of face!*" MIST's JOURN. *June* 8. This *Genius* and *man of worth* whom an honest mind should love, is Mr. *Curl.* True it is, he stood in the Pillory; an accident which will lengthen the face of any man tho' it were ever so comely, therefore is no reflection on the natural beauty of Mr. *Curl.* But as to reflections on any man's Face, or Figure, Mr. *Dennis* saith excellently; " Natural deformity comes not by " our fault, 'tis often occasioned by calamities " and diseases, which a man can no more help, " than a monster can his deformity. There is " no one misfortune, and no one disease, but " what all the rest of men are subject to. —— " But the deformity of this Author is visible, " present, lasting, unalterable, and peculiar to " himself: it is the mark of God and Nature " upon him, to give us warning that we should " hold no society with him, as a creature not " of our original, nor of our species: And they " who have refused to take this warning which " God and Nature have given them, and have " in spite of it by a senseless presumption, ven- " tur'd to be familiar with him, have severely " suffer'd, &c. 'Tis certain his original is not " from *Adam,* but from the Devil," &c. DENNIS *and* GILDON: *Charact.* of Mr. P. 8°. 1716.

It is admirably observ'd by Mr. *Dennis* against Mr. *Law,* p. 33. " That the language of *Bil-* " *lingsgate* can never be the language of Charity, " nor consequently of Christianity." I should else be tempted to use the language of a Critick: For what is more provoking to a Commentator, than to behold his author thus pourtrayed? Yet I consider it really hurts not *Him*; whereas ma- liciously to call some *others* dull, might do them prejudice with a world too apt to believe it. Therefore tho' Mr. *D.* may call another a *little ass* or a *young toad,* far be it from us to call him a *toothless lion,* or an *old serpent.* Indeed, had I

written these notes (as was once my intent) in the learned language, I might have given him the appellations of *Balatro, Calceatum caput,* or *Scurra in triviis,* being phrases in good esteem, and frequent usage among the best learned: But in our mother-tongue were I to tax any Gentle- man of the Dunciad, surely it should be in words not to the vulgar intelligible, whereby christian charity, decency, and good accord among au- thors, might be preserved. SCRIBLERUS.

VERSE 135. *A shaggy Tap'stry.*] A sorry kind of Tapestry frequent in old Inns, made of worsted or some coarser stuff: like that which is spoken of by Doctor *Donne* — *Faces as frightful as theirs who whip Christ in old hangings.* The imagery woven in it alludes to the mantle of *Cloanthus* in *Æn.* 5.

VERSE 136. *On Codrus' old, or Dunton's modern bed.*] Of *Codrus* the Poet's bed see *Ju- venal,* describing his *poverty* very copiously. *Sat.* 3. *v.* 203, &c.

Lectus erat Codro, &c.

Codrus *had but one bed, so short to boot,*
That his short Wife's short legs hung dangling out:
His cupboard's head six earthen pitchers grac'd,
Beneath them was his trusty tankard plac'd;
And to support this noble Plate, there lay
A bending Chiron, cast from honest clay.
His few Greek books a rotten chest contain'd,
Whose covers much of mouldiness complain'd,
Where mice and rats devour'd poetic bread,
And on Heroic Verse luxuriously were fed.
'Tis true, poor Codrus *nothing had to boast,*
And yet poor Codrus *all that nothing lost.*
Dryd.

But Mr. *C.* in his dedication of the Letters, Advertisements, &c. to the Author of the *Dun- ciad,* assures us, that " *Juvenal* never satyrized the poverty of *Codrus.*"

John Dunton was a broken Bookseller and abu- sive scribler: he writ *Neck or Nothing,* a vio- lent satyr on some Ministers of State; *The dan-*

Earless on high, stood un-abash'd Defoe,
140 And Tutchin flagrant from the scourge, below:
There Ridpath, Roper, cudgell'd might ye view;
The very worsted still look'd black and blue:
Himself among the storied Chiefs he spies,
As from the blanket high in air he flies,
145 And oh! (he cry'd) what street, what lane, but knows
Our purgings, pumpings, blanketings and blows?
In ev'ry loom our labours shall be seen,
And the fresh vomit run for ever green!
See in the circle next, Eliza plac'd;
150 Two babes of love close clinging to her waste.

REMARKS.

gur of a death-bed repentance, a libel on the late Duke of Devonshire and on the Rt. Rev. Bishop of Peterborough, &c.

VERSE 140. And Tutchin flagrant from the scourge.] John Tutchin, author of some vile verses, and of a weekly paper call'd the Observator: He was sentenc'd to be whipp'd thro' several towns in the west of England, upon which he petition'd King James II. to be hanged. When that Prince died in exile, he wrote an invective against his memory, occasioned by some humane Elegies on his death. He liv'd to the time of Queen Anne.

VERSE 141. There Ridpath, Roper.] Authors of the Flying-Post and Post-Boy, two scandalous papers on different sides, for which they equally and alternately were cudgell'd, and deserv'd it.

VERSE 143. Himself among the storied chiefs he spies, &c.] The history of Curl's being toss'd in a blanket, and whipp'd by the scholars of Westminster, is ingeniously and pathetically related in a poem entituled Neck or Nothing. Of his purging and vomiting, see A full and true account of a horrid revenge on the body of Edm. Curl, &c.

VERSE 149. See in the circle next, Eliza plac'd.] In this game is expos'd in the most contemptuous manner, the profligate licenciousness of those shameless scriblers (for the most part of That sex, which ought least to be capable of such malice or impudence) who in li-

IMITATIONS.

VERSE 143. Himself among the storied chiefs he spies, &c.] Virg. Æn. 1.
Se quoq; principibus permixtum agnovit Achivis —
Constitit & lacrymans. Quis jam locus, inquit,
    Achate!
Quæ regio in terris nostri non plena laboris?
VERSE 148. And the fresh vomit run for ever green.] A parody on these of a late noble author,
His bleeding arm had furnish'd all their rooms,
And run for ever purple in the looms.
VERSE 150. Two babes of love close clinging to her waste.] Virg. Æn. 5.
Cressa genus, Pholoe, geminique sub ubere nati.

Fair as before her works she stands confess'd,
In flow'rs and pearls by bounteous Kirkall dress'd.
153 The Goddess then : " Who best can send on high
" The salient spout, far-streaming to the sky ;
" His be yon Juno of majestic size,
" With cow-like-udders, and with ox-like eyes.
" This China-Jordan, let the chief o'ercome
158 " Replenish, not ingloriously, at home.
    Chetwood and Curl accept the glorious strife,
    (Tho' one his son dissuades, and one his wife)

REMARKS.

bellous Memoirs and Novels, reveal the faults and misfortunes of both sexes, to the ruin or disturbance, of publick fame or private happiness. Our good Poet, (by the whole cast of his work being obliged not to take off the Irony) where he cou'd not show his Indignation, hath shewn his Contempt as much as possible : having here drawn as vile a picture, as could be represented in the colours of Epic poesy.

              SCRIBLERUS.

VERSE 149. *Eliza Haywood.*] This woman was authoress of those most scandalous books, call'd *The Court of Carimania*, and *The new Utopia*. For the *two Babes of Love*, See CURL, *Key*, p. 22. But whatever reflection he is pleas'd to throw upon this Lady, surely 'twas what from him she little deserv'd, who had celebrated his undertakings for *Reformation of Manners*, and declared her self " to be so perfectly acquaint-

" ed with the *sweetness of his disposition*, and " that *tenderness with which he consider'd the* " *errors of his fellow-creatures* ; that tho' she " should find the *little inadvertencies of her own* " *life* recorded in his papers, she was certain " it would be done in such a manner as she " could not but approve," Mrs. HAYWOOD, Hist. of *Clar.* printed in the *Female Dunciad*, p. 18.

VERSE 152. *Kirkall*, the Name of a Graver. This Lady's Works were printed in four Volumes duod. with her picture thus dress'd up, before them.

VERSE 159. *Chetwood* the name of a Bookseller, whose Wife was said to have as great an influence over her husband, as *Boilsau's Perruquiere*. See *Lutrin.* Cant. 2. — *Henry Curl*, the worthy son of his father *Edmund*.

IMITATIONS.

VERSE 155. —— *This* Juno ——
With cow-like udders, and with ox-like eyes]
In allusion to *Homer's* Βοῶπις πότνια Ἥρη.
    VERSE 157. *This* China *Jordan*, &c.]
Virg. Æn. 5.
Tertius, Argolica hac galea contentus abito.
    VERSE ibid. *This* China *Jordan*.] In the

games of *Homer Il.* 23, there are set together as prizes, a Lady and a Kettle ; as in this place Mrs. *Haywood* and a Jordan. But there the preference in value is given to the *Kettle*, at which Mad. *Dacier* is justly displeas'd : Mrs. *H.* here is treated with distinction, and acknowledg'd to be the more valuable of the two.

This on his manly confidence relies,

That on his vigor and superior size.

165 First Chetwood lean'd against his letter'd post;

It rose, and labour'd to a curve at most:

So Jove's bright bow displays its watry round,

(Sure sign, that no spectator shall be drown'd)

A second effort brought but new disgrace,

170 For straining more, it flies in his own face;

Thus the small jett which hasty hands unlock,

Spirts in the gard'ners eyes who turns the cock.

Not so from shameless Curl: Impetuous spread

The stream, and smoaking, flourish'd o'er his head.

175 So, (fam'd like thee for turbulence and horns,)

Eridanus his humble fountain scorns,

Thro' half the heav'ns he pours th' exalted urn;

His rapid waters in their passage burn.

REMARKS.

VERSE 177. *Thro' half the heavens he pours th' exalted urn.*] In a manuscript Dunciad (where are some marginal corrections of some gentlemen some time deceas'd) I have found another reading of these lines, thus;

And lifts his urn thro' half the heav'ns to flow:
His rapid waters in their passage glow.
This I cannot but think the right: For first, that the difference between *burn* and *glow* may seem not very material to others, to me I confess the.

IMITATIONS.

VERSE 163. *This on his manly confidence relies, That on his vigor.*] Virg. Æn. 5.
Ille melior motu, fretusque juventa,
Hic membris & mole valens——
VERSE 167. *So Jove's bright bow — Sure sign——*] The words of *Homer* of the Rainbow, in *Iliad* 11.

—— ἅς τε Κρονίων

Ἐν νέφει στήριξε, τέρας μερόπων ἀνθρώπων.
Which Mad. *Dacier* thus renders, *Arcs merveilleux, que le fils de Saturn à fondez dans les nües, pour etre dans tous les âges un signe à tous les mortels.*

VERSE 175. *So (fam'd like thee for turbulence and horns) Eridanus.*] *Virgil* mentions these two qualifications of *Eridanus.* Geor. 4.
Et gemina auratus taurino cornua vultu,
Eridanus, quo non alius per pinguia culta
In mare purpureum violentior effluit amnis.
The Poets fabled of this River *Eridanus*, that it flow'd thro' the skies. *Denham, Cooper's Hill.*
Heav'n her Eridanus no more shall boast,
Whose Fame like thine in lesser currents lost,
Thy nobler stream shall visit Jove's abodes,
To shine among the stars, and bathe the Gods.

Swift as it mounts, all follow with their eyes;
180 Still happy Impudence obtains the prize.

Thou triumph'st, victor of the high-wrought day,
And the pleas'd dame soft-smiling leads away.
Chetwood, thro' perfect modesty o'ercome,
Crown'd with the Jordan, walks contented home.

185   But now for Authors nobler palms remain:
Room for my Lord! three Jockeys in his train;
Six huntsmen with a shout precede his chair;
He grins, and looks broad nonsense with a stare.
His honour'd meaning, Dulness thus exprest;
190 " He wins this Patron who can tickle best."

He chinks his purse, and takes his seat of state:
With ready quills the dedicators wait;
Now at his head the dext'rous task commence,
And instant, fancy feels th' imputed sense;
195 Now gentle touches wanton o'er his face,
He struts Adonis, and affects grimace:

REMARKS.

latter has an elegance, a *Jenesçay quoy*, which is much easier to be conceiv'd than explain'd. Secondly, every reader of our Poet must have observ'd how frequently he uses this word *glow* in other parts of his works: To instance only in his *Homer.*

(1.) Iliad 9. v. 726.—*With one resentment glows.*
(2.) Iliad 11. v. 626.—*There the battle glows.*
(3.) Ibid. 985.—*The closing flesh that instant ceas'd to glow.*
(4.) Il. 12. v. 55.—*Encompass'd Hector glows.*
(5.) Ibid. 475.—*His beating breast with gen'rous ardour glows.*
(6.) Iliad 18. v. 591.—*Another part glow'd with refulgent arms.*
(7.) Ibid. v. 654.—*And curl'd on silver props in order glow.*

I am afraid of growing too luxuriant in examples, or I could stretch this catalogue to a great extent, but these are enough to prove his fondness for this *beautiful word*, which therefore let all future Editions re-place here.

I am aware after all, that *burn* is the proper word to convey an idea of what was said to be Mr. *Curl's* condition at that time. But from that very reason I infer the direct contrary. For surely every lover of our author will conclude he had more humanity, than to insult a man on such a misfortune or calamity, which could never befal him purely by his *own fault*, but from an unhappy communication with another. *This Note is partly Mr.* THEOBALD, *partly* SCRIBLERUS.

Rolli the feather to his ear conveys,

Then his nice taste directs our Operas:

Welsted his mouth with Classic flatt'ry opes,

200 And the puff'd Orator bursts out in tropes.

But Oldmixon the Poet's healing balm

Strives to extract from his soft, giving palm;

Unlucky Oldmixon! thy lordly master

The more thou ticklest, gripes his fist the faster.

205   While thus each hand promotes the pleasing pain,

And quick sensations skip from vein to vein,

A youth unknown to Phœbus, in despair,

Puts his last refuge all in Heav'n and Pray'r.

REMARKS.

VERSE 197. *Paolo Antonio Rolli*, an *Italian* Poet, and writer of many Operas in that language, which, partly by the help of his genius, prevail'd in *England* near ten years.

VERSE 199. *Welsted.*] See Note on verse 295 of this Book.

VERSE 201. *But Oldmixon, &c.*] Mr. *John Oldmixon* (next to Mr. *Dennis* the most ancient Critick of our Nation) not so happy as laborious in Poetry, and therefore perhaps characteriz'd by the *Tatler*, Nº. 62. by the name of *Omicron* the *unborn Poet.* CURL, Key to the D. p. 13. An unjust censurer of Mr. *Addison*, whom in his imitation of *Bouhours* (call'd the *Arts of Logic and Rhetoric*) he misrepresents in plain matter of fact. In p. 45. he cites the *Spectator* as abusing Dr. *Swift* by name, where there is not the least hint of it: And in p. 304. is so injurious as to suggest, that Mr. *Addison* himself writ that *Tatler* Nº. 43. which says of his *own* Simile, that " 'tis as great as ever en-" ter'd into the mind of man." This person wrote numbers of books which are not come to our knowledge. " Dramatick works, and a " volume of Poetry, consisting of heroic Epi-

" stles, &c. some whereof are very well done," saith that great Judge Mr. JACOB. *Lives of Poets, Vol.* 2. *p.* 303.

I remember a *Pastoral* of his on the *Battle of Blenheim*; a Critical History of *England*; Essay on Criticism, in prose; The Arts of Logic and Rhetoric, in which he frequently reflects on our Author. We find in the *Flying-Post* of *Apr.*13. 1728. some very flat verses of his against him and Dr. *Sew.* He was all his life a hired writer for a Party, and received his reward in a small place which he yet enjoys.

VERSE 207. *A youth unknown to Phœbus, &c.*] The satire of this Episode being levelled at the base flatteries of authors to worthless wealth or greatness, concludeth here with an excellent lesson to such men; That altho' their pens and praises were as exquisite as they conceit of themselves, yet (even in their own mercenary views) a creature unlettered, who serveth the passions, or pimpeth to the pleasures of such vain, braggart, puft Nobility, shall with those patrons be much more inward, and of them much higher rewarded.

SCRIBLERUS.

What force have pious vows? the Queen of Love
210 His Sister sends, her vot'ress, from above.
　　As taught by Venus, Paris learnt the art
　　To touch Achilles' only tender part;
　　Secure, thro' her, the noble prize to carry,
　　He marches off, his Grace's Secretary.

215　　Now turn to diff'rent sports (the Goddess cries)
　　And learn, my sons, the wond'rous pow'r of Noise.
　　To move, to raise, to ravish ev'ry heart,
　　With Shakespear's nature, or with Johnson's art,
　　Let others aim: 'Tis yours to shake the soul
220 With thunder rumbling from the mustard-bowl,
　　With horns and trumpets now to madness swell,
　　Now sink in sorrows with a tolling Bell.
　　Such happy arts attention can command,
　　When fancy flags, and sense is at a stand.
225 Improve we these. Three cat-calls be the bribe
　　Of him, whose chatt'ring shames the Monkey tribe;
　　And his this Drum, whose hoarse heroic base
　　Drowns the loud clarion of the braying Ass.

REMARKS.

VERSE 220. *With Thunder rumbling from the mustard-bowl.*] The old way of making Thunder and Mustard were the same; but since it is more advantagiously perform'd by troughs of wood with stops in them. Whether Mr. *Dennis* was the inventor of that improvement, I know not; but it is certain, that being once at a Tragedy of a new Author with a friend of his, he fell into a great passion at hearing some, and cry'd, " S'death! that is " *my* Thunder."

IMITATIONS.

VERSE 217. *To move, to raise, &c. — Let others aim — 'Tis yours to shake, &c.* —] Virgil, Æn 6.
Excudent alii spirantia mollius æra,

Credo equidem, vivos ducant e marmore vultus, &c.
Tu, regere imperio populos, Romane, memento,
Hæ tibi erunt artes ———

　　Now thousand tongues are heard in one loud din:
230　The Monkey-mimicks rush discordant in.
　　'Twas chatt'ring, grinning, mouthing, jabb'ring all,
　　And Noise, and Norton, Brangling, and Breval,
　　Dennis and Dissonance; and captious Art,
　　And Snip-snap short, and Interruption smart.
235　Hold (cry'd the Queen) A Catcall each shall win,
　　Equal your merits! equal is your din!
　　But that this well-disputed game may end,
　　Sound forth, my Brayers, and the welkin rend.
　　As when the long-ear'd milky mothers wait
240　At some sick miser's triple-bolted gate,
　　For their defrauded, absent foals they make
　　A moan so loud, that all the Guild awake,
　　Sore sighs Sir G * *, starting at the bray
　　From dreams of millions, and three groats to pay!
245　So swells each Windpipe; Ass intones to Ass,
　　Harmonic twang! of leather, horn, and brass.
　　Such, as from lab'ring lungs th' Enthusiast blows,
　　High sounds, attempred to the vocal nose.
　　But far o'er all, sonorous Blackmore's strain,
250　Walls, steeples, skies, bray back to him again:

REMARKS.

Verse 225. *Three Catcalls.*) Certain musical instruments used by one sort of Criticks to confound the Poets of the Theatre.

Verse 232. *Norton.*[See verse 383. *J. Durant Breval*, Author of a very extraordinary Book of Travels, and some Poems. See before, V. 118.

IMITATIONS.

Verse 235. ——*A Catcall each shall win,* &c.] Virg. Ecl. 3.
*Non inter nos est tantas componere lites,
Et vitula tu dignus, & hic* ——
Verse 240.] A *Simile* with a long tail, in the manner of *Homer.*

Verse 250. — *bray back to him again* [A figure of speech taken from *Virgil.*
Et vox assensu nemorum ingeminata remugit.
　　　　　　　　　　　　Geor. 3.

L

In Tot'nam fields, the brethren with amaze
Prick all their ears up, and forget to graze;
Long Chanc'ry-lane retentive rolls the found,
And courts to courts return it round and round:
255 Thames wafts it thence to Rufus' roaring hall,
And Hungerford re-ecchoes, bawl for bawl.
All hail him victor in both gifts of Song,
Who fings fo loudly, and who fings fo long.

REMARKS.

VERSE 253. *Long* Chanc'ry-lane.] The place where the Courts of Chancery are kept: The long detention of Clients in thofe Courts, and the difficulty of getting out of them, is humouroufly allegoriz'd in thefe lines.

VERSE 258. *Who fings fo loudly, and who fings fo long.*] A juft character of Sir *Richard Blackmore*, Kt. who (as Mr. *Dryden* exprefs'd it) *Writ to the rumbling of his Coach's wheels*, and whofe indefatigable Mufe produced no lefs that fix Epic poems : *Prince* and *King Arthur*, 20 Books; *Eliza*, 10; *Alfred*, 12; *The Redeemer*, 6 : befides *Job* in folio, the whole *Book of Pfalms*, *The Creation*, 7 Books, *Nature of Man*, 3 Books, and many more. "Tis in this fenfe he is ftiled afterwards, the *Everlafting Blackmore*. Notwithftanding all which, Mr. *Gildon* feems affured, that " this admirable author did not think himfelf upon the *fame foot* " with *Homer*." *Comp. Art of Poetry*, Vol. 1. p. 108.

But how different is the judgment of the author of *Characters of the Times?* p. 25. who fays, " Sir *Richard* is unfortunate in happening " to miftake his proper talents, and that he has " not for many years been *fo much as named*, or " even *thought of* among writers." Even Mr. *Dennis* differs greatly from his friend Mr. *Gildon* : " *Blackmore*'s Action (faith he) has neither " unity, nor integrity, nor morality, nor uni- " verfality; and confequently he can have no " *Fable*, and no *Heroic Poem* : His Narration " is neither probable, delightful, nor wonder- " ful : His Characters have none of the necef- " fary qualifications. —— The things contain'd " in his narration are neither in their own na- " ture delightful, nor numerous enough, nor " rightly difpofed, nor furprifing, nor pathe- " tic. —— Nay he proceeds fo far as to fay Sir *Richard* has *no Genius*; firft laying down " that Genius is caufed by a *furious joy* and " *pride of foul*, on the conception of an *ex- " traordinary Hint*. Many men (fays he) have " their *Hints*, without thefe motions of *fury* " and *pride of foul*, becaufe they want fire " enough to agitate their fpirits; and thefe we

IMITATIONS.

He hears his num'rous herds low o'er the plain, While neighb'ring hills low back to them again.
Cowley.

The poet here celebrated, Sir *R. B.* delighted much in the word *Bray*, which he endeavour'd to ennoble by applying it to the found of *Armour*, *War*, &c. In imitation of him, and ftrengthen'd by his authority, our author has here admitted it into Heroic poetry.

VERSE 252. *Prick all their ears up, and forget to graze.*] Virg. Ecl. 8.
Immemor herbarum quos eft mirata juvenca.
The progrefs of the found from place to place, and the fcenary here of the bordering regions, *Tot'nam fields*, *Chancery-lane*, the *Thames*, *Weftminfter-hall*, and *Hungerford-ftairs*, are imitated from *Virg. Æn. 7.* on the founding the horn of *Alecto*.
Audiit & Trivia longè lacus, audiit amnis Sulphurea Nar albus aqua, fontefque Velini, &c.

This labour paſt, by Bridewell all deſcend,

260 (As morning-pray'r and flagellation end.)

To where Fleet-ditch with diſemboguing ſtreams

Rolls the large tribute of dead dogs to Thames,

REMARKS.

" call cold writers: Others who have a great " deal of fire, but have not excellent organs, " feel the foremention'd *motions*, without the " *extraordinary hints*; And theſe we call fu- " ſtian writers. But he declares, that Sir " *Richard* had neither the *Hints*, nor the *Mo*- " *tions*." *Remarks on Pr. Arth.* 8º. 1696. *Preface.*

This gentleman in his firſt works abuſed the character of Mr. *Dryden*, and in his laſt of Mr. *Pope*, accuſing him in very high and ſober terms of prophaneneſs and immorality *(Eſſay on polite writing*, Vol. 2. p. 270.) on a meer report from *Edm. Curl*, that he was author of a Tra- veſtie on the firſt Pſalm. Mr. *Dennis* took up the ſame report, but with the addition of what Sir *Richard* had neglected, an *Argument to prove it*; which being very curious, we ſhall here tranſcribe. *(Remarks on Homer.* 8º. p. 27.) " It *was* he who burleſqu'd the Pſalm of *Da*- " *vid*. It is *apparent* to me that Pſalm was " burleſqu'd by a *Popiſh* rhymeſter. Let rhy- " ming perſons who have been brought up " *Proteſtants* be otherwiſe what they will, let " them be Rakes, let 'em be Scoundrels, let " 'em be *Atheiſts*, yet education has made an " invincible impreſſion on them in behalf of " the ſacred writings. But a *Popiſh rhymeſter* " has been brought up with a contempt for " thoſe ſacred writings. Now ſhow me ano- " ther Popiſh rhymeſter but he."——— This manner of argumentation is uſual with Mr. *Den*- *nis*; he has employ'd the ſame againſt Sir *Richard* himſelf in a like charge of *Impiety* and *Irreligion*. " All Mr. *Blackmore*'s cele- " ſtial Machines, as they cannot be defended ſo " much as by common receiv'd opinion, ſo are " directly contrary to the doctrine of the Church " of *England*: For the viſible deſcent of an An- " gel muſt be a miracle. Now it is the doctrine

" of the Church of *England* that miracles had " ceas'd a long time before Prince *Arthur* came " into the world. Now if the doctrine of the " Church of *England* be true, as we are oblig'd " to believe, then are all the celeſtial machines " in Prince *Arthur* unſufferable, as wanting not " only human but divine probability. But if " the machines are ſufferable, that is if they " have ſo much as divine probability, then it " follows of neceſſity that the doctrine of the " Church is falſe: So I leave it to every im- " partial Clergyman to conſider, &c." *Pre- face to the Remarks on Prince* Arthur.

It has been ſuggeſted in the Character of Mr. *P.* that he had Obligations to Sir *R. B.* He never had any, and never ſaw him but twice in his Life.

VERSE 260. *As morning pray'r and flagella- tion end.*] It is between eleven and twelve in the morning, after church ſervice, that the cri- minals are whipp'd in *Bridewell*.—This is to mark punctually the Time of the day: *Homer* does it by the circumſtance of the Judges riſing from court, or of the Labourers dinner; our au- thor by one very proper both to the *Perſons* and the *Scene* of his Poem; which we may re- member commenc'd in the evening of the Lord- mayor's day: The firſt book paſſed in that night; the next morning the games begin in the *Strand*, thence along *Fleetſtreet* (places inhabited by Bookſellers) then they proceed by *Bridewell* to- ward *Fleetditch*, and laſtly thro' *Ludgate* to the City and the Temple of the Goddeſs.

VERSE 261. *The* Diving.] This I fancy (ſays a great Enemy to the Poem) is a Game which no body could ever think of but the Au- thor: however it is work'd up admirably well, eſpecially in thoſe lines where he deſcribes *Euſden* (he ſhould ſay *Smedley*) riſing up again. ESSAY on the DUNCIAD, p. 19.

The King of Dykes! than whom, no sluice of mud
With deeper sable blots the silver flood.
265 " Here strip my children! here at once leap in!

   " Here prove who best can dash thro' thick and thin,

   " And who the most in love of dirt excel,

   " Or dark dexterity of groping well.

   " Who flings most filth, and wide pollutes around

270 " The stream, be his the Weekly Journals, bound.

   " A pig of lead to him who dives the best.

   " A peck of coals a-piece shall glad the rest.

   In naked majesty great Dennis stands,

   And, Milo-like, surveys his arms and hands.

REMARKS.

VERSE 266, 267, 268.] The three chief qualifications of Party-writers; to stick at nothing, to delight in flinging dirt, and to slander in the dark by guess.

VERSE 270. *The* Weekly Journals.] Papers of news and scandal intermix'd, on different sides and parties and frequently shifting from one side to the other, call'd the *London Journal, Miss's Journal, British Journal, Daily Journal,* &c. the writers of which for some time were *Welsted, Roome, M'Loy, Concanen,* and others; persons never seen by our author.

VERSE 272. *A peck of coals a-piece.*] Our indulgent Poet, whenever he has spoken of any dirty or low work, constantly puts us in mind of the Poverty of the offenders, as the only extenuation of such practices. Let any one but remark, when a Thief, a Pickpocket, a Highwayman or a Knight of the Post is spoken of, how much our hatred to those characters is lessen'd, if they add, a *needy* Thief, a *poor* Pickpocket, a *hungry* Highwayman, a *starving* Knight of the Post, &c.

VERSE 273. *In naked majesty great Dennis stands.*] The reader, who hath seen in the course

of these notes, what a constant attendance Mr. *Dennis* paid to our author, might here expect a particular regard to be shewn him; and consequently may be surprized at his sinking at once, in so few lines, never to rise again! But in truth he looked upon him with some esteem, for having, more generously than the rest, set his *name* to such works. He was not only a formidable Critick who for many years had written against every thing that had success, (the Antagonist of Sir *Richard Blackmore*, Sir *Richard Steele*, Mr. *Addison,* and Mr. *Pope)* but a zealous Politician (not only appearing in his works, where *Poetry* and the *State* are always equally concerned, but in many secret Hints and sage advices given to the Ministers of all reigns.) He is here likened to *Milo*, in allusion to that verse of *Ovid.*

  — *Fletque Milon senior, cum spectat inanes*
   Herculeis similes, fluidos pendere lacertos;
either with regard to his great Age, or because he was undone by trying to pull to pieces an Oak that was too strong for him.

  —— *Remember Milo's End,*
  Wedg'd in that timber which he strove to rend.
               Lord *Rosc.*

IMITATIONS.

VERSE 263. *The King of* Dykes, *&c.*]
Virg.

  Eridanus, rex fluviorum ——

  —— *quo non alius, per pinguia culta,*
  In mare purpureum violentior effluit amnis.

275 Then fighing, thus. " And am I now threefcore?
   " Ah why, ye Gods! fhould two and two make four?
   He faid, and climb'd a ftranded Lighter's height,
   Shot to the black abyfs, and plung'd down-right.
   The Senior's judgment all the crowd admire,
280 Who but to fink the deeper, rofe the higher.
   Next Smedley div'd; flow circles dimpled o'er
   The quaking mud, that clos'd, and ope'd no more.
   All look, all figh, and call on Smedley loft;
   Smedley in vain refounds thro' all the coaft.
285   Then * * try'd, but hardly fnatch'd from fight,
   Inftant buoys up, and rifes into light;

REMARKS.

VERSE 275. —— And am I now three-fcore?] I fhall here, to prove my impartiality, remark a great overfight in our author as to the age of Mr. Dennis. He muft have been fome years above threefcore in the Mayoralty of Sir George Thorold, which was in 1720, and Mr. Dennis was born (as he himfelf inform'd us in Mr. Jacob's Lives before-mentioned) in 1657; fince when he has happily liv'd eight years more, and is already fenior to Mr. Durfey, who hither-to of all our Poets, enjoy'd the longeft, bodily, Life.

VERSE 281. Next Smedley div'd.] In the furreptitious editions this whole Epifode was apply'd to an initial letter E —, by whom if they meant the Laureate, nothing was more ab-furd, no part agreeing with his character. The Allegory evidently demands a perfon dipp'd in fcandal, and deeply immers'd in dirty work: whereas Mr. Eufden's writings rarely offended but by their length and multitude, and accord-ingly are tax'd of nothing elfe in book 1. verfe 102. But the perfon here mention'd, an Irifh-

man, was author and publifher of many fcurri-lous pieces, a weekly Whitehall Journal in the year 1722, in the name of Sir James Baker, and particularly whole Volumes of Billingfgate againft Dr. Swift and Mr. Pope, call'd Gulliveriana and Alexandriana, printed in 8°. 1728.

VERSE 285. Then * * try'd.] This is an inftance of the Tendernefs of our author. The perfon here intended writ an angry preface againft him, grounded on a Miftake, which he afterwards honourably acknowledg'd in another printed pre-face. Since when, he fell under a fecond mi-ftake, and abus'd both him and his Friend.

He is a writer of Genius and Spirit, tho' in his youth he was guilty of fome pieces bor-dering upon bombaft. Our Poet here gives him a Panegyric inftead of a Satire, being edify'd beyond meafure, at this only inftance he ever met with in his life, of one who was much a Poet, confeffing himfelf in an Error: And has fuppreft his name, as thinking him capable of a fecond repentance.

IMITATIONS.

VERSE 283. —— and call on Smedley loft, &c.] Lord Rofcommon's tranflation of Vir-gil's 6th Eclog.

Alcides wept in vain for Hylas loft,
Hylas in vain refounds thro' all the coaft:

He bears no token of the fabler streams, •

And mounts far off, among the fwans of Thames.

True to the bottom, fee Concanen creep,

290 A cold, long-winded, native of the deep!

If perfeverance gain the Diver's prize,

Not everlasting Blackmore this denies:

No noife, no stir, no motion can'ft thou make,

Th' unconfcious flood fleeps o'er thee like a lake.

295   Not Welsted fo: drawn endlong by his fcull,

Furious he finks; precipitately dull.

Whirlpools and storms his circling arm inveft,

With all the Might of gravitation bleft.

No crab more active in the dirty dance,

300 Downward to climb, and backward to advance;

He brings up half the bottom on his head,

And boldly claims the Journals and the Lead.

Sudden, a burst of thunder fhook the flood.

Lo Smedley rofe, in majefty of mud!

REMARKS.

VERSE 289. *Concanen.*] In the former editions there were only Afterisks in this place; this name was fince inferted merely to fill up the verfe, and give eafe to the ear of the reader.

VERSE 295. *Welfted.*] Leonard Welfted, author of the *Triumvirate*, or a Letter in verfe from *Palæmon* to *Celia* at *Bath*, which was meant for a Satire on Mr. *P.* and fome of his friends about the year 1718. The ftrength of the metaphors in this paffage is to exprefs the great fcurrility and fury of this writer, which may be feen, One day, in a Piece of his, call'd (as I think) *Labeo.* He writ other things which we cannot remember. *Smedley* in his *Metam. of Scrib.* mentions one, the *Hymn of a Gentleman* to the *Creator.* L. W. characteris'd in the treatife περὶ βάθες or the Art of finking as a *Didapper*, and after as an *Eel*, is faid to be this perfon, by DENNIS *Daily Journal* of *May* 11, 1728. He is mentioned again in book 3.

IMITATIONS.

VERSE 292. *Not everlafting* Blackmore.]
Virg. Æn. 5.
Nec bonus Eurytion prælato invidit honori, &c.

VERSE 304. —— *in Majefty of mud.*]
Milton,
—— *in majefty of darknefs round*
Circled ——

305 Shaking the horrors of his ample brows,

And each ferocious feature grim with ooze.

Greater he looks, and more than mortal stares;

Then thus the wonders of the Deep declares.

First he relates, how sinking to the chin,

310 Smit with his mien, the Mud-nymphs suck'd him in:

How young Lutetia, softer than the down,

Nigrina black, and Merdamante brown,

Vy'd for his love in jetty bow'rs below;

As Hylas fair was ravish'd long ago.

315 Then sung, how shown him by the nutbrown maids,

A branch of Styx here rises from the Shades,

That tinctur'd as it runs, with Lethe's streams,

And wafting vapours from the Land of Dreams,

(As under seas Alphæus' sacred sluice

320 Bears Pisa's offerings to his Arethuse)

REMARKS.

VERSE 314. *As Hylas fair.*] Who was ravish'd by the water-nymphs and drawn into the river. The story is told at large by *Valerius Flaccus, Lib. 3. Argon.* See *Virg. Ecl. 6.*

VERSE 316, &c. *A branch of Styx, &c.*] Homer, *Il. 2. Catal.*

Οι τ' αμφ' ιμερτον Τιλαρησιον εργ' ενεμον]ο,
Ος ρ' ις Πλωειον προιει καλλιρροον υδωρ,
Ουδ' ογε Πλωειω συμμιςγε]αι αργυρεδινη,
Αλλά τε μιν καθύπερθεν επιρρέει ηυτ' ελαιον.
Ορχυ δ' εινυ, Στυγος υδατ⊙, εςιν απορρωξ.

Of the land of Dreams in the same region, he makes mention, *Odyss. 24.* See also *Lucian's* true History. *Lethe* and the *Land of Dreams* allegorically represent the *Stupefaction* and *visionary Madness* of Poets equally dull and extravagant. Of *Alphæus* his waters gliding secretly under the sea of *Pisa,* to mix with those of *Arethuse* in *Sicily,* vid. *Moschus Idyl. 8. Virg. Ecl. 10,*

Sic tibi, cum fluctus subter labere Sicanos,
Doris amara suam non intermisceat undam.
And again, *Æn. 3.*
— *Alphæum, fama est, huc Elidis amnem*
Occultas egisse vias, subter mare, qui nunc
Ore Arethusa tuo, Siculis confunditur undis.

IMITATIONS.

VERSE 307. *Greater he looks, and more than mortal stares.*] Virg. 6. of the Sybil.

——— *majorque videri*
Nec mortale sonans ——

Pours into Thames: Each city-bowl is full
Of the mixt wave, and all who drink grow dull.
How to the banks where bards departed doze,
They led him soft; how all the bards arose;
325 Taylor, sweet bird of Thames, majestic bows,
And Shadwell nods the poppy on his brows;
While Milbourn there, deputed by the rest,
Gave him the caffock, furcingle, and vest;
And " Take (he said) these robes which once were mine,
330 " Dulness is facred in a found Divine.

He ceas'd, and show'd the robe; the crowd confefs
The rev'rend Flamen in his lengthen'd drefs.
Slow moves the Goddefs from the fable flood,
(Her Prieft preceding) thro' the gates of Lud.

REMARKS.

VERSE 325. Taylor, *sweet bird of* Thames.]
John Taylor the Water Poet, an honeft man,
who owns he learn'd not fo much as his *Acci-
dence*: a rare example of modefty in a Poet!
  I muft confefs I do want eloquence,
  And never fcarce did learn my Accidence,
  For having got from Poffum *to* Poffet,
  I there was gravell'd, could no farther get.
He wrote fourfcore books in the reign of *James* I.
and *Charles* I. and afterwards (like Mr. *Ward*)
kept a Publick-houfe in *Long Acre*. He died
in 1654.
  VERSE 326. *And* Shadwell *nods the poppy*.]
Shadwell took Opium for many years, and died
of too large a dofe of it, in the year 1692.

VERSE 327. *While* Milbourn] *Luke Mil-
bourn* a Clergyman, the faireft of Criticks; who
when he wrote againft Mr. *Dryden's Virgil*, did
him juftice, in printing at the fame time his
own tranflations of him, which were intolerable.
His manner of writing has a great refemblance
with that of the Gentlemen of the *Dunciad* againft
our author, as will be feen in the Parallel of
Mr. *Dryden* and him. *Attend.*
  VERSE 334. *Gates of* Lud.] " King *Lud*
" repairing the City, call'd it after his own
" name, *Lud's* Town; the ftrong gate which
" he built in the Weft part, he likewife for
" his own honour named *Ludgate*. In the year
" 1260, this gate was beautified with images

IMITATIONS.

VERSE 323. *How to the banks,* &c.] Virg.
Ecl. 6.
  Tum canit errantem Permeffi ad flumina Gallum,,
  Utque viro Phœbi chorus affurexerit omnis:

  Ut Linus hæc illi divino carmine paftor,
  Floribus atque apio crines ornatus amaro,
  Dixerit, Hos tibi dant calamos, en accipe, Mufæ,
  Afcræo quos ante feni ———— *&c.*

335 Her Criticks there she summons, and proclaims
    A gentler exercise to close the games.

        Hear you! in whose grave heads, as equal scales,
    I weigh what author's heaviness prevails,
    Which most conduce to sooth the soul in slumbers,
340 My Henley's periods, or my Blackmore's numbers?
    Attend the trial we propose to make:
    If there be man who o'er such works can wake,
    Sleep's all-subduing charm who dares defy,
    And boasts Ulysses' ear with Argus' eye;
345 To him we grant our amplest pow'rs to sit
    Judge of all present, past, and future wit,
    To cavil, censure, dictate, right or wrong,
    Full, and eternal privilege of tongue.

        Three Cambridge Sophs and three pert Templars came,
350 The same their talents, and their tastes the same,
    Each prompt to query, answer, and debate,
    And smit with love of Poesy and Prate.
    The pond'rous books two gentle readers bring;
    The heroes sit; the vulgar form a ring.

REMARKS.

" of *Lud* and other Kings. Those images in
" the reign of *Edward* VI. had their heads
" smitten off, and were otherwise defaced by
" unadvised folks. Queen *Mary* did set new
" heads on their old bodies again. The 28th of

" Q. *Eliz.* the same gate was clean taken down,
" and newly and beautifully builded with images
" of *Lud* and others as afore." S T O W's Sur-
vey of *London*.
    VERSE 344.] See *Hom. Odyss.* 12. *Ovid, Met.* 1.

IMITATIONS.

VERSE 350. *The same their talents——Each
prompt, &c.*] Virg. Ecl. 7.
    *Ambo florentes ætatibus, Arcades ambo,
    Et certare pares, & respondere parati.*

VERSE 354, *The heroes sit; the vulgar form
a ring.*] Ovid M. 3.
    Consedere duces, & vulgi stante corona.
    VERSE 353.] *Smit with the love of sacred song——*
                                                Milton.

M

355 The clam'rous crowd is hufh'd with mugs of Mum,

     'Till all tun'd equal, fend a gen'ral hum.

     Then mount the clerks; and in one lazy tone,

     Thro' the long, heavy, painful page, drawl on;

     Soft, creeping, words on words, the fenfe compofe,

360 At ev'ry line, they ftretch, they yawn, they doze.

     As to foft gales top-heavy pines bow low

     Their heads, and lift them as they ceafe to blow,

     Thus oft they rear, and oft the head decline,

     As breathe, or paufe, by fits, the airs divine :

365 And now to this fide, now to that, they nod,

     As verfe, or profe, infufe the drowzy God.

     Thrice Budgel aim'd to fpeak, but thrice fuppreft

     By potent Arthur, knock'd his chin and breaft.

     Toland and Tindal, prompt at Priefts to jeer,

370 Yet filent bow'd to Chrift's No kingdom here.

REMARKS.

VERSE 358. *Thro' the long, heavy, painful page,* &c.] All thefe lines very well imitate the flow drowzinefs with which they proceed. It is impoffible for any one who has a poetical ear to read them, without perceiving the heavinefs that lags in the verfe to imitate the action it defcribes. The Simile of the Pines is very juft and well adapted to the fubject. ESSAY on the DUNC. p. 21.

VERSE 367. *Thrice* Budgel *aim'd to fpeak.*] Famous for his fpeeches on many occafions about the *South Sea* Scheme, &c. " He is a very inge-" nious gentleman, and hath written fome excel-" lent Epilogues to Plays, and one fmall piece on " Love, which is very pretty." JACOB Lives of Poets, vol. 2. p. 289. But this Gentleman has fince made himfelf much more eminent, and perfonally well-known to the greateft ftatefmen of all parties, in this nation.

VERSE 369. Toland *and* Tindal.] Two perfons not fo happy as to be obfcure, who writ againft the Religion of their Country. The furreptitious editions placed here the name of a Gentleman, who, tho' no great friend to the Clergy, is a perfon of Morals and Ingenuity. *Tindal* was Author of the *Rights of the Chriftian Church :* He alfo wrote an abufive pamphlet againft Earl *Stanhope,* which was fupprefs'd while yet in manufcript by an eminent Perfon then out of the Miniftry, to whom he fhow'd it expecting his approbation. This Doctor afterwards publifh'd the fame piece, *mutatis mutandis,* againft that very Perfon when he came into the Adminiftration.

VERSE 370. *Chrift's No kingdom,* &c.] This is fcandaloufly faid by CURL, Key to *Dunc.* to allude to a Sermon of a reverend Bifhop. But the context fhows it to be meant of a famous publick Orator, not more remarkable for his long-winded periods, than his Difaffection to Ecclefiaftical Hierarchy, and to the doctrine that Chrift's Kingdom is of *this world.*

Who fate the neareft, by the words o'ercome

Slept firft, the diftant nodded to the hum.

Then down are roll'd the books; ftretch'd o'er 'em lies,

Each gentle clerk, and mutt'ring feals his eyes.

375 At what a Dutchman plumps into the lakes,

One circle firft, and then a fecond makes,

What Dulnefs dropt among her fons impreft

Like motion, from one circle to the reft;

So from the mid-moft the nutation fpreads

380 Round, and more round, o'er all the fea of heads.

At laft Centlivre felt her voice to fail,

Old James himfelf unfinifh'd left his tale,

Boyer the State, and Law the Stage gave o'er,

Nor Motteux talk'd, nor Nafo whifper'd more;

REMARKS.

VERSE 381. *Centlivre.*] Mrs. *Sufanna Cent-livre*, wife to Mr. *Centlivre*, Yeoman of the Mouth to his Majefty. She writ many Plays, and a fong (fays Mr. *Jacob*, vol. 1. p. 32.) before fhe was feven years old. She alfo writ a Ballad againft Mr. *Pope's Homer* before he begun it.

VERSE 383. Boyer *the State, and* Law *the Stage gave o'er.*] A. *Boyer*, a voluminous compiler of Annals, Political Collections, &c.—— *William Law*, A. M. wrote with great zeal againft the Stage, Mr. *Dennis* anfwer'd with as great. Their books were printed in 1726. Mr. *Law* affirm'd that " the Playhoufe is " the Temple of the Devil, the pecu- " liar pleafure of the Devil, where all they " who go, yield to the Devil, where all the " Laughter is a laughter among Devils, and " that all who are there are hearing Mufick " in the very Porch of Hell." To which Mr. *Dennis* replied, that " there is every jot as " much difference between a true Play, and one " made by a Poetafter, as between *Two religious* " *books*, the *Bible* and the *Alcoran*." Then he demonftrates that " all thofe who had written " againft the Stage were *Jacobites* and *Nonjurors*, " and did it always at a time when fomething " was to be done for the *Pretender*. Mr. *Collier* " publifh'd his *Short View* when *France* declar'd " for the *Chevalier*; and his *Diffuafive* juft " at the *great Storm*, when the devaftation " which that Hurricane wrought had amazed " and aftonifhed the minds of men, and made " them obnoxious to melancholy and defponding " thoughts. Mr. *Law* took the opportunity to " attack the Stage upon the great preparations " he heard were making abroad, and which the " *Jacobites* flatter'd themfelves were defign'd in " their favour. And as for Mr. *Bedford's* Scri-

IMITATIONS.

VERSE 380. O'er all the fea of heads.] Blackm. Job.

A waving fea of heads was round me fpread, *And ftill frefh ftreams the gazing deluge fed.*

385 Norton, from Daniel and Oſtræa ſprung,
 Bleſt with his father's front, and mother's tongue,
 Hung ſilent down his never-bluſhing head;
 And all was huſh'd, as Folly's ſelf lay dead.
  Thus the ſoft gifts of Sleep conclude the day,
390 And ſtretch'd on bulks, as uſual, Poets lay.
 Why ſhou'd I ſing what bards the nightly Muſe
 Did ſlumbring viſit, and convey to ſtews?
 Who prouder march'd, with magiſtrates in ſtate,
 To ſome fam'd round-houſe, ever open gate!
395 How Laurus lay inſpir'd beſide a ſink,
 And to mere mortals ſeem'd a Prieſt in drink?

REMARKS.

" ous *Remonſtrance,* tho' I know nothing of the
" time of publiſhing it, yet I dare to lay odds
" it was either upon the Duke *D'Aumont's* be-
" ing at *Somerſet-houſe,* or upon the *late Rebel-*
" *lion.*" DENNIS, Stage defended againſt Mr.
Law, pag. *ult.*

VERSE 385. Norton.] *Norton de Foe,* ſaid to be
the natural offspring of the famous *Daniel. Fortes
creantur fortibus.* One of the authors of the
Flying-Poſt, in which well-bred work Mr. *P.*
had ſometime the honour to be abus'd with his
betters, and of many hired ſcurrilities and daily
papers to which he never ſet his name, in a due
fear of Laws and Cudgels. He is now writing
the *Life of Colonel* Charteris.

VERSE 395. *How* Laurus *lay* inſpir'd *beſide
a ſink,
And to* meer mortals, ſeem'd *a Prieſt in drink.*]
This line preſents us with an excellent Moral;
that we are never to paſs judgment merely by
appearances; a Leſſon to all men who may hap-
pen to ſee a reverend perſon in the like ſitua-
tion, not to determine too raſhly, ſince not only
the Poets frequently deſcribe a Bard inſpir'd in
this poſture,
(*On* Cam's *fair bank where* Chaucer *lay* inſpir'd,
and the like) but an eminent Caſuiſt tells us, that
if a Prieſt be ſeen in any indecent action, we
ought to account it a deception of ſight, or illu-
ſion of the Devil, who ſometimes takes upon

IMITATIONS.

VERSE 388. *And all was huſh'd, as Folly's
ſelf lay dead.*] Alludes to Dryden's verſe in | the *Indian Emperor,
All things are huſh'd, as Nature's ſelf lay dead.*

While others timely, to the neighbouring Fleet
(Haunt of the Muſes) made their ſafe retreat.

REMARKS.

upon him the ſhape of Holy men on purpoſe to cauſe ſcandal. How little the prophane author of the *Characters of the Times* printed 8°. 1728. regarded this admonition, appears from theſe words pag. 26. (ſpeaking of the reverend Mr. *Laurence Eusden*) "A moſt worthy ſucceſſor of "*Tate* in the Laureatſhip, a man of inſupe- "rable modeſty, ſince certainly it was not his "Ambition that led him to ſeek this illuſtrious "poſt, but his affection to the Perquiſite of *Sack*." A reflection as mean as it is ſcandalous!

SCRIBLERUS.

VERSE 397. *Fleet.*] A Priſon for inſolvent Debtors on the bank of the Ditch.

End of the Second Book

THE

DUNCIAD.

Book the Third.

B<small>UT</small> in her Temple's laſt receſs inclos'd,
On Dulneſs lap th'Anointed head repos'd.
Him cloſe ſhe curtain'd round with vapors blue,
And ſoft beſprinkled with Cimmerian dew.
5 Then raptures high the ſeat of ſenſe o'erflow,
Which only heads, refin'd from reaſon, know.
Hence, from the ſtraw where Bedlam's Prophet nods,
He hears loud Oracles, and talks with Gods.

REMARKS.

V<small>ERSE</small> 5, 6, &c.] Hereby is intimated that the following Viſion is no more than the Chimera of the Dreamer's brain, and not a real or intended ſatire on the Preſent Age, doubtleſs more learned, more inlighten'd, and more abounding with great Genius's in Divinity, Politics, and whatever Arts and Sciences, than all the preceding. For fear of any ſuch miſtake of our Poet's honeſt meaning, he hath again at the end of this Viſion, repeated this monition, ſaying that it all paſt thro' the *Ivory gate*, which (according to the Ancients) denoteth Falſity.
S<small>CRIBLERUS.</small>

IMITATIONS.

V<small>ERSE</small> 8. *Hence from the ſtraw where Bed-*
lam's Prophet nods,
He hears loud Oracles, and talks with Gods.

Virg. Æn. 7.
Et varias audit voces, fruiturque deorum
Colloquio ——

Hence the Fool's paradise, the Statesman's scheme,
10 The air-built Castle, and the golden Dream,
The Maids romantic wish, the Chymists flame,
And Poets vision of eternal fame.

And now, on Fancy's easy wing convey'd,
The King descended to th' Elyzian shade.
15 There, in a dusky vale where Lethe rolls,
Old Bavius sits, to dip poetic souls,
And blunt the sense, and fit it for a scull
Of solid proof, impenetrably dull.

REMARKS.

VERSE 16. *Old* Bavius *sits.*] *Bavius* was an ancient Poet, celebrated by *Virgil* for the like cause as *Tibbald* by our author, tho' in less christian-like manner : For heathenishly it is declared by *Virgil* of *Bavius*, that he ought to be *hated* and *detested* for his evil works ; *Qui Bavium non* odit —— Whereas we have often had occasion to observe our Poet's great good nature and mercifulness, thro' the whole course of this Poem.

Mr. *Dennis* warmly contends that *Bavius* was no inconsiderable author ; nay, that " he and " *Mævius* had (even in *Augustus's* days) a very " formidable Party at *Rome*, who thought them " much superior to *Virgil* and *Horace* : For (faith he) " I cannot believe they would have " fix'd that eternal brand upon them, if they " had not been coxcombs in more than ordinary " credit." An argument which (if this Poem should last) will conduce to the honour of the Gentlemen of the *Dunciad.* In like manner he tells us of Mr. *Settle*, that " he was once a formi- " dable Rival to Mr. *Dryden*, and that in the Uni- " versity of *Cambridge* there were those who gave " him the *preference.*" Mr. *Welsted* goes yet far- ther in his behalf. " Poor *Settle* was formerly " the *Mighty Rival* of *Dryden* : nay, *for many* " *years*, bore his Reputation *above* him." [*Pref.* *to his Poems*, 8⁰. *p.* 51.] And Mr. *Milbourn* cry'd out, " How little was *Dryden* able, even " when his blood run high, to defend himself " against Mr. *Settle* !" *Notes on* Dryd. Virg. *p.* 175. These are comfortable opinions ! and no wonder some authors indulge them.

SCRIBLERUS.

IMITATIONS.

VERSE 15. *There in a dusky vale,* &c.] Virg. Æn. 6.
—— *Videt Æneas in valle reducta*
Seclusum nemus ——
Lethæumque domos placidas qui prænatat am-
nem, &c.
Hunc circum innumeræ gentes, &c.

VERSE 16. *Old* Bavius *sits, to dip poetic* *souls.*] Alluding to the story of *Thetis* dipping *Achilles* to render him impenetrable.
At pater Anchises penitus convalle virenti
Inclusas animes, superumque ad lumen ituras,
Lustrabat ——
Virg. Æn. 6.

Inſtant when dipt, away they wing their flight,
20 Where Brown and Mears unbar the gates of Light,
Demand new bodies, and in Calf's array
Ruſh to the world, impatient for the day.
Millions and millions on theſe banks he views,
Thick as the ſtars of night, or morning dews,
25 As thick as bees o'er vernal bloſſoms fly,
As thick as eggs at Ward in Pillory.

Wond'ring he gaz'd: When lo! a Sage appears,
By his broad ſhoulders known, and length of ears,
Known by the band and ſuit which Settle wore,
30 (His only ſuit) for twice three years before:

REMARKS.

VERSE 20. Brown *and* Mears.] Bookſellers, Printers for *Tibbald*, Mrs. *Haywood*, or any body.—The Allegory of the ſouls of the Dull coming forth in the form of Books, and being let abroad in vaſt numbers by Bookſellers, is ſufficiently intelligible.

VERSE 26. Ward *in Pillory*.] *John Ward* of *Hackney*, Eſq; Member of Parliament, being convicted of Forgery, was firſt expelled the Houſe, and then ſentenc'd to the Pillory on the 17th of *Febr.* 1727. Mr. *Curl* looks upon the mention of ſuch a Gentleman in a Satire, as a *great act of Barbarity. Key to the* Dunc. 3d *Edit. p.* 16. And another Author thus reaſons upon it. *Durgen,* 8°. pag. 11, 12. " How " unworthy is it of *Chriſtian Charity* to animate " the *rabble* to abuſe a *worthy man* in ſuch a " ſituation? It was in vain! he had no *Eggs* " thrown at him; his *Merit* preſerv'd him. " What cou'd move the Poet thus to mention a " *brave Sufferer*, a *gallant Priſoner*, expos'd to " the view of all mankind! It was laying aſide " his *Senſes*, it was committing a *Crime* for " which the *Law is deficient* not to puniſh him! " nay a Crime which *Man can ſcarce forgive*, " nor *Time efface!* Nothing ſurely could have " induced him but being bribed to it by a great " Lady," (to whom this brave, honeſt, worthy Gentleman was guilty of no offence but Forgery proved in open Court, &c.)

VERSE 28. *And length of Ears*.] This is a *ſophiſticated* reading. I think I may venture to affirm all the Copyiſts are miſtaken here: I believe I may ſay the ſame of the Criticks; *Dennis, Oldmixon, Welſted*, have paſs'd it in ſilence: I have always ſtumbled at it, and wonder'd how an error ſo manifeſt could eſcape ſuch accurate perſons? I dare aſſert it proceeded originally from the inadvertency of ſome Tranſcriber, whoſe head run on the *Pillory* mention'd two lines before: It is therefore amazing that Mr. *Curl* himſelf ſhould overlook it! Yet that Scholiaſt takes not the leaſt notice hereof. That the learned *Miſt* alſo read it thus,

IMITATIONS.

VERSE 20. *Unbar the gates of Light*.] Milton.
VERSE 25. *Millions and millions — Thick as the Stars*, &c.] Virg. 6.

Quam multa in ſylvis autumni frigore primo
Lapſa cadunt folia, aut ad terram gurgite ab alto
Quam multæ glomerantur aves, &c.

All as the vest, appear'd the wearer's frame,
Old in new state, another yet the same.
Bland and familiar as in life, begun
Thus the great Father to the greater Son.
35   Oh born to fee what none can fee awake!
Behold the wonders of th' Oblivious Lake.
Thou, yet unborn, haft touch'd this facred fhore;
The hand of Bavius drench'd thee o'er and o'er.
But blind to former, as to future Fate,
40 What mortal knows his pre-exiftent ftate?
Who knows how long, thy tranfmigrating foul
Did from Bœotian to Bœotian roll?
How many Dutchmen fhe vouchfaf'd to thrid?
How many ftages thro' old Monks fhe rid?
45 And all who fince, in mild benighted days,
Mix'd the Owl's ivy with the Poet's bays?
As man's mæanders to the vital fpring
Roll all their tydes, then back their circles bring;

REMARKS.

i
s plain, from his ranging this paffage among thofe in which our Author was blamed for *perfonal Satire* on a *Man's Face* (whereof doubtlefs he might take the *Ear* to be a part;) So likewife *Concanen, Ralph,* the *Flying-Poft,* and all the Herd of Commentators.—*Tota armenta fequuntur.*

A very little Sagacity (which all thefe Gentlemen therefore wanted) will reftore to us the true fenfe of the Poet, thus,

By his broad fhoulders known, and length of years.
See how eafy a change! of one fingle letter! That Mr. *Settle* was old is moft certain, but he was (happily) a ftranger to the Pillory. *This Note partly Mr.* THEOBALD, *partly* SCRIBLERUS.
VERSE 42. *Did from Bœotian, &c.*] See the Remark on Book 1. V. 23.

IMITATIONS.

VERSE 46, *Mix'd the Owl's Ivy with the Poet's Bays.*] Virg. Ec. 8.

——— *fine tempora circum*
Inter victrices Hederam tibi ferpere lauros.

N

Or whirligigs, twirl'd round by skilful swain,
50 Suck the thread in, then yield it out again:
All nonsense thus, of old or modern date,
Shall in thee centre, from thee circulate.
For this, our Queen unfolds to vision true
Thy mental eye, for thou haft much to view:
55 Old scenes of glory, times long cast behind,
Shall first recall'd, run forward to thy mind;
Then stretch thy sight o'er all her rising reign,
And let the past and future fire thy brain.

    Ascend this hill, whose cloudy point commands
60 Her boundless Empire over seas and lands.
See round the Poles where keener spangles shine,
Where spices smoke beneath the burning Line,
(Earth's wide extreams) her sable flag display'd;
And all the nations cover'd in her shade!
65   Far Eastward cast thine eye, from whence the Sun
And orient Science at a birth begun.
One man immortal all that pride confounds,
He, whose long Wall the wand'ring Tartar bounds.

REMARKS.

VERSE 61, 62. *See round the Poles*, &c.] Almost the whole Southern and Northern Continent wrapt in Ignorance.

VERSE 65] Our Author favours the opinion that all Sciences came from the Eastern nations.

IMITATIONS.

VERSE 53. *For this, our Queen unfolds to vision true Thy mental eye, for thou haft much to view.*] This has a resemblance to that passage in *Milton*, *l.* 11. where the Angel,

To nobler fights from Adam's eye remov'd
The film; then purg'd with Euphrasie and Rue
The visual nerve—For he had much to see.
There is a general allusion in what follows to that whole passage.

Heav'ns! what a pyle? whole ages perish there:
70 And one bright blaze turns Learning into air.

Thence to the South extend thy gladden'd eyes;
There rival flames with equal glory rise,
From shelves to shelves see greedy Vulcan roll,
And lick up all their Physick of the Soul.

75 How little, mark! that portion of the ball,
Where, faint at best, the beams of Science fall.
Soon as they dawn, from Hyperborean skies,
Embody'd dark, what clouds of Vandals rise!
Lo where Mœotis sleeps, and hardly flows
80 The freezing Tanais thro' a waste of Snows,
The North by myriads pours her mighty sons,
Great nurse of Goths, of Alans, and of Huns.
See Alaric's stern port, the martial frame
Of Genseric! and Attila's dread name!
85 See, the bold Ostrogoths on Latium fall;
See, the fierce Visigoths on Spain and Gaul.
See, where the Morning gilds the palmy shore,
(The soil that arts and infant letters bore)
His conqu'ring tribes th' Arabian prophet draws,
90 And saving Ignorance enthrones by Laws.

REMARKS.

VERSE 69.] *Chi Ho-am-ti*, Emperor of *China*, the same who built the great wall between *China* and *Tartary*, destroyed all the books and learned men of that empire.

VERSE 73, 74.] The *Caliph, Omar* I. having conquer'd *Ægypt*, caus'd his General to burn the *Ptolomæan* library, on the gates of which was this inscription, *Medicina Animæ, The Physick of the Soul.*

VERSE 88. *The Soil that arts and infant letters bore.*] *Phœnicia, Syria*, &c. where *Letters* are said to have been invented. In these Countries *Mahomet* began his Conquests.

N 2

See Chriſtians, Jews, one heavy ſabbath keep;
And all the Weſtern World believe and ſleep.

Lo Rome herſelf, proud miſtreſs now no more
Of arts, but thund'ring againſt Heathen lore;
95 Her gray-hair'd Synods damning books unread,
And Bacon trembling for his brazen head:
Padua with ſighs beholds her Livy burn;
And ev'n th' Antipodes Vigilius mourn.
See, the Cirque falls! th' unpillar'd Temple nods!
100 Streets pav'd with Heroes, Tyber choak'd with Gods!
Till Peter's Keys ſome chriſten'd Jove adorn,
And Pan to Moſes lends his Pagan horn;
See graceleſs Venus to a Virgin turn'd,
Or Phidias broken, and Apelles burn'd.

REMARKS.

VERSE 94. *Thund'ring againſt Heathen lore.*] A ſtrong inſtance of this pious rage is plac'd to Pope *Gregory*'s account. *John of Salisbury* gives a very odd Encomium to this Pope, at the ſame time that he mentions one of the ſtrangeſt effects of this exceſs of zeal in him. *Doctor ſanctiſſimus ille Gregorius, qui melleo prædicationis imbre totam rigavit & inebriavit eccleſiam, non modo* Matheſin *juſſit ab aulâ; ſed, ut traditur a majoribus, incendio dedit probatæ lectionis ſcripta, Palatinus quæcunque tenebat Apollo.* And in another place: *Fertur beatus Gregorius bibliothecam combuſſiſſe gentilem; quo divinæ paginæ gratior eſſet locus, & major authoritas, & diligentia ſtudioſior. Deſiderius* Archbiſhop of *Vienna* was ſharply reproved by him for teaching Grammar and Literature, and explaining the Poets; Becauſe (ſays this Pope) *in uno ſe ore cum Jovis laudibus, Chriſti laudes non capiunt: Et quan gravæ neſandumque ſit, Epiſcopis canere quod ne Laico religioſo conveniat, ipſe conſidera.* He is ſaid, among the reſt, to have burn'd *Livy; Quia in ſuperſtitionibus & ſacris Romanorum perpetuò verſatur.* The ſame Pope is accuſed by *Voſſius* and others of having caus'd the noble monuments of the old *Roman* magnificence to be deſtroyed, leſt thoſe who came to *Rome* ſhou'd give more attention to Triumphal Arches, &c. than to Holy Things. BAYLE, *Dict.*

VERSE 101. '*Till* Peter's *Keys ſome chriſten'd* Jove *adorn,* &c.] After the Government of *Rome* devolved to the Popes, their zeal was for ſome time exerted in demoliſhing the Heathen Temples and Statues, ſo that the *Goths* ſcarce deſtroyed more Monuments of Antiquity out of Rage, than theſe out of Devotion. At length they ſpar'd ſome of the Temples by converting them to Churches, and ſome of the Statues, by modifying them into Images of Saints. In much later times, it was thought neceſſary to change the Statues of *Apollo* and *Pallas* on the tomb of *Sannazarius,* into *David* and *Judith;* the Lyre eaſily became a Harp, and the Gorgon's Head turn'd to that of *Holoſernes.*

105   Behold yon' Ifle, by Palmers, Pilgrims trod,
        Men bearded, bald, cowl'd, uncowl'd, fhod, unfhod,
        Peel'd, patch'd, and pyebald, linfey-woolfey brothers,
        Grave mummers! fleevelefs fome, and fhirtlefs others.
        That once was Britain —Happy! had fhe feen
110 No fiercer fons, had Eafter never been.
        In peace, great Goddefs! ever be ador'd;
        How keen the war, if Dulnefs draw the fword?
        Thus vifit not thy own! on this blefs age
        Oh' fpread thy Influence, but reftrain thy Rage!
115   And fee! my fon, the hour is on its way,
        That lifts our Goddefs to imperial fway:
        This fav'rite Ifle, long fever'd from her reign,
        Dove-like, fhe gathers to her wings again.
        Now look thro' Fate! behold the fcene fhe draws!
120 What aids, what armies, to affert her caufe?
        See all her progeny, illuftrious fight!
        Behold, and count them, as they rife to light.
        As Berecynthia, while her offspring vye
        In homage, to the mother of the fky,

REMARKS.

VERSE 110. *Happy—had* Eafter *never been.*] Wars in *England* anciently, about the right time of celebrating *Eafter.*

IMITATIONS.

VERSE 110. *Happy—had* Eafter *never been.*] Virg. Ecl. 6.
Et fortunatam, fi nunquam armenta fuiffent.
VERSE 119, 121. *Now look thro' Fate——See all her Progeny——* &c.] Virg. Æn. 6.
Nunc age, Dardanium prolem quæ deinde fequatur Gloria, qui maneant Itala de gente nepotes,

Illuftres animas, noftrumque in nomen ituras Expediam ——
VERSE 123. *As* Berecynthia, *&c.*] Virg. ib.
Felix prole virum, qualis Berecynthia mater Invehitur curru Phrygias turrita per urbes, Læta deum partu, centum complexa nepotes, Omnes cælicolas, omnes fupera alta tenentes.

125 Surveys around her in the bleſt abode

A hundred ſons, and ev'ry ſon a God:

Not with leſs glory mighty Dulneſs crown'd,

Shall take thro' Grubſtreet her triumphant round,

And Her Parnaſſus glancing o'er at once,

130 Behold a hundred ſons, and each a dunce.

Mark firſt the youth who takes the foremoſt place,

And thruſts his perſon full into your face.

With all thy Father's virtues bleſt, be born!

And a new Cibber ſhall the Stage adorn.

135 A ſecond ſee, by meeker manners known,

And modeſt as the maid that ſips alone:

From the ſtrong fate of drams if thou get free,

Another Durfey, Ward! ſhall ſing in thee.

Thee ſhall each Ale-houſe, thee each Gill-houſe mourn,

140 And anſw'ring Gin-ſhops ſowrer ſighs return!

Lo next two ſlip-ſhod Muſes traipſe along,

In lofty madneſs, meditating ſong,

With treſſes ſtaring from poetic dreams,

And never waſh'd, but in Caſtalia's ſtreams:

REMARKS.

VERSE 138. Ward.] *Vid.* Book 1. Ver. 200.

IMITATIONS.

VERSE 131. *Mark firſt the youth,* &c.] Virg. Æn. 6.
Ille vides, pura juvenis qui nititur baſta
VERSE 133. *With all thy Father's virtues bleſt, be born!*] A manner of expreſſion uſed by *Virgil,*
Naſcere! præque diem veniens, age Lucifer——
As alſo that of *Patriis virtutibus.* Ecl. 4.

VERSE 137. *From the ſtrong fate of drams if thou get free,* &c.] Virg. Æn. 6.
——— *ſi qua fata aſpera rumpas,*
Tu Marcellus eris! ———
VERSE 139. *For thee each Ale-houſe,* &c.] *Virgil* again, Ecl. 10.
Illum etiam lauri, illum flevere myricæ, &c.

145 Haywood, Centlivre, Glories of their race!

Lo Horneck's fierce, and Roome's funereal face;

Lo sneering G * * de, half malice and half whim,

A Fiend in glee, ridiculously grim.

Jacob, the Scourge of Grammar, mark with awe,

150 Nor less revere him, Blunderbuss of Law.

Lo Bond and Foxton, ev'ry nameless name,

All crowd, who foremost shall be damn'd to Fame?

Some strain in rhyme; the Muses, on their racks,

Scream, like the winding of ten thousand Jacks:

155 Some free from rhyme or reason, rule or check,

Break Priscian's head, and Pegasus's neck;

Down, down they larum, with impetuous whirl,

The Pindars, and the Miltons, of a Curl.

REMARKS.

VERSE 143. *Haywood, Centlivre.*] See book 2.

VERSE 146. Lo Horneck's *fierce and* Roome's *funeral face.*] This stood in one edition *And M — s ruful face.* But the person who suppos'd himself meant applying to our author in a modest manner, and with declarations of his innocence, he removed the occasion of his uneasiness.

VERSE 146. Horneck *and* Roome.] These two are worthily coupled, being both virulent Party-writers; and one wou'd think prophetically, since immediately after the publishing of this Piece the former dying, the latter succeeded him in Honour and *Employment.* The first was *Philip Horneck*, Author of a Billingsgate paper call'd *The High German Doctor*, in the 2d Vol. of which Nº. 14. you may see the regard he had for Mr. P: — *Edward Roome*, Son of an Undertaker for Funerals in *Fleet-street*, writ some of the papers call'd *Pasquin*, and Mr. *Ducket* others, where by malicious Innuendos, it was endeavour'd to represent him guilty of malevolent practices with a great man then under prosecution of Parliament.

VERSE 147. G ª * *dè.*] An ill-natur'd Critick who writ a Satire on our Author, yet unprinted, call'd *The mock Æsop.*

VERSE 149. Jacob, *the Scourge of Grammar, mark with awe.*] This Gentleman is Son of a *considerable Malster of Romsey* in *Southampton-shire*, and bred to the Law under a *very eminent Attorney:* who, between his *more laborious* Studies, has *diverted* himself with Poetry. He is a great admirer of Poets and their works, which has occasion'd him to try his genius that way— He has writ in prose the *Lives of the Poets,* *Essays*, and a great many Law-Books, *The Accomplish'd Conveyancer, Modern Justice*, &c. GILES JACOB of himself, *Lives of Poets*, Vol. 1.

VERSE 151. Bond *and* Foxton.] Two inoffensive offenders against our poet; persons unknown, but by being mention'd by Mr. *Curl.*

IMITATIONS.

VERSE 150.] Virg. Æn. 6.

——————— *duo fulmina belli*
| *Scipiadas, cladem Lybiæ !* ———

Silence, ye Wolves! while Ralph to Cynthia howls,
160 And makes Night hideous — Anſwer him ye Owls!

Senſe, ſpeech, and meaſure, living tongues and dead,

Let all give way — and Durgen may be read.

Flow Welſted, flow! like thine inſpirer, Beer,

Tho' ſtale, not ripe; tho' thin, yet never clear;

165 So ſweetly mawkiſh, and ſo ſmoothly dull;

Heady, not ſtrong, and foaming tho' not full.

Ah Dennis! Gildon ah! what ill-ſtarr'd rage

Divides a friendſhip, long confirm'd by age?

Blockheads with reaſon wicked wits abhor,

170 But fool with fool is barb'rous civil war.

Embrace, embrace my Sons! be foes no more!

Nor glad vile Poets with true Criticks gore.

Behold yon Pair, in ſtrict embraces join'd;

How like their manners, and how like their mind!

REMARKS.

VERSE 159. *Ralph.*] A name inſerted after the firſt Editions, not known to our Author till he writ a Swearing-piece call'd *Sawney*, very abuſive of Dr. *Swift*, Mr. *Gay*, and himſelf. Theſe lines allude to a thing of his, intituled *Night a Poem.* Shakeſpear, Hamlet.

— *Viſit thus the glimpſes of the Moon,*
Making Night hideous —

This low writer conſtantly attended his own works with Panegyricks in the Journals, and once in particular prais'd himſelf highly above Mr. *Addiſon*, in wretched remarks upon that Author's Account of Engliſh Poets, printed in a *London Journal*, Sept. 1728. He was wholly illiterate, and knew no Language not even *French*: Being adviſed to read the Rules of Dramatick Poetry before he began a Play, he ſmiled and reply'd, *Shakeſpear writ without Rules.*

VERSE 162. *Durgen.*] A ridiculous thing of *Ward*'s.

IMITATIONS.

VERSE 163. *Flow,* Welſted, *flow!* &c.] Parody on *Denham, Cooper's Hill.*
O could I flow like thee, and make thy ſtream
My great example, as it is my theme.
Tho' deep, yet clear; tho' gentle, yet not dull;
Strong, without rage; without o'erflowing, full.
VERSE 169. *Embrace, embrace my Sons! be foes no more.*] Virg. Æn. 6.
—— *Ne tanta animis aſſueſcite bella,*

Neu patriæ validas in viſcera vertite vires:
Tuq; prior, tu parce —— *ſanguis meus!* ——
VERSE 145. *Behold yon pair, in ſtrict embraces join'd.*] Virg. Æn. 6.
Illæ autem paribus quas fulgere cernis in armis,
Concordes animæ ——
And in the fifth,
Euryalus, forma inſignis viridique juventa,
Niſus amore pio pueri.

175 Fam'd for good-nature, B** and for truth;

D** for pious paſſion to the youth.

Equal in wit, and equally polite,

Shall this a Paſquin, that a Grumbler write;

Like are their merits, like rewards they ſhare,

180 That ſhines a Conſul, this Commiſſioner.

REMARKS.

VERSE 175. *Fam'd for good nature* B**, *&c.* D**, *for pious paſſion to the youth.*] The firſt of theſe was Son of the late Biſhop of S. Author of a weekly paper called *The Grumbler*, as the other was concern'd in another call'd *Paſquin*, in which Mr. *Pope* was abuſed (particularly with the late Duke of *Buckingham* and Biſhop of *Rocheſter.*) They alſo join'd in a piece againſt his firſt undertaking to tranſlate the *Iliad*, intituled *Homerides*, by Sir *Iliad Dogrel*, printed by *Wilkins* 1715. And Mr. *D.* writ an Epilogue for *Powel's* Puppet-ſhow, reflecting on the ſame work. Mr. *Curl* gives us this further account of Mr. *B.* "He did *himſelf write* a Letter to "the E. of *Halifax*, *informing his Lordſhip* "(as he tells him) *of what he knew much* "*better before*: And he *publiſh'd in his own* "*name* ſeveral political pamphlets, A cer- "tain information of a certain diſcourſe, A ſe- "cond Tale of a Tub, *&c. All which* it is "ſtrongly affirmed *were written by* Colonel "*Ducket.*" CURL, Key, p. 17. But the author of the *Characters of the Times* tells us, theſe political pieces were not approv'd of by his *own Father*, the Reverend Biſhop.

Of the other works of theſe Gentlemen, the world has heard no more, than it wou'd of Mr. *Pope's*, had their united laudable endeavours diſcourag'd him from his undertakings. How few good works had ever appear'd (ſince men of true merit are always the leaſt preſuming) had there been always ſuch champions to ſtifle them in their conception? And were it not better for the publick, that a million of monſters came in-

to the world, than that the Serpents ſhould have ſtrangled one *Hercules* in his cradle?

VERSE 174. —— *for pious paſſion to the youth.*] The verſe is a literal tranſlation of *Virgil, Niſus amore pio pueri* — and here, as in the original, apply'd to Friendſhip: That between *Niſus* and *Euryalus* is allow'd to make one of the moſt amiable Epiſodes in the world, and ſurely was never interpreted in a perverſe ſenſe: But it will aſtoniſh the Reader to hear, that on no other occaſion than this line, a Dedication was written to this Gentleman to induce him to think ſomething farther. " Sir, you are known to have "all that affection for the beautiful part of the "creation which God and Nature deſign'd.— "Sir, you have a very fine Lady — and, Sir, "you have eight very fine Children,"—*&c.* [*Dedic. to* Dennis *Rem. on the Rape of the Lock.*] The truth is, the poor Dedicator's brain was turn'd upon this article; he had taken into his head that ever ſince ſome *Books* were written againſt the *Stage*, and ſince the *Italian Opera* had prevail'd, the nation was infected with a vice not fit to be nam'd. He went ſo far as to print upon this ſubject, and concludes his argument with this remark, "that he cannot help thinking the Ob- "ſcenity of Plays excuſable at this juncture, "ſince, when that execrable ſin is ſpread "ſo wide, it may be of uſe to the reducing "mens minds to the natural deſire of women." DENNIS, *Stage defended* againſt Mr. *Law*, p. 20. Our author has ſolemnly declared to me, he ne- ver heard any creature but the Dedicator men- tion that Vice and this Gentleman together.

O

" But who is he, in closet close y-pent,

" Of sober face, with learned dust besprent?

Right well mine eyes arede the myster wight,

On parchment scraps y-fed, and Wormius hight.

REMARKS.

VERSE 184. Wormius *hight*.] Let not this name, purely fictitious, be conceited to mean the learned *Olaus Wormius*; much less (as it was unwarrantably foisted into the surreptitious editions) our own Antiquary Mr. *Thomas Herne*, who had no way aggrieved our Poet, but on the contrary published many curious tracts which he hath to his great contentment perused.

Most rightly are ancient words here imployed in speaking of such who so greatly delight in the same: We may say not only rightly, but *wisely*, yea *excellently*, inasmuch as for the like practise the like praise is given to *Hopkins* and *Sternhold* by Mr. *Herne* himself. [*Glossar*. to *Rob*. of *Gloucester*] *Artic*. BEHETT; others say BEHIGHT, *promised*, and so it is used *excellently well* by *Tho. Norton* in his translation into metre of the 116th Psalm, verse 14.

   I to the Lord will pay my vows,

   That I to him BEHIGHT.

Where the modern innovators, not understanding the propriety of the word (which is *Truly English*, from the *Saxon*) have most unwarrantably alter'd it thus,

   I to the Lord will pay my vows,

   With joy and great delight.

VERSE ibid.—HIGHT.] " In *Cumberland* " they say to *hight*, for to *promise* or *vow*; " but HIGHT usually signifies *was call'd*: and " so it does in the North even to this day, " notwithstanding what is done in *Cumberland*. HERNE, ibid.

VERSE 183. AREDE.] *Read* or *peruse*; tho' sometimes used for *counsel*, " READE " THY READ, *take thy counsaile. Thomas Stern-*

" *holde* in his translation of the first Psalm into " *English* metre, hath *wisely* made use of this " word,

   The man is blest that hath not bent

   To wicked READ *his ear.*

" But in the last spurious editions of the Sing- " ing Psalms the word READ is changed into " *men*. I say spurious editions, because not " only here, but quite throughout the whole " book of Psalms, are strange alterations, all for " the worse! And yet the title-page stands as " it us'd to do! and all (which is abominable in " any book, much more in a sacred work) is " ascribed to *Thomas Sternhold*, *John Hopkins*, " *and others!* I am confident, were *Sternhold* " and *Hopkins* now living, they would proceed " against the innovators as cheats——A liberty " which, to say no more of their intolerable al- " terations, ought by no means to be permitted. " or approved of, by such as are for *Unifor-* " *mity*, and have any regard for the old *English* " *Saxon* tongue. HERNE, *Gloss*. on Rob. of Gloc. *Art*. rede.

I do herein agree with Mr. *H*. Little is it of avail to object that such words are become *unintelligible*. Since they are *Truly English*, Men ought to understand them; and such as are for *Uniformity* should think all alterations in a Language, *strange*, *abominable*, and *unwarrantable*. Rightly therefore, I say again, hath our Poet used ancient words, and poured them forth, as a precious ointment, upon good old *Wormius* in this place.   SCRIBLERUS.

VERSE ibid. *Myster wight*.]. Uncouth mortal.

IMITATIONS.

VERSE 181. *But who is he*, &c.] Virg. Æn. 6. questions and answers in this manner, of *Numa*,

   Quis procul ille autem ramis insignis olivæ

   Sacra ferens? — *nosco crines, incanaq; menta*, &c.

185 To future ages may thy dulneſs laſt,

As thou preſerv'ſt the dulneſs of the paſt!

There, dim in clouds, the poreing Scholiaſts mark,

Wits, who like Owls ſee only in the dark,

A Lumberhouſe of Books in ev'ry head,

190 For ever reading, never to be read.

But, where each Science lifts its modern Type,

Hiſt'ry her Pot, Divinity his Pipe,

While proud Philoſophy repines to ſhow

Diſhoneſt ſight! his breeches rent below;

195 Imbrown'd with native Bronze, lo Henley ſtands,

Tuning his voice, and balancing his hands.

REMARKS.

VERSE 188. *Wits, who like Owls, &c.*] Theſe few lines exactly deſcribe the right verbal Critick: He is to his Author as a Quack to his Patients, the more they ſuffer and complain, the better he is pleas'd; like the famous Doctor of that ſort, who put up in his bills, *He delighted in matters of difficulty.* Some-body ſaid well of theſe men, that their heads were *Libraries out of order.*

VERSE 195 —— *Lo! Henley ſtands, &c.*] *J. Henley,* the Orator; he preach'd on the Sun-days Theological matters, and on the Wedneſ-days upon all other ſciences. Each Auditor paid one ſhilling. He declaim'd ſome years un-puniſh'd againſt the greateſt perſons, and occa-ſionally did our author that honour. WEL-STED, in Oratory Tranſactions, N° 1. publiſh'd by *Henley* himſelf, gives the following account of him. " He was born at *Melton Mowbry* in *Lei-*" *ceiſterſhire.* From his own Pariſh ſchool he " went to St. *John*'s College in *Cambridge.*" He began there to be uneaſy; for it *ſhock'd*" him to find he was *commanded to believe* againſt " his judgment in points of Religion, Philoſo-" phy, *&c.* for his genius leading him freely " to *diſpute all propoſitions, and call all points to*

" *account,* he was impatient under thoſe fetters " of the free-born mind. —— Being admitted " to Prieſt's orders, he found the examination " very ſhort and ſuperficial, and that it was *not* " *neceſſary to conform to the Chriſtian Religion* " *in order either to Deaconſhip or Prieſthood.*" He came to Town, and after having for ſome years been a writer for Bookſellers, he had an ambition to be ſo for Miniſters of State. The only reaſon he did not riſe in the Church we are told " was the envy of others, and a diſ-" reliſh entertain'd of him, becauſe *he was not* " *qualify'd to be a compleat Spaniel.*" However he offer'd the ſervice of his pen, in one morning, to two Great men of opinions and intereſts di-rectly oppoſite; by both of whom being re-jected, he ſet up a new Project, and ſtiled him-ſelf the *Reſtorer of ancient Eloquence.* He thought " it as lawful to take a licence from the King " and Parliament at one place, as another; at " *Hick*'s Hall, as at Doctors Commons; ſo ſet up his Oratory in *Newport*-Market, Butcher-Row. There (ſays his friend) " he had the " *aſſurance* to form a Plan which no mortal " ever thought of; he had ſucceſs againſt all " oppoſition; challenged his adverſaries to fair

O 2

How fluent nonfenfe trickles from his tongue !
How fweet the periods, neither faid nor fung !
Still break the benches, Henley ! with thy ftrain,
200 While K**, B**, W**, preach in vain.
Oh great Reftorer of the good old Stage,
Preacher at once, and Zany of thy Age !
Oh worthy thou of Ægypt's wife abodes,
A decent Prieft, where monkeys were the Gods !
205 But Fate with Butchers plac'd thy prieftly Stall,
Meek modern faith to murder, hack, and mawl ;
And bade thee live, to crown Britannia's praife,
In Toland's, Tindal's, and in Woolfton's days.

Thou too, great Woolfton ! here exalt thy throne,
210 And prove, no Miracles can match thy own.

Yet oh my fons ! a father's words attend :
(So may the fates preferve the ears you lend)
'Tis yours, a Bacon, or a Locke to blame,
A Newton's Genius, or a Seraph's flame :
215 But O ! with one, immortal One difpenfe,
The fource of Newton's Light, of Bacon's Senfe !

REMARKS.

" difputations, and *none would difpute with* " *him* ; writ, read and ftudied twelve hours a " day ; compos'd three differtations a week on " all fubjects ; undertook to teach in *one year* " what Schools and Univerfities teach in " *five* ; was not terrify'd by menaces, infults " or fatyrs, but ftill proceeded, matured his " bold fcheme, and put the *Church* and *all* " *that*, in *danger.*" WELSTED, *Narrative*, in *Orat. Tranfact.* Nº. 1

After having ftood fome Profecutions, he turned his Rhetorick to Buffoonry upon all publick and private occurrences. All this paffed in the fame room ; where fometimes he broke Jefts, and fometimes that Bread which he call'd the *Primitive Eucharift.* —— This wonderful perfon ftruck Medals, which he difperfed as Tickets to his fubfcribers : The device, a Star rifing to the Meridian, with this Motto, AD SUMMA ; and below, INVENIAM VIAM AUT FACIAM.

VERSE 208. Of *Toland* and *Tindal*, fee book 2. *Tho. Woolfton*, an impious madman, who wrote in a moft infolent ftyle againft the Miracles of the Gofpel ; in the years 1726, 27, &c.

Content, each Emanation of his fires

That beams on earth, each Virtue he inspires,

Each Art he prompts, each Charm he can create,

220 What-e'er he gives, are giv'n for You to hate.

Persist, by all divine in Man un-aw'd,

But learn, ye Dunces! not to scorn your GOD.

Thus he, for then a ray of Reason stole

Half thro' the solid darkness of his soul;

225 But soon the Cloud return'd—and thus the Sire:

See now, what Dulness and her sons admire;

See! what the charms, that smite the simple heart:

Not touch'd by Nature, and not reach'd by Art.

He look'd, and saw a sable Sorc'rer rise,

230 Swift to whose hand a winged volume flies:

All sudden, Gorgons hiss, and Dragons glare,

And ten-horn'd fiends and Giants rush to war.

Hell rises, Heav'n descends, and dance on Earth,

Gods, imps, and monsters, music, rage, and mirth,

235 A fire, a jig, a battle, and a ball,

Till one wide Conflagration swallows all.

REMARKS.

VERSE 222. *But learn, ye Dunces ! not to scorn your God.*] *Virg. Æn.* 6. puts this precept into the mouth of a wicked man, as here of a stupid one,
Discite justitiam moniti, & non temnere divos !

VERSE 229. —— *a sable Sorc'rer.*] Dr. *Faustus*, the subject of a set of Farces which lasted in vogue two or three seasons, in which both Play-houses strove to outdo each other in the years 1726, 27. All the extravagancies in the sixteen lines following were introduced on the Stage, and frequented by persons of the first quality in *England* to the twentieth and thirtieth time.

VERSE 233. *Hell rises, Heav'n descends, and dance on earth.*] This monstrous absurdity was actually represented in *Tibbald's Rape of Proserpine.*

Thence a new world, to Nature's laws unknown,

Breaks out refulgent, with a heav'n its own:

Another Cynthia her new journey runs,

240 And other planets circle other suns:

The forests dance, the rivers upward rise,

Whales sport in woods, and dolphins in the skies,

And last, to give the whole creation grace,

Lo! one vast Egg produces human race.

245   Joy fills his soul, joy innocent of thought:

What pow'r, he cries, what pow'r these wonders wrought?

Son! what thou seek'st is in thee. Look, and find

Each monster meets his likeness in thy mind.

Yet would'st thou more? In yonder cloud, behold!

250 Whose sarcenet skirts are edg'd with flamy gold,

A matchless youth: His nod these worlds controuls,

Wings the red lightning, and the thunder rolls.

Angel of Dulness, sent to scatter round

Her magic charms o'er all unclassic ground:

REMARKS.

Verse 244. *Lo! one vast Egg.*] In another of these Farces *Harlequin* is hatch'd upon the Stage, out of a large Egg.

IMITATIONS.

Verse 240. *And other planets.*] Virg. Æn. 6.
—— *solemque suum, sua sydera norunt.*
Verse 242. *Whales sport in woods, and dolphins in the skies.*] Hor.
Delphinum sylvis appingit, fluctibus aprum.
Verse 247. *Son! what thou seek'st is in thee.*]
Quod petis in te est ——
Ne te quæsiveris extra.   Pers.
Verse 252. *Wings the red lightning, &c.*]
Like *Salmoneus* in Æn. 6.

Dum flammas Jovis, & sonitus imitatur olympi.
— *Nimbos, & non imitabile fulmen,*
Ære & cornipedum cursu simularat æquorum.
Verse 254. —— *o'er all unclassic ground,*]
alludes to Mr. *Addison's* verse in the praises of *Italy,*
Poetic fields incompass me around,
And still I seem to tread on Classic ground.
As verse 260 is a Parody on a noble one of the same Author in the *Campaign*; and verse 255, 256. on two sublime verses of Dr. *Y.*

255 Yon ſtars, yon ſuns, he rears at pleaſure higher,
    Illumes their light, and ſets their flames on fire.
    Immortal Rich! how calm he ſits at eaſe
    Mid ſnows of paper, and fierce hail of peaſe;
    And proud his miſtreſs' orders to perform,
260 Rides in the whirlwind, and directs the ſtorm.
    But lo! to dark encounter in mid air
    New wizards riſe: here Booth, and Cibber there:
    Booth in his cloudy tabernacle ſhrin'd,
    On grinning dragons Cibber mounts the wind:
265 Dire is the conflict, diſmal is the din,
    Here ſhouts all Drury, there all Lincoln's-Inn;
    Contending Theatres our empire raiſe,
    Alike their labours, and alike their praiſe.
    And are theſe wonders, Son, to thee unknown?
270 Unknown to thee? Theſe wonders are thy own.
    For works like theſe let deathleſs Journals tell,
    " None but Thy ſelf can be thy parallel.
    Theſe, Fate reſerv'd to grace thy reign divine,
    Foreſeen by me, but ah! with-held from mine.

REMARKS.

VERSE 257. *Immortal* Rich.] Mr. *John Rich*, Maſter of the Theatre in *Lincolns-Inn-Fields*, was the firſt that excell'd this way.

VERSE 262 *Booth* and *Cibber*, two of the managers of the Theatre in *Drury-Lane*.

VERSE 272. *None but thy ſelf can be thy parallel.*] A marvellous line of *Theobald*; unleſs the Play call'd the *Double Falſhood* be, (as he would have it believed) *Shakeſpear's*: But whether this line be his or not, he proves *Shakeſpear* to have written as bad, (which methinks in an author for whom he has a Veneration almoſt riſing to idolatry, might have been concealed) as for example,

   Try what *Repentance* can: What can it not?
   But what can it, when one cannot *repent?*
   —— For *Cogitation*
Reſides not in the Man who does not *think*, &c.
            MIST's JOURN.

It is granted they are all of a piece, and no man doubts but herein he is able to imitate *Shakeſpear.*

V. id.] The former Annotator ſeeming to be of opinion that the *Double Falſhood* is not *Shakeſpear's*; it is but juſtice to give Mr. *Theobald's*

275 In Lud's old walls, tho' long I rul'd renown'd,

Far, as loud Bow's stupendous bells resound;

Tho' my own Aldermen conferr'd my bays,

To me committing their eternal praise,

REMARKS.

Arguments to the contrary: First that the MS. was above sixty years old; secondly, that once Mr. *Betterton* had it, or he hath heard so; thirdly, that some-body told him the author gave it to a bastard-daughter of his: But fourthly and above all, " that he has a *great mind* every thing " that is good in our tongue *should be* Shake-speare's." I allow these reasons to be truly critical; but what I am infinitely concern'd at is, that so many Errors have escaped the learned Editor: a few whereof we shall here amend, out of a much greater number, as an instance of our regard to this *dear Relick.*

ACT I. SCENE I.

I have his letters of a modern date,
Wherein by *Julio,* good *Camillo*'s son
(Who as he says, [ ] shall follow hard upon,
And whom I with the growing hour [ ] expect)
He doth follicit the return of gold,
To purchase certain horse that *like him well.*

This place is corrupted: the epithet *good* is a meer insignificant expletive, but the alteration of that single word restores a clear light to the whole context, thus,

I have his letters of a modern date,
Wherein, by *July,* (by *Camillo*'s son,
Who, as he *saith,* shall follow hard upon,
And whom I with the growing hours expect)
He doth follicit the return of gold.

Here you have not only the *Person* specify'd, by whose hands the return was to be made, but the most necessary part, the *Time,* by which it was required. *Camillo*'s son was to follow hard upon — What? Why upon *July.* — Horse that *like him well,* is very absurd: Read it, without contradiction,

— Horse, that *he likes well.*

ACT I. at the end.

— I must stoop to gain her,
Throw all my gay *Comparisons* aside,
And turn my proud additions out of service:
faith *Henriquez* of a maiden of low condition, objecting his high quality: What have his *Comparisons* here to do? Correct it boldly,

Throw all my gay *Caparisons* aside,
And turn my proud additions out of service.

ACT 2. SCENE I.

All the verse of this Scene is confounded with prose. —— O that a man
Could reason down this *Feaver* of the blood,
Or footh with *words* the tumult in his heart!
Then *Julio,* I might be *indeed* thy friend.
Read —— this *fervor* of the blood,
Then *Julio* I might be in *deed* thy friend.
marking the just opposition of deeds and words.

ACT 4. SCENE I.

How his eyes *shake* fire! — said by *Violante,* observing how the lustful shepherd looks at her. It must be, as the sense plainly demands,
—— How his eyes *take* fire!
And measure every piece of youth about me!
Ibid. That, tho' I *wore disguises* for some *ends.* She had but one disguise, and wore it but for one end. Restore it, with the alteration but of two letters,
That, tho' I *were disguised* for some *end.*

ACT 4. SCENE 2.

— To oaths no more give credit,
To tears, to vows; false *both !* —
False Grammar I'm sure. *Both* can relate but to *two* things: And see! how easy a change sets it right ?
To tears, to vows, false *troth* —
I could shew you that very word troth, in *Shakespear* a hundred times.
Ib. For there is nothing left thee now to look for,
That can bring *comfort,* but a *quiet grave.*
This I fear is of a piece with *None but itself can be its parallel:* for the grave *puts an end* to all sorrow, it can then need no *comfort.* Yet let us vindicate *Shakespear* where we can: I make no doubt he wrote thus,
For there is nothing left thee now to look for,
Nothing that can bring *quiet,* but the grave.
Which reduplication of the word gives a much stronger emphasis to *Violante*'s concern. This figure is call'd *Anadyplosis.* I could shew you a hundred just such in him, if I had nothing else to do.

SCRIBLERUS.

Their full-fed Heroes, their pacific May'rs,
280 Their annual trophies, and their monthly wars.
Tho' long my Party built on me their hopes,
For writing pamphlets, and for burning Popes;
(Diff'rent our parties, but with equal grace
The Goddess smiles on Whig and Tory race,
285 'Tis the same rope at sev'ral ends they twist,
To Dulness, Ridpath is as dear as Mist.)
Yet lo! in me what authors have to brag on!
Reduc'd at last to hiss in my own dragon.
Avert it, Heav'n! that thou or Cibber e'er
290 Should wag two serpent tails in Smithfield fair.
Like the vile straw that's blown about the streets
The needy Poet sticks to all he meets,
Coach'd, carted, trod upon, now loose, now fast,
In the Dog's tail his progress ends at last.

REMARKS.

VERSE 280. *Annual trophies*, on the *Lord Mayor's Day*; and *monthly wars*, in the *Artillery Ground.*

VERSE 281. *Tho' long my Party.*] *Settle*, like most Party-writers, was very uncertain in his political principles. He was employ'd to hold the pen in the *Character* of a *Popish successor*, but afterwards printed his *Narrative* on the contrary side. He had managed the Ceremony of a famous Pope-burning on *Nov.* 17, 1680: then became a Trooper of King *James*'s army at *Hounslow-heath*: After the Revolution he kept a Booth at *Bartlemew-fair*, where in his Droll call'd St. *George for England*, he acted in his old age in a Dragon of green leather of his own invention. He was at last taken into the Charter-house, and there dyed, aged about 60 years.

V. 285. *To Dulness*, Ridpath *is as dear as* Mist.] *George Ridpath*, author for several years of the *Flying-Post*, a Whig-paper; *Nathaniel Mist*, publisher of the Weekly Journal, a Tory-paper.

IMITATIONS.

VERSE 283-84. —— *With equal grace Our Goddess smiles on Whig and Tory race.*] Virg. Æn. 10.

Tros Rutulusve fuat, nullo discrimine habebo.
—— *Rex Jupiter omnibus idem.*

P.

295 Happier thy fortunes! like a rolling ftone,
     Thy giddy dulnefs ftill fhall lumber on,
     Safe in its heavinefs, can never ftray,
     And licks up every blockhead in the way.
     Thy dragons Magiftrates and Peers fhall tafte,
300 And from each fhow rife duller than the laft:
     Till rais'd from Booths to Theatre, to Court,
     Her feat imperial, Dulnefs fhall tranfport.
     Already, Opera prepares the way,
     The fure fore-runner of her gentle fway.
305 To aid her caufe, if heav'n thou can'ft not bend,
     Hell thou fhalt move; for Fauftus is thy friend:
     Pluto with Cato thou for her fhalt join,
     And link the Mourning-Bride to Proferpine.
     Grubftreet! thy fall fhould men and Gods confpire,
310 Thy ftage fhall ftand, enfure it but from Fire.

REMARKS.

Verse 299. *Thy dragons Magiftrates and Peers fhall tafte.*] It ftood in the firft edition with blanks, *Thy dragons* ** *and* ***. *Concanen* was fure, " they " muft needs mean no-body but the *King* and " *Queen*, and faid he would infift it was fo, till " the Poet clear'd himfelf by filling up the " blanks otherwife agreeably to the context, and " confiftent with his *allegiance*. [Pref. to a Col-lection of Verfes, Effays, Letters, &c. againft Mr. *P.* printed for *A. Moore*, pag. 6.]

Verse 307. ——— *Fauftus is thy friend*, Pluto *with* Cato, &c.] Names of miferable Farces of *Tibbald* and others, which it was their cuftom to get acted at the end of the beft Tragedies, to fpoil the digeftion of the audience.

Verse 310. ——— *enfure it but from fire.*] In *Tibbald's* Farce of *Proferpine* a Corn-field was fet on fire; whereupon the other Playhoufe had a Barn burnt down for the recreation of the fpectators. They alfo rival'd each other in fhowing the Burnings of Hell-fire, in Dr. *Fauftus.*

IMITATIONS.

Verse 305. — *If heav'n thou canft not bend,*
Hell thou fhalt move ——]

Virg. Æn. 7.
Flectere fi nequeo fuperos, acheronta movebo.

Another Æschylus appears! prepare
For new Abortions, all ye pregnant Fair!
In flames, like Semeles, be brought to bed,
While opening Hell spouts wild-fire at your head.
315   Now Bavius, take the poppy from thy brow,
And place it here! here all ye Heroes bow!
This, this is He, foretold by ancient rhymes,
Th' Augustus born to bring Saturnian times:
Beneath his reign, shall Eusden wear the bays,
320 Cibber preside Lord-Chancellor of Plays,

REMARKS.

VERSE 311. *Another Æschylus appears!* &c.] It is reported of *Æschylus*, that when his Tragedy of the *Furies* was acted, the audience were so terrify'd that the children fell into fits, and the big-bellied women miscarried. *Tibbald* is translating this author: he printed a specimen of him many years ago, of which I only remember that the first Note contains some comparison between *Prometheus* and *Christ crucify'd*.

VERSE 319. Eusden *wear the bays.*] Laurence Eusden, Poet-Laureate: Mr. *Jacob* gives a catalogue of some few only of his works, which were very numerous. Mr. *Cook* in his *Battle of Poets* saith of him,

Eusden, *a laurel'd Bard, by fortune rais'd,*
By very few was read, by fewer prais'd.

Mr. *Oldmixon* in his Arts of Logic and Rhetoric, p. 413, 414. affirms, "That of all the Ga-
" limatia's he ever met with, none comes up to
" some verses of this Poet, which have as much
" of the Ridiculum and the Fustian in 'em
" as can well be jumbled together, and are of
" that sort of nonsense which so perfectly con-
" founds all Ideas, that there is no distinct one
" left in the mind. Further he says of him, that
" he hath prophesy'd his own poetry shall be
" sweeter than *Catullus, Ovid,* and *Tibullus,*
" but we have little hope of the accomplishment
" of it from what he hath lately publish'd."
Upon which Mr. *Oldmixon* has not spar'd a re-
flection, " That the putting the Laurel on the
" head of one who writ such verses, will give
" futurity a very lively idea of the Judgment
" and Justice of those who bestow'd it." *Ibid.*
p. 417. But the well-known learning of that
Noble Person who was then Lord Chamberlain,
might have screen'd him from this unmannerly
reflection. Mr. *Eusden* was made *Laureate* for the
same reason that Mr. *Tibbald* was made *Hero* of
This Poem, because there was *no better to be
had.* Nor ought Mr. *Oldmixon* to complain, so
long after, that the Laurel would better have be-

IMITATIONS.

VERSE 313. —— *Like Semeles* ——] See *Ovid, Met. 3.*
VERSE 317. *This, this is he, foretold by ancient rhymes,*
Th' Augustus, *&c.*] Virg. Æn. 6.
Hic vir, hic est! tibi quem promitti sæpius audis,

Augustus Cæsar, divum genus; aurea condet
Sæcula qui rursus Latio, regnata per arva
Saturno quondam ——
Saturnian here relates to the age of *Lead,* mention'd book 1. ver. 26.

P 2

B * * fole Judge of Architecture fit,
And Namby Pamby be prefer'd for Wit!
While naked mourns the Dormitory wall,
And Jones and Boyle's united labours fall,

REMARKS.

come his own brows, or any other's: It were decent to acquiesce in the opinion of the Duke of *Buckingham* upon this matter.
—*In rush'd Eusden, and cry'd, Who shall have it.*
But I the true Laureate to whom the King gave it?
Apollo begg'd pardon, and granted his claim,
But vow'd, that till then he ne'er heard of his name.
Seffion of Poets.

VERSE 321. B * * *fole judge of Architecture fit,*] W——n B—nf—n (late Surveyor of the Buildings to his Majesty King *George* I.) gave in a report to the *Lords,* that Their House and the Painted Chamber adjoining were in immediate danger of falling. Whereupon the Lords met in a Committee to appoint fome other place to fit in, while the House should be taken down. But it being proposed to caufe fome other Builders first to infpect it, they found it in very good condition. The Lords, upon this, were going upon an addrefs to the King against B—nf—n, for fuch a mifreprefentation; but the Earl of *Sunderland,* then Secretary, gave them an affurance that his Majesty would remove him, which was done accordingly. In favour of this man, the famous Sir *Christopher Wren,* who had been Architect to the Crown for above fifty years, who laid the first stone of St. *Paul's,* and lived to finish it, had been difplac'd from his employment at the age of near ninety years.

VERSE 322. *And* Namby Pamby.] An author whofe eminence in the Infantine stile obtain'd him this name. He was (faith Mr. JACOB) " one of the Wits at *Button's,* and a Justice of " the Peace." But fince he hath met with higher preferment, in *Ireland:* and a much greater character we have of him in Mr. GILDON's Compleat Art of Poetry, vol. 1. p. 157. " Indeed " he confeffes, he dares not fet him *quite on the* " *fame foot* with *Virgil,* left it should *feem* Flat- " tery: but he is much mistaken if posterity " does not afford him a *greater esteem* than " he *at present enjoys.*" This is faid of his

Pastorals, of which fee in the Appendix the *Guardian,* at large. He endeavour'd to create fome mif-understanding between our author and Mr. *Addison,* whom. also foon after he abufed as much. His constant cry was, that Mr. *P.* was an Enemy to the government; and in particular he was the avowed author of a report very industriously spread, that he had a hand in a Party-paper call'd the *Examiner:* A falshood well known to thofe yet living, who had the direction and publication of it.

Qui meprise Cotin, *n'estime point fon* Roy,
Et n'a, (felon Cotin,) *ni* Dieu, *ni* Foy, *ni* Loy.

VERSE 323. *Dormitory wall.*] The Dormitory in *Westminster* was a building intended for the lodging of the King's Scholars; toward which a fum was left by Dr. *Edw. Hannes,* the rest was raifed by contributions procured from feveral eminent perfons by the interest of *Francis* late Bishop of *Rochester,* and Dean of *Westminster:* He requested the Earl of *Burlington* to be the Architect, who carry'd on the work till the Bill against that learned Prelate was brought in, which ended in his banifhment. The shell being finished according to his Lordship's defign, the fucceeding Dean and Chapter employ'd a common builder to do the infide, which is perform'd *accordingly.*

VERSE 324. *And* Jones *and* Boyle's *united labours fall.*] At the time when this Poem was written, the Banquetting-house of *Whitehall,* the Church and Piazza of *Covent-garden,* and the Palace and Chappel of *Somerfet-house,* the works of the famous *Inigo Jones,* had been for many years fo neglected, as to be in danger of ruin. The Portico of *Covent-garden* Church had been just then restored and beautify'd at the expence of *Richard* Earl of *Burlington;* who, at the fame time, by his publication of the defigns of that great Master and *Palladio,* as well as by many noble buildings of his own, revived the true Taste of Architecture in this Kingdom.

325 While Wren with sorrow to the grave descends,
   Gay dies un-pension'd with a hundred Friends,
   Hibernian Politicks, O Swift, thy doom,
   And Pope's, translating three whole years with Broome.
   Proceed great days! till Learning fly the shore,
330 Till Birch shall blush with noble blood no more.

REMARKS.

VERSE 326. Gay *dies un-pension'd, &c.*] See Mr. *Gay's* Fable of the *Hare* and *Many Friends.* This gentleman was early in the friendship of our author, which has continued many years. He wrote several works of humour with great success, the *Shepherd's Week, Trivia,* the *What d'ye call it,* &c. (printed together in 4°. by *J. Tonson) Fables*; and lastly, the celebrated *Beggars Opera*; a piece of Satire which hit all tastes and degrees of men, from those of the highest Quality to the very Rabble: That verse of *Horace*

Primores populi arripuit, populumque tributim,

could never be so justly applied as to this. The vast success of it was unprecedented, and almost incredible: What is related of the wonderful effects of the ancient Music or Tragedy hardly came up to it: *Sophocles* and *Euripides* were less follow'd and famous. It was acted in *London* sixty-three days, uninterrupted; and renew'd the next season with equal applauses. It spread into all the great towns of *England,* was play'd in many places to the 30th, and 40th time, at *Bath* and *Bristol* 50, *&c.* It made its progress into *Wales, Scotland,* and *Ireland,* where it was performed 24 days together. The fame of it was not confin'd to the author only; the Ladies carry'd about with 'em the favourite songs of it in Fans; and houses were furnish'd with it in Screens. The person who acted *Polly,* till then obscure, became all at once the favourite of the town; her *Pictures* were ingraved and sold in great numbers; her *Life* written; books of *Let-*ters and *Verses* to her publish'd; and pamphlets made even of her *Sayings* and *Jests.*

Furthermore, it drove out of *England* the *Italian Opera,* which had carry'd all before it for ten years: That Idol of the Nobility and the people, which the great Critick Mr. *Dennis* by the labours and outcries of a whole life could not overthrow, was demolish'd in one winter by a single stroke of this gentleman's pen. This remarkable period happen'd in the year 1728. Yet so great was his modesty, that he constantly prefixed to all the editions of it this Motto, *Nos hæc novimus esse nihil.*

VERSE 327. Hibernian *politicks, O Swift! thy doom.*] The Politicks of *England* and *Ireland* at this time were thought by some to be opposite or interfering with each other. Dr. *Swift* of course was in the interests of the latter.

VERSE 328. *And* Pope's, *translating three whole years with* Broome.] He concludes his Irony with a stroke upon himself: For whoever imagines this a sarcasm on the other ingenious person is greatly mistaken. The opinion our author had of him was sufficiently shown, by his joining him in the undertaking of the *Odyssey:* in which Mr. *Broome* having ingaged without any previous agreement, discharged his part so much to Mr. *Pope's* satisfaction, that he gratified him with the full sum of *Five hundred pounds,* and a present of all those books for which his own interest could procure him Subscribers, to the value of *One hundred more.* The author only seems to lament, that he was imploy'd in Translation at all.

IMITATIONS.

VERSE 329. *Proceed great days*] Virg. Ecl. 4.
——*Incipiunt magni procedere menses.*

Q

Till Thames fee Eton's fons for ever play,

Till Weftminfter's whole year be holiday;

Till Ifis' Elders reel, their Pupils fport;

And Alma Mater lye diffolv'd in Port!

335   Signs following figns lead on the Mighty Year;

See! the dull ftars roll round and re-appear.

She comes! the Cloud-compelling Pow'r, behold!

With Night Primæval, and with Chaos old.

Lo! the great Anarch's ancient reign reftor'd,

340   Light dies before her uncreating word:

As one by one, at dread Medæa's ftrain,

The fick'ning Stars fade off the a'thereal plain;

As Argus' eyes, by Hermes wand oppreft,

Clos'd one by one to everlafting reft;

REMARKS.

VERSE 337, &c. *She comes! the Cloud-compelling pow'r, behold!* &c.] Here the Mufe, like *Jove*'s Eagle, after a fudden ftoop at ignoble game, foareth again to the fkies. As Prophecy hath ever been one of the chief provinces of Poefy, our poet here foretells from what we feel, what we are to fear; and in the ftyle of other Prophets, hath ufed the future tenfe for the preterit: fince what he fays fhall be, is already to be feen, in the writings of fome even of our moft adored authors, in Divinity, Philofophy, Phyfics, Metaphyfics, &c. (who are too good indeed to be named in fuch company.) Do not gentle reader, reft too fecure in thy contempt of the Inftruments for fuch a revolution in learning, or defpife fuch weak agents as have been defcribed in our poem, but remember what the *Dutch* ftories fomewhere relate, that a great part of their Provinces was once overflow'd, by a fmall opening made in one of their dykes by a fingle *Water-Rat.*

However, that fuch is not ferioufly the judgment of our Poet, but that he conceiveth better hopes from the diligence of our Schools, from the regularity of our Univerfities, the difcernment of our Great men, the encouragement of our Patrons, and the genius of our Writers in all kinds, (notwithftanding fome few exceptions in each) may plainly be feen from his conclufion; where by caufing all this Vifion to pafs thro' the *Ivory Gate*, he exprefly in the language of poefy declares all fuch imaginations to be wild, ungrounded, and fictitious.

SCRIBLERUS.

IMITATIONS.

VERSE 343. *As Argus eyes by Hermes wand oppreft*] Ovid Met. I.

Et quamvis fopor eft oculorum parte receptus,
Parte tamen vigilat—Vidit Cyllenius omnes
Succubuiffe oculos, &c. ibid.

345 Thus at her felt approach, and fecret might,
     Art after Art goes out, and all is Night.
     See fculking Truth in her old cavern lye,
     Secur'd by mountains of heap'd cafuiftry:
     Philofophy, that touch'd the Heavens before,
350 Shrinks to her hidden caufe, and is no more:
     See Physic beg the Stagyrite's defence!
     See Metaphyfic call for aid on Sence!
     See Myftery to Mathematicks fly!
     In vain! they gaze, turn giddy, rave, and die.
355 Thy hand great Dulnefs! lets the curtain fall,
     And univerfal Darknefs covers all.

       Enough! enough! the raptur'd Monarch cries;
     And thro' the Ivory Gate the Vifion flies.

R E M A R K S.

VERSE 347. *Truth in her old cavern lye*] Alludes to the faying of *Democritus*, that Truth lay at the bottom of a deep well.

I M I T A T I O N S.

VERSE 358. *And thro' the Ivory Gate the Vifion flies*] Virg. Æn. 6.
     Sunt geminæ fomni portæ; quarum altera fertur
     Cornea, qua veris facilis datur exitus umbris;
     Altera, candenti perfecta nitens elephanto,
     Sed falfa ad cœlum mittunt infomnia manes.

F I N I S.

M. SCRIBLERUS Lectori.

THE *Errata* of this Edition we thought (gentle reader) to have trusted to thy candor and benignity, to correct with thy pen, as accidental Faults escaped the press: But seeing that certain Censors do give to such the name of *Corruptions of the Text* and *false Readings*, charge them on the Editor, and judge that correcting the same is to be called *Restoring*, and an *Atchievement that brings Honour to the Critic*; we have in like manner taken it upon ourselves.

Book i. Verse 8. *E'er Pallas issu'd from the Thund'rers head.* *E'er* is the contraction of *ever*, but that is by no means the sense in this place: Correct it, without the least scruple, *E're*, the contraction of *or-ere*, an old *English* word for *before.* What Ignorance of our mother tongue!

Verse 6. *Still Dunce* [ ] *second reigns like Dunce the first.* Read infallibly, still Dunce *the* second—Want of knowledge in the very Measure!

Verse 23, 24. ——*tho' her power* retires,
Grieve not at ought our sister realms acquire.
Read,—*our sister realm acquires.* Want of Ear even in Rhime!

Verse 38. —— *Lintot's rubric's post.* Read, *rubric post.* I am aware, there is such a Substantive as *Rubric*, *The Rubric*; but here (I can assure the Editor) it is an Adjective.

Verse 189. Remarks. *C'est le mem quem* Marc Tulle. Correct it boldly, *le meme que* Marc Tulle. Ignorance in the *French* !

Book ii. verse 79. Imitations.—Terrasque *fretamque.* Read *fretumque*, Neut. Unskilfulness in *Latin !*

Ibid. verse 88.—ῥεε δ᾽Ἀμβροτον, correct the Accents thus, ῥεε δ᾽Ἀμβροτον—περ]ε, Corr. περ τε. Want of understanding in *Greek !*

Book i. verse 58. Rem. Tenderness for *a*

bad writer, read *the bad writers.* Plur. False *English:* No Relative!

Verse 197. Rem. *Incensa* [.,] make it a plain Comma; [,] a strange sort of Punctuation this, [.,] invented sure by the Editor!

Verse 208. Imit. *Ut, alegon.* Monstrous Division ! away with that Comma !

Book ii. verse 369. Leave out these words—*When he came into the Administration;* For these Gentlemen never write against any man *in power.* This betrays great want of knowledge in Authors !

After so shameful ignorance in *Greek, Latin, French, English,* Quantity, Accent, Rhyme, Grammar, we cannot wonder at such Errors as the following. Book i. verse 101. *Rem.* for 254, read 258. and for 300, read 281.——Book ii. verse 75, for *Here* r. *Hear,* Verse 118. Rem. col. 2. for *Libel,* read *silly book,* it deserves not the name of a Libel. Verse 258, for *Courts* of *Chancery* r. *Offices,* for *those Courts,* r. *that Court,* and for *them* r. *it.* Verse 319. for *sacred* r. *secret.* Book iii. verse 46. Imit. for *hedæram* r. *hederam.* Verse 56. for *run forward* r. *rush forward.* We must also observe the careless manner of spelling sometimes *Satyr,* sometimes *Satire,* in the Notes, probably from the different Orthography of the various Annotators; however no excuse for the Editor, who ought constantly to have spelled it *Satire.*

In our Prolegomena likewise, pag. 12. line 6. where it is said, certain Verses were *never made publick till by Curl their own Bookseller;* Correct and strengthen the passage thus, *never made publick till in* their own Journals, *and by Curl* their own Bookseller, &c. But this, gentle reader, be so candid as to believe the Error only of the Printer.

Vale & fruere.

INDEX

INDEX

OF

PERSONS celebrated in this POEM.

OGIL-

INDEX

OF THE

AUTHOR's of the NOTES.

Authors of Lives of Poets.
MR. Winstanley, } Book i. Verse 121, 122,
Mr. Giles Jacob, } 126, 134. b. i. v. 104,
106, 200, 240, *ibid.*
ii. 201, 367. iii. 149.
Mr. Edm. Curl, b. i. v. 48, 240. ii. 46, 66,
116, 149, 370, 111, 26.
Mr. Charles Gildon, ii. 258, 134, iii. 322.
Mr. Lewis Theobald, b. i. v. 48, 104, 106, 129,
162, 221. ii. 177. iii. 28.
Mr. John Dennis, b. i. v. 61, 88, 104, 106, 162.

ii. 111, 134, 258, 295, 382. iii. 16.
Mr. Mist, *Publisher of the Journal,* b, i. v. 106,
129. ii. 134.
Flying-Post, b. ii.
London Journal, b. ii. and iii.
Daily Journal, b. i. 61. &c.
Mr. Jonathan Smedley, b. ii. 130, 295.
Mr. John Oldmixon, b. i. 102. iii. 319.
Mr. J. Ralph, b. i. v. 1, 28, 31. ii. 111.
Mr. Welstede, b. iii. 16, 195.
The learned Martinus Scriblerus, *and others.* passim.

APPEN-

APPENDIX.

PIECES contained in the APPENDIX.

PREFACE of the Publisher, prefixed to the five imperfect Editions of the *Dunciad*, printed at *Dublin* and *London*.

A List of Books, Papers, &c. in which our Author was abused: with the Names of the (hitherto conceal'd) Writers.

WILLIAM CAXTON his Proeme to *Æneidos*.

VIRGIL RESTORED: Or a Specimen of the Errors in all the Editions of the *Æneid*, by M. SCRIBLERUS.

A Continuation of the GUARDIAN (N° 40) on Pastoral Poetry.

A Parallel of the Characters of Mr. DRYDEN and Mr. POPE, as drawn by certain of their Cotemporary Authors.

A List of all our Authors Genuine Works hitherto published.

INDEX of Memorable things in this Book.

APPENDIX.

I.

PREFACE *prefix'd to the five imperfect* Editions *of the* DUNCIAD, *printed at* Dublin *and* London, *in Octavo &* Duod.

(a) The Publisher to the Reader.

IT will be found a true obfervation, tho' fomewhat furprizing, that when any fcandal is vented againft a man of the higheft diftinction and character, either in the State or in Literature, the publick in general afford it a moft quiet reception; and the larger part accept it as favourably as if it were fome kindnefs done to themfelves: Whereas if a known fcoundrel or blockhead chance but to be touch'd upon, a whole legion is up in arms, and it becomes the common caufe of all Scriblers, Bookfellers, and Printers whatfoever.

(a) The Publifher.] Who he was is uncertain; but *Edward Ward* tells us in his Preface to *Durgen*, that " moft Judges are of opinion this Preface is not of *Englifh* Extraction but *Hiber-* " *nian*, &c. He means Dr. *Swift*, who whether Publifher or not, may be faid in a fort to be Author of the Poem: For when He, together with Mr. *Pope*, (for reafons fpecify'd in their Preface to the Mifcellanies) determin'd to own the moft trifling pieces in which they had any hand, and to deftroy all that remain'd in their power, the firft fketch of this poem was fnatch'd from the fire by Dr. *Swift*, who perfuaded his friend to proceed in it, and to him it was therefore Infcribed.

Not

Not to search too deeply into the *Reason* hereof, I will only observe as a *Fact*, that every week for these two Months past, the town has been persecuted with (b) Pamphlets, Advertisements, Letters, and weekly Essays, not only against the Wit and Writings, but against the Character and Person of Mr. *Pope.* And that of all those men who have received pleasure from his Writings (which by modest computation may be about a (c) hundred thousand in these Kingdoms of *England* and *Ireland,* not to mention *Jersey, Guernsey,* the *Orcades,* those in the *New world,* and *Foreigners* who have translated him into their languages) of all this number, not a man hath stood up to say one word in his defence.

The only exception is the (d) Author of the following Poem, who doubtless had either a better insight into the grounds of this clamour, or a better opinion of Mr. *Pope's* integrity, join'd with a greater personal love for him, than any other of his numerous friends and admirers.

Further, that he was in his peculiar intimacy, appears from the knowledge he manifests of the most *private* Authors of all the *anonymous* pieces against him, and from his having in this Poem attacked (e) no man living, who had not before printed or published some scandal against this particular Gentlemen.

How I became possest of it, is of no concern to the Reader ; but it would have been a wrong to him, had I detain'd this publication : since those *Names* which are its chief ornaments, die off daily so fast, as must render it too soon unintelligible. If it provoke the Author to give us a more perfect edition, I have my end.

Who he is, I cannot say, and (which is great pity) there is certainly (f) nothing in his style and manner of writing, which can distinguish, or discover him. For if it bears any resemblance to that of Mr. *P.* 'tis not improbable

---

(b) *Pamphlets, Advertisements,* &c.] See the List of these anonymous papers, with their dates and Authors thereunto annexed. N° 2.

(c) *About a hundred thousand*] It is surprizing with what stupidity this Preface, which is almost a continued Irony, was taken by these Authors. This passage among others they understood to be serious :

(d) *The Author of the following Poem,* &c.] A very plain Irony, speaking of Mr. *Pope* himself.

(e) The Publisher in these words went a little too far : but it is certain whatever Names the Reader finds that are unknown to him, are of such : and the exception is only of two or three, whose dulness or scurrility all mankind agree to have justly entitled them to a place in the Dunciad.

(f) *There is certainly nothing in his Style,* &c.] This Irony had small effect in concealing the Author. The Dunciad, imperfect as it was, had not been publish'd two days, but the whole Town gave it to Mr. *Pope.*

but

but it might be done on purpofe, with a view to have it pafs for his. But by the frequency of his allufions to *Virgil*, and a *labor'd* (not to fay *affected*) *fhortnefs* in imitation of him, I fhould think him more an admirer of the *Roman* Poet than of the *Grecian*, and in that not of the fame tafte with his Friend.

I have been well inform'd, that this work was the labour of full (g) *fix* years of his life, and that he retired himfelf entirely from all the avocations and pleafures of the world, to attend diligently to its correction and perfection ; and fix years more he intended to beftow upon it, as it fhould feem by this verfe of *Statius*, which was cited at the head of his manufcript.

Oh mihi biffenos multum vigilata per annos,
(h) *Duncia !*

Hence alfo we learn the true *Title* of the Poem ; which with the fame certainty as we call that of *Homer* the *Iliad*, of *Virgil* the *Æneid*, of *Camoens* the *Lufiad*, of *Voltaire* the *Henriad* (i), we may pronounce could have been, and can be no other, than

The DUNCIAD.

It is ftyled *Heroic*, as being *doubly* fo ; not only with refpect to its nature, which according to the beft Rules of the Ancients and ftricteft ideas of the Moderns, is critically fuch ; but alfo with regard to the Heroical difpo-

---

(g) *The Labour of full* fix *years*, &c.] This alfo was honeftly and ferioufly believ'd, by divers of the Gentlemen of the Dunciad. *J. Ralph*, Pref. to *Sawney*, " We are told it was the " labour of *fix years*, with the utmoft *affiduity* and *application*: It is no great compliment to " the Author's fenfe, to have employed fo *large a part* of his *Life*, &c." So alfo *Ward*, Pref. to *Durg*. " The Dunciad, as the Publifher very *wifely* confeffes, coft the Author *fix years retire- " ment from all the pleafures of life*, to but half finifh his abufive undertaking——tho' it is fome- " what difficult to conceive, from either its Bulk or Beauty, that it cou'd be fo long in hatch- " ing, &c. But the *length of time* and *clofenefs of application* were mentioned to prepoffefs the " reader with a good opinion of it."
Neverthelefs the Prefacer to Mr. *Curl's Key* (a great Critick) was of a different fentiment, and thought it might be written in *fix days*.
It is to be hoped they will as well underftand, and write as gravely upon what *Scriblerus* hath faid of this Poem.
(h) The fame learned Prefacer took this word to be really in *Statius*. " By a quibble on the " word *Duncia*, the Dunciad is formed," *pag.* 3. Mr. *Ward* alfo follows him in the fame opinion.
(i) *The Henriad*.] The French Poem of Monfieur *Voltaire*, entitled *La Henriade*, had been publifh'd at *London* the year before.

fition and high courage of the Writer, who dar'd to ftir up fuch a formidable, irritable, and implacable race of mortals.

The time and date of the Action is evidently in the laft reign, when the office of City Poet expir'd upon the death of *Elkanab Settle*, and he has fix'd it to the Mayoralty of Sir *Geo. Thorold*. But there may arife fome obfcurity in Chronology from the *Names* in the Poem, by the inevitable removal of fome Authors, and infertion of others, in their Niches. For whoever will confider the Unity of the whole defign, will be fenfible, that the *Poem was not made for thefe Authors, but thefe Authors for the Poem:* And I fhould judge they were clapp'd in as they rofe, frefh and frefh, and chang'd from day to day, in like manner as when the old boughs wither, we thruft new ones into a chimney.

I would not have the reader too much troubled or anxious, if he cannot decypher them ; fince when he fhall have found them out, he will probably know no more of the Perfons than before.

Yet we judg'd it better to preferve them as they are, than to change them for *fictitious names*, by which the Satyr would only be multiplied, and applied to many inftead of one. Had the Hero, for inftance, been called *Codrus*, how many would have affirm'd him to be Mr. *W——* Mr. *D——* Sir *R—— B——*, &c. but now, all that unjuft fcandal is faved, by calling him *Theobald*, which by good luck happens to be the name of a real perfon.

I am indeed aware, that this name may to fome appear too *mean*, for the Hero of an Epic Poem : But it is hoped, they will alter that opinion, when they find, that an Author no lefs eminent than *la Bruyere* has thought him worthy a place in his Characters.

Voudriez vous, THEOBALDE, *que je crufe que vous êtes baiffe? que vous n'êtes plus Poete, ni bel efprit? que vous êtes prefentement auff: mauvais Juge de tout genre d'Ouvrage, que mechant Auteur? Votre air libre & prefumptueux me raffure, & me perfuade tout le contraire,* &c. Characteres, Vol. I. *de la Societe & de la Converfation, pag.* 176. Edit. Amft, 1720.

A Lift

II.

A List of Books, Papers, and Verses, in which our Author was abused, printed before the Publication of the Dunciad : *With the true Names of the Authors.*

REFLECTIONS Critical and Satyrical on a late Rhapsody called an Essay on Criticism. By Mr. *Dennis.* Printed for *B. Lintot.* Price 6 *d.*

A New Rehearsal, or Bays the Younger, Containing an Examen of Mr. *Rowe's* Plays, and a word or two upon Mr. *Pope's* Rape of the Locke. Anon. [*Charles Gildon.*] Printed for *J. Roberts,* 1714. Price 1 *s.*

Homerides, or a Letter to Mr. *Pope,* occasion'd by his intended Translation of Homer. By Sir *Iliad Doggrel.* [*T. Burnet* and *G. Ducket* Esquires] Printed for *W. Wilkins,* 1715. Price 6 *d.*

Æsop at the Bear-garden. A Vision in imitation of the Temple of Fame. By Mr. *Preston.* Sold by *John Morphew,* 1715. Price 6 *d.*

The Catholic Poet, or Protestant Barnabys sorrowful Lamentation, a Ballad about Homer's Iliad [by Mrs. *Centlivre* and others] 1715. Price 1 *d.*

An Epilogue to a Puppet-show at Bath, concerning the said Iliad, by *George Ducket* Esq; Printed by *E. Curl.*

A compleat Key to the What-d'ye-call-it, Anon. [Mr. *Th——*] Printed for *J. Roberts,* 1715.

A true character of Mr. *Pope* and his Writings, in a Letter to a Friend, Anon. [Messieurs *Gildon* and *Dennis.*] Printed for *S. Popping,* 1716. Price 3 *d.*

The Confederates, a Farce. By *Joseph Gay* [*J. D. Breval.*] Printed for *R. Burleigh,* 1717. Price 1 *s.*

Remarks upon Mr. *Pope's* Translation of Homer, with two Letters concerning the Windsor Forrest and the Temple of Fame. By Mr. *Dennis.* Printed for *E. Curl,* 1717. Price 1 *s.* 6 *d.*

Satires on the Translators of Homer, Mr. *P.* and Mr. *T.* Anon. [*Bez. Morris*] 1717. Price 6 *d.*

The

The Triumvirate, or a Letter from Palæmon to Celia at Bath. Anon. [*Leonard Welfted.*] Price 1 *s.* 1718. Folio.

The Battle of Poets, a Heroic Poem. [By *Tho. Cooke*] Printed for *J. Roberts.* Folio. 1725.

Memoirs of Lilliput, Anon. [Mrs. *Eliz. Haywood.*] 8º. Printed 1727.

An Effay on Criticifm, in Profe, by the Author of the Critical Hiftory of England [*J. Oldmixon*] 8º 1728.

Gulliveriana, and Alexandriana. With an ample Preface and Critique on *Swift* and *Pope*'s Mifcellanies [By *Jonathan Smedley.*] Printed for *J. Roberts* 8ᵛ 1728. Advertifed before the publication of the Dunciad in the Daily Journal, *April 13.* 1728.

Characters of the Times, or an Account of the Writings, Characters, &c. of feveral Gentlemen libell'd by *S—* and *P—* in a late Mifcellany, 8º 1728. [*C—l* and *W—d.*]

Remarks on Mr. *Pope*'s Rape of the Lock, in Letters to a Friend. [By Mr. *Dennis.*] Written in 1714, tho' not printed till 1728. 8º.

Verfes, Letters, Effays, or Advertifements in the publick Prints.

Britifh Journal, *Nov.* 25, 1727. A Letter on *Swift* and *Pope*'s Mifcellanies. [Writ by *Concanen.*]

Daily Journal, *March* 18, 1728. A Letter by *Philomauri.* [*James Moore Smyth.*]

Id. *March* 29. A Letter about *Therfites* and accufing the Author of Difaffection to the Government. [*James Moore Smyth.*]

Mift's Weekly Journal, *March* 30. An Effay on the Arts of a Poets finking in reputation, Or a fupplement to the Art of finking in Poetry [fuppofed by Mr. *Theobald.*]

Daily Journal, *April* 3. A Letter under the name of *Philo-ditto* [by *James Moore Smyth.*]

Flying-Poft, *April* 4. A Letter againft *Gulliver* and Mr. *P.* [Mr. *Oldmixon*]

Daily Journal, *April* 5. An Auction of Goods at *Twickenham,* [by *J. Moore Smyth.*]

Flying-Poft. *April* 6. A Fragment of a Treatife upon *Swift* and *Pope,* [by Mr. *Oldmixon.*]

The Senator, *April* 9. On the fame, [by *Edward Room.*]

Daily

Daily Journal, *April* 8. Advertifement [by *James Moore Smyth.*]

Daily Journal, *April* 9. Letter and Verfes againft Dr. *Swift*, [by * * Efq;]

Flying-Poft, *April* 13. Verfes againft the fame, and againft Mr. *P—'*s *Homer*, [by *J. Oldmixon.*]

Daily Journal, *April* 16. Verfes on Mr. *P.* [by * * Efq;.]

Id. *April* 23. Letter about a Tranflation of the character of *Therfites* in *Homer*, [*J—D—*, &c.]

*Mift'*s Weekly Journal, *April* 27. A Letter of *Lewis Theobald.*

Daily Journal, *May* 11. A Letter againft Mr. *P.* at large, Anon. [*John Dennis.*]

All thefe were afterwards reprinted in a Pamphlet entitled, A collection of all the Verfes, Effays, Letters and Advertifements occafion'd by *Pope* and *Swift'*s Mifcellanies. Prefaced by *Concanen*, Anonymous. 8°. Printed for *A. Moore*, 1728. Price 1 *s.* Others of an elder date, having layn as wafte paper many years, were upon the publication of the Dunciad brought out, and their Authors betrayed by the mercenary Bookfellers (in hope of fome poffibility of vending a few) by advertifing them in this manner——*The Confederates*, a Farce, By Capt. *Breval*, (for which he is *put into the Dunciad.*) An *Epilogue to Powel's Puppetfhow*, by Col. *Ducket*, (for which he is *put into the Dunciad.*) Effays, *&c.* by Sir *Rich. Blackmore. N. B.* It is for a paffage in pag. —— of this book that Sir *Richard* was *put into the Dunciad.*) And fo of others.

After the DUNCIAD, 1728.

AN Effay on the Dunciad, 8°. Printed for *J. Roberts.* [In this book, pag. 9. it was formally declared " That the complaint of the aforefaid " Pieces, Libels, and Advertifements, was forged and untrue, that all mouths " had been filent except in Mr. *Pope'*s praife, and nothing againft him pub- " lifh'd, but, by Mr. THEOBALD. *Price* 6 *d.*

Sawney, in blank Verfe, occafion'd by the Dunciad, with a Critique on that Poem. [By *J. Ralph*, a perfon never mention'd in it at firft, but inferted after this.] Printed for *J. Roberts.* 8°. Price 1 *s.*

A compleat Key to the Dunciad, by *E. Curl.* 12°. Price 6 *d.*

A fecond and third Edition of the fame, with Additions. 12°.

The

The Popiad, by *E. Curl*, extracted from *J. Dennis*, Sir *R. Blackmore*, &c. 12°. Price 6 *d.*

The Female Dunciad, collected by the same Mr. *Curl.* 12°. Price 6 *d.* With the Metamorphosis of *P——* into a stinging Nettle, [by Mr. *Foxton.*] 12°.

The Metamorphosis of *Scriblerus* into *Snarlerus*, [by *J. Smedley.*] Printed for *A. Moore.* Folio. Price 6 *d.*

The Dunciad dissected, or Farmer *P.* and his Son, by *Curl.* 12°.

An Essay on the Taste and Writings of the present times, said to be writ by a Gentleman of C. C. C. *Oxon.* Printed for *J. Roberts,* 8°.

The Arts of Logic and Rhetorick, partly taken from *Bouhours,* with new Reflections, *&c.* [by *John Oldmixon.*] 8°:

A Supplement to the Profund, Anon. [By *Matthew Concanen.*] 8°.

Mist's Weekly Journal, *June* 8. A long Letter sign'd *W. A.* [*Dennis, Theobald,* and others.]

Daily Journal, *June* 11. A Letter sign'd *Philoscriberus,* on the name of *Pope.* —— Letter to Mr. *Theobald* in Verse, sign'd *B. M.* against Mr. *P.* —— Many other little Epigrams about this time in the same papers, [by *James Moore* and others.]

Mist's Journal, *June* 22. A Letter by *Lewis Theobald.*

Flying-Post, *August* 8. Letter on *Pope* and *Swift.*

Daily Journal, *August* 8. Letter charging the Author of the Dunciad with Treason.

Durgen, A plain Satyr on a pompous Satyrist. [By *Edw. Ward,* with a little of *James Moore.*]

Labeo, [a Paper of Verses written by *Leonard Welsted.*]

Gulliveriana Secunda, Being a collection of many of the Libels in the News papers, like the former Volume under the same title, by *Smedley.* Advertised in the Craftsman *November* 9, 1728. with this remarkable promise, that " *any thing* which *any body* shou'd send as Mr. *Pope*'s or Dr. *Swift*'s, shou'd " be inserted and published as Theirs."

A

III.

A Copy of CAXTON's Preface to his
Tranflation of VIRGIL.

AFTER dyuerfe Werkes, made tranflated and achieued, hauyng
noo werke in hande I fittyng in my ftudye where as laye many
dyuerfe paunflettes and bookys. happened that to my hande cam
a lytlyl booke in frenfhe. whiche late was tranflated oute of latyn by fome
noble clerke of fraunce whiche booke is named *Eneydos* (made in latyn
by that noble poete & grete clerke *Vyrgyle*) whiche booke I fawe over and
redde therein. How after the generall deftruccyon of the grete *Troye, Eneas*
departed berynge his olde fader *anchifes* upon his fholdres, his lytyl fon
yolas on his hande. his wyfe wyth moche other people followynge, and how
he fhipped and departed wyth alle thyftorye of his aduentures that he had
er he cam to the atchieuement of his conqueft of ytalye as all a longe fhall be
fhewed in this prefent boke. In whiche booke I had grete playfyr. by caufe
of the fayr and honeft termes & wordes in frenfhe Whyche I neuer fawe to
fore lyke. ne none fo playfaunt ne fo wel ordred. whiche booke as me femed
fholde be moche requyfyte to noble men to fee as wel for the eloquence as the
hiftoryes. How wel that many hondred yerys paffed was the fayd booke
of *Eneydos* wyth other workes made and lerned dayly in fcolis fpecyally
in *ytalye* and other places, whiche hiftorye the fayd *Vyrgyle* made in metre,
And whan I had aduyfed me in this fayd booke. *I delybered and concluded*
to tranflate it in to englyfhe. And forthwyth toke a penne and ynke and
wrote a leef or tweyne, whyche I ouerfawe agayn to corecte it, And whan
I fawe the fayr & ftraunge termes therein, I doubted that it fholde not pleafe
fome gentylmen whiche late blamed me fayeng that in my tranflacyons I
had ouer curyous termes whiche coude not be vnderftande of comyn peple,
and defired me to vfe olde and homely termes in my tranflacyons. and fayn
wolde I fatysfye euery man, and fo to doo toke an olde boke and redde

therein, and certaynly the englyfhe was fo rude and brood that I coude not wele vnderftande it. And alfo my lorde *Abbot* of *Weftmynfter* ded do fhewe to me late certayn euydences wryton in olde englyfhe for to reduce it in to our englyfhe now vfid, And certaynly it was wryton in fuche wyfe that it was more lyke to dutche than englyfhe I coude not reduce ne brynge it to be vnderftonden, And certaynly our langage now vfed varyeth ferre from that whiche was vfed and fpoken whan I was borne, For we englyfhe men, ben borne vnder the domynacyon of the mone. whiche is neuer ftedfafte, but euer wauerynge, wexynge one feafon, and waneth & dyfcreafeth another feafon, And that comyn englyfhe that is fpoken in one fhyre varyeth from another. In fo moche that in my dayes happened that certayn marchants were in a fhip in Tamyfe for to haue fayled ouer the fee into Zelande, and for lacke of wynde thei taryed atte forlond. and wente to lande for to re-frefhe them And one of theym named *Sheffelde* a mercer cam in to an hows and axed for mete. and fpecyally he axyd after eggys And the goode wyf anfwerde. that fhe coude fpeke no frenfhe. And the merchant was angry. for he alfo coude fpeke no frenfhe. but wolde haue hadde egges, and fhe vnderftode hym not, And thenne at lafte another fayd that he wolde haue eyren, then the good wyf fayd that fhe vnderftod hym wel, Loo what fholde a man in thyfe dayes now wryte. egges or eyren, certaynly it is harde to playfe every man, by caufe of dyuerfite & change of langage. For in thefe dayes euery man that is in ony reputacyon in his contre. wyll vtter his comynycacyon and maters in fuche maners & termes, that fewe men fhall vnderftonde theym, And fom honeft and grete clerkes haue ben wyth me and defired me to wryte the mofte curyous termes that I coude fynde, And thus bytwene playn rude, & curyous I ftande abafhed. but in my Judge-mente, the comyn termes that be dayli vfed ben lyghter to be vnderftonde than the olde and ancyent englyfhe, And for as moche as this prefent booke is not *for a rude vplondyfhe man* to laboure therein, ne rede it, but onely for a clerke & a noble gentylman that feleth and vnderftondeth in faytes of armes in loue & in noble chyualrye, Therefore in a meane betwene bothe I haue reduced & tranflated this fayd booke in to our englyfhe not ouer rude ne curyous but in fuche termes as fhall be vnderftanden by goddys grace accordynge to my copye. And yf ony man wyll enter mete in redyng of hit and fyndeth fuche termes that he can not vnderftande late

hym.

hym goo rede and lerne *Vyrgyll*, or the pyſtles of *Ouyde*, and ther he ſhall
ſee and vnderſtonde lyghtly all, Yf he haue a good redar & enformer,
For this booke is not for euery rude and vnconnynge man to ſee, but
to clerkys & very gentylmen that underſtande gentylnes and ſcyence.
Thenne I praye alle theym that ſhall rede in this lytyl treatys to holde me
for excuſed for the tranſlatynge of hit. For I knowleche my ſelfe ignorant
of connynge to enpryſe on me ſo hie and noble a werke, But I praye
Mayſter *John Skelton* late created poete laureate in the vnyuerſite of *Oxen-
forde* to ouerſee and correcte this ſayd booke. And t'addreſſe and expowne
where as ſhall be founde faulte to theym that ſhall requyre it. For hym I
knowe for ſuffycyent to expowne and englyſhe euery dyffyculte that is
therein, For he hath late tranſlated the epyſtlys of *Tulle*, and the boke
of *Dyodorus Syculus*. and diuerſe others werkes oute of latyn in to eng-
lyſhe not in rude and olde langage. but in *polyſſhed and ornate termes*
craftely, as he that hath redde *Vyrgyle*, *Ouyde*, *Tullye*, and all the other
noble poetes and oratours, to me unknown: And alſo he hath redde
the ix muſes and vnderſtande theyr muſicalle ſcyences. and to whom of
theym eche ſcyence is appropred, I ſuppoſe he hath dronken of Elycons
well. Then I praye hym & ſuche other to correcte adde or mynysſhe
where as he or they ſhall fynde faulte, For I haue but folowed my copye
in frenſhe as nygh as me is poſſyble, And yf ony worde be ſayd therein
well, I am glad. and yf otherwyſe I ſubmytte my ſayd boke to theyr
correctyon, Whiche boke I preſente vnto the hye born my *tocomynge*
naturall & ſouerayn lord *Arthur* by the grace of God Prynce of *Walys*,
Duke of *Cornewayll*. & Erle of *Cheſter* firſt bygoten Son and heyer vnto
our moſt dradde naturall & ſouerayn lorde & moſt cryſten kynge, *Henry*
the vij. by the grace of God kynge of *Englonde* and of *Fraunce* & lord
of *Irelonde*, byſeeching his noble grace to receyve it in thanke of me
his moſte humble ſubget & ſeruant, And I ſhall praye vnto almyghty
God for his proſperous encreaſyng in vertue, wyſedom, and humanyte
that he may be egal wyth the moſt renômed of alle his noble progenytours.
And ſo to lyue in this preſent lyf, that after this tranſitorye lyſe he and
we alle may come to euerlaſtynge lyf in heuen, *Amen :*

AT.

At the end of the Book.

Here fynyssheth the boke of *Eneydos*, compyled by *Vyrgyle*, whiche hathe be tranflated out of *latyne* in to *frenfhe*, and out of *frenfhe* reduced in to *Englysfhe* by me *Wyllm. Caxton*, the xxij daye of *Juyn*. the yere of our lorde. M. iiij C lxxxx. The fythe yere of the Regne of kyng *Henry* the feuenth.

VIRGI.

IV.

VIRGILIUS RESTAURATUS:

SEU

MARTINI SCRIBLERI

Summi Critici

CASTIGATIONUM in ÆNEIDEM

SPECIMEN:

ÆNEIDEM totam, Amice Lector, innumerabilibus pœne mendis fca-
turientem, ad priftinum fenfum revocabimus. In fingulis ferè ver-
fibus fpuriæ occurrunt lectiones, in omnibus quos unquam vidi co-
dicibus aut vulgatis aut ineditis, ad opprobrium ufque Criticorum, in
hunc diem exiftentes. Interea adverte oculos, & his paucis fruere. At
fi quæ fint in hifce caftigationibus de quibus non fatis liquet, fylla-
barum quantitates, προλιϛωμϟϞ noftra Libro ipfi præfigenda, ut con-
fulas, moneo.

I. SPECIMEN LIBRI PRIMI, VERS. I. *(a)*

ARMA Virumque cano, Trojæ qui primus ab *oris*
Italiam, *fato* profugus, Lavinaque venit
Litora: multum ille & terris *jactatus* & alto,
Vi fuperum———

II. VERS. 52. *(b)*

—Et quifquis *Numen* Junonis adoret?

(a) Arma Virumque cano, Trojæ qui primus ab
Italiam, *flatu* profugus, *Latinaque* venit [*Aris*
Litora: multum ille & terris *vexatus*, & alto,
Vi fuperum———
Ab *aris*, nempe Hercæi Jovis, vide lib. 2.
vers. 512, 550.—*Flatu*, ventorum Æoli, ut fequi-
tur—*Latina* certè littora cum Æneas aderat,
Lavina non nifi poftea ab ipfo nominata, Lib. 12.
vers. 193—*Jactatus, terris* non convenit.
(b) —Et quifquis *Nomen* Junonis adoret?
Longè melius, quam ut antea, *Namen.*
Et Procul dubiò fic Virgilius.

III. Vers. 86. (c)

—Venti velut *agmine facto*
Qua data porta ruunt—

IV. Vers. 117. (d)

Fidumque vehebat *Orontem.*

V. Vers. 119. (e)

Excutitur, pronusque *magister*
Volvitur in caput———

VI. Vers. 122. (f)

Apparent rari nantes in gurgite vasto
Arma virùm———

VII. Vers. 151. (g)

Atque rotis *summas* leviter perlabitur *undas.*

VIII. Vers. 154. (b)

Jamque *faces* & saxa volant, *furor arma ministrat.*

IX. Vers. 170. (i)

Fronte sub adversa *scopulis pendentibus* antrum,
Intus aquæ dulces, vivoque sedilia saxo.

(c) —Venti velut *aggere fracto*
Qua data porta ruunt———
Sic corrige, meo periculo.

(d) *Fortemque* vehebat *Orontem* :
Non *fidum*, quia Epitheton *Achatæ* notissimum,
Oronti nunquam datur.

(e) —Excutitur : pronusque magis tèr
Volvitur in caput———
Aio Virgilium aliter non scripsisse, quod planè
confirmatur ex sequentibus—*Ast illam* ter *fluctus*
ibidem Torquet———

(f) *Armi hominum* : Ridicule anteà *Arma virùm*
quæ ex ferro conflata, quomodo possunt *natare?*

(g) Atque rotis *spumas* leviter perl.bitur *udas.*
Summas, & *leviter perlabere*, pleonasinus est: Mi-

rificè alter lectio Neptuni agilitatem & celerita-
tem exprimit; simili modo Noster de Camilla,
Æn. 11.—*intacta segetis per summa volaret,* &c.
hyperbolicè.

(h) Jamque *faces* & saxa volant, *fugiuntque*
Ministri : Uti solent, instanti periculo.—*Faces,*
facibus longe præstant, quid enim nisi fæces jac-
tarent vulgus sordidum ?

(i) Fronte sub adversa *populis prandentibus*
[antrum.
Sic malim, longe potiùs quam *scopulis pendenti-*
bus: Nugæ! Nonne vides versu sequenti *dulces*
aquas ad potandum & sedilia ad discubitum dari?
In quorum usum? prandentium.

X. Vers. 188. *(k)*

———— Tres littore *cervos*
Prospicit errantes : hos *tota armenta* sequuntur
A tergo———

XI. Vers. 748.

Arcturum pluviasque Hyades, *geminosque Triones*;
Error gravissimus. Corrige,———*septemque Triones.*

XII. Vers. 631. *(l)*

Quare agite O juvenes, *tectis* succedite nostris.

LIBER SECUNDUS. Vers. 1. *(a)*

CONTICUERE omnes, intentique ora tenebant,
Inde toro *Pater Æneas* sic orsus ab alto :

Vers. 3. *(b)*

Infandum Regina jubes renovare dolorem.

(k) ———Tres litore *cervos*
Aspicit errantes : hos *agmina tota* sequuntur
A tergo—*Cervi,* lectio vulgata, absurditas notissima : hæc animalia in Africa non inveniri, quis nescit ? At motus & ambulandi ritus Corvorum, quis non agnovit hoc loco ? Litore, locus ubi errant Corvi, uti Noster alibi,
Et sola secum sicca spaciatur arena.
Omen præclarissimum, immo et *agminibus* Militum frequentèr observatum, ut patet ex Historicis.
(l) Quare agite O Juvenes, *tectis* succedite nostris.

Lectis potius dicebat Dido, posita magis oratione, & quæ unica voce et Torum & Mensam exprimebat : Hanc lectionem probe confirmat appellatio O *Juvenes!* Duplicem hunc sensum alibi etiam Maro lepidè innuit,
Æn. 4. vers. 19. Huic uni forsan potui succùmbere *culpæ :*
Anna ! fatebor enim———
Corrige, *Huic uni* [*Viro* scil.] potui succùmbere ; Culpas
Anna ? fatebor enim, *&c.* Vox *succumbere* quàm eleganter ambigua !

LIB. II. Vers. 1. *&c.*

(a) Concubuere omnes, intentèque ora tenebant ; Inde toro *satur* Æneas sic orsus ab alto.
Concubuere, quia toro Æneam vidimus accumbentem : quin & altera ratio, scil. *Conticuere & ora tenebant,* tautologicè' dictum. In Manuscripto perquam rarissimo in Patris Musæo, legitur *ore gemebant* ; sed magis ingeniosè quam verè. *Satur* Æneas, quippe qui jam-jam a prandio surrexit :

Pater nihil ad rem attinet.
(b) Infantum regina jubes renovare dolorem. Sic haud dubito veterrimis codicibus scriptum fuisse : hoc satis constat ex perantiqua illa Brittannorum Cantilena vocata *Chevy-Chace,* cujus autor hunc locum sibi ascivit in hæc verba,
The Child may rue that is unborn.

T

VERS. 4. *(c)*

Trojanas ut *opes*, & lamentabile regnum.

VERS. 5. *(d)*

Eruerint Danai, Quæque ipse *miserrima vidi*
Et quorum pars magna fui.

VERS. 7. *(e)*

——Quis talia *fando*
Temperet *a* lacrymis?

VERS. 9. *(f)*

Et jam nox *humida* cœlo
Præcipitat, suadentque *cadentia* sydera somnos.
Sed si tantus amor *casus* cognoscere *nostras*, *(g)*
Et *breviter* Trojæ *supremum* audire laborem,
Quanquam animus meminisse horret, *luctuque refugit*, *(b)*
Incipiam.

(c) Trojanas ut *Oves* & lamentabile regnum *Diruerint*—Mallem *oves* plusquam *opes*, quoniam in antiquissimis illis temporibus oves & armenta divitiæ regum fuere. Vel fortasse *Oves Paridis* innuit, quas super Idam nuperrime pascebat, & jam in vindictam pro Helenæ raptu, a Menelao, Ajace aliisque ducibus, merito occisas.

(d) — Quæque ipse *miserrimus audi*,
Et quorum pars magna fui——
Omnia tam *audita* quam *visa* recta distinctione enarrare hic Æneas profitetur: Multa quorum nox ea fatalis sola conscia fuit, Vir probus & pius tanquam *visa* referre non potuit.

(e) ——Quis talia *flendo*,
Temperet *in* lachrymis?——Major enim doloris indicatio, absque modo lachrymare, quam solummodo *a* lachrymis non temperare?

(f) Et jam nox *lumina* cœlo
Præcipitat, suadentque *latentia* sydera somnos.
Lectio, *humida*, vespertinum rorem solum innuere videtur: magis mi arridet *Lumina*, quæ *latentia* postquam *præcipitantur*, Auroræ adventum annunciant.

(g) Sed si tantus amor *curas* cognoscere *noctis*,
Et *brevi ter* Trojæ, *supernmque* audire *labores*,
Curæ Noctis (scilicet Noctis Excidii Trojani) magis compendiose (vel ut dixit ipse *breviter*) totam Belli catastrophen denotat, quam diffusa illa & indeterminata lectio, *casus nostras.* Ter audire gratum esse Didoni, patet ex libro quarto, ubi dicitur, *Iliacosque iterum demens audire labores Exposcit:* Ter enim pro *sæpe* usurpatur. *Trojæ, superumque labores*, recte, quia non tantum homines sed & Dii sese his laboribus immiscuerunt. Vide Æn. 2. vers. 610, &c.

(b) Quamquam animus meminisse horret, *luctusque resurgit. Resurgit* multò proprius dolorem renascentem notat, quam ut huctenus, *refugit.*

VERS. 13. (i)

Fracti bello, fatifque repulfi,
Ductores Danaûm, tot jam labentibus annis,
Inftar montis *Equum*, divina Palladis arte,
Ædificant——*&c.*

(i) *Tracti* bello, fatifque repulfi. *Tracti & Repulfi*, Antithefis perpulcra ! *Fracti* frigidè & vulgaritèr.

Equum jam *Trojanum*, (ut vulgus loquitur) adeamus; quem fi *Equam Græcam* vocabis Lector, minimè pecces : Solæ enim femellæ utero geftiunt. Uterumque *armato milite complent*——Uteroque *recufo Infonuere cavæ*——*Atque* utero *fonitum quater arma dedere*.——*Inclufos utero Danaos*

&c. Vox *fœta* non convenit maribus,——*Scandit fatalis machina muros, Fœta armis*——Palladem Virginem, Equo mari fabricando invigilare decuiffe quis putat? Incredibile prorfus! Quamobrem exiftimo veram *Equæ* lectionem paffim reftituendam, nifi ubi forte metri cauffa, *Equum* potius quam *Equam*, *Genus* pro *Sexu*, dixit Maro. Vale! dum hæc paucula corriges, majus opus moveo.

V.

A Continuation of the GUARDIAN: *On the Subject of* PASTORALS.

Compulerantque greges Corydon & Thyrfis in unum.
Ex illo Corydon, Corydon eft tempore nobis.

Monday, April 27, 1713.

1. I Defigned to have troubled the Reader with no farther Difcourfes of *Paftorals,* but being informed that I am taxed of Partiality in not mentioning an Author whofe Eclogues are publifhed in the fame Volume with Mr. *Philips's* ; I fhall employ this Paper in Obfervations upon him, written in the *free Spirit of Criticifm,* and without apprehenfion of offending that Gentleman, whofe character it is that he takes the greateft care of his Works before they are publifhed, and has the leaft concern for them afterwards.

2. I have laid it down as the firft rule of Paftoral, that its Idea fhould be taken from the manners of the *Golden Age,* and the Moral form'd upon the reprefentation of *Innocence* ; 'tis therefore plain that any Deviations from that defign degrade a Poem from being true Paftoral. In this view it will appear that *Virgil* can only have *two* of his Eclogues allowed to be fuch : His firft and ninth muft be rejected, becaufe they defcribe the ravages of Armies, and oppreffions of the Innocent; *Corydon's* criminal Paffion for *Alexis* throws out the fecond ; the calumny and railing in the third are not proper to that ftate of Concord ; the eighth reprefents unlawful ways of procuring Love by Inchantments, and introduces a Shepherd whom an inviting Precipice tempts to Self-Murder. As to the fourth, fixth, and tenth, they

are

are given up by *(a) Heinſius, Salmaſius, Rapin*, and the Criticks in general. They likewiſe obſerve that but *eleven* of all the *Idyllia* of *Theocritus* are to be admitted as Paſtorals; and even out of that number the greater part will be excluded for *one* or *other* of the *Reaſons abovementioned.* So that when I remark'd in a former paper, that *Virgil*'s Eclogues taken all together are rather *ſelect Poems* than *Paſtorals*; I might have ſaid the ſame thing with no leſs truth of *Theocritus.* The reaſon of this I take to be yet unobſerved by the Criticks, *viz. They never meant them all for Paſtorals.*

Now it is plain *Philips* hath done this, and *in that Particular* excelled both *Theocritus* and *Virgil.*

3. As *Simplicity* is the diſtinguiſhing Characteriſtick of Paſtoral, *Virgil* hath been thought guilty of too courtly a Stile; his Language is *perfectly pure*, and he often forgets he is among Peaſants. I have frequently wonder'd, that ſince he was ſo converſant in the writings of *Ennius*, he had not imitated the *Ruſticity* of the *Doric*, as well by the help of the *old obſolete Roman* Language, as *Philips* hath by the *antiquated Engliſh*: For example, might he not have ſaid *Quoi* inſtead of *Cui*; *quoijum* for *cujum*; *volt* for *vult*, &c. as well as our Modern hath *Welladay* for *Alas*, *whilome* for *of old*, *make mock* for *deride*, and *witleſs Younglings* for *ſimple Lambs*, &c. by which means he had attained as much of the Air of *Theocritus*, as *Philips* hath of *Spencer?*

4. Mr. *Pope* hath fallen into the *ſame error with Virgil.* His Clowns do not converſe in *all the Simplicity* proper to the Country: His names are borrow'd from *Theocritus* and *Virgil*, which are improper to the Scene of his Paſtorals. He introduces *Daphnis, Alexis* and *Thyrſis* on *Britiſh* Plains, as *Virgil* had done before him on the *Mantuan*: Whereas *Philips*, who hath the ſtricteſt regard to Propriety, makes choice of names *peculiar to the Country*, and more agreeable to a Reader of *Delicacy*; ſuch as *Hobbinol, Lobbin, Cuddy*, and *Colin Clout.*

5. So eaſie as Paſtoral Writing may ſeem, (in the *Simplicity* we have deſcribed it) yet it requires great *Reading*, both of the *Ancients* and *Moderns*, to be a maſter of it. *Philips* hath given us manifeſt proofs of his *Knowledge of Books*: It muſt be confeſſed his competitor hath imitated ſome *ſingle thoughts* of the Ancients well enough, (if we conſider he had not the happineſs of an

---

(a) See Rapin *de* Carm. Paſt. *pars* 3.

Univerſity Education) but he hath diſperſed them, *here* and *there*, without that order and method which Mr. *Philips* obſerves, whoſe *whole* third Paſtoral is an inſtance how well he hath ſtudied the fifth of *Virgil*, and how judiciouſly *reduced Virgil*'s thoughts to the ſtandard of Paſtoral ; as his contention of *Colin Clout* and the *Nightingale* ſhows with what *exaƐtneſs* he hath imitated *every line* in *Strada.*

6 When I remarked it as a principal fault, to introduce *Fruits* and *Flowers* of a *Foreign growth,* in deſcriptions where the Scene lies in our *own Country,* I did not deſign that obſervation ſhould extend alſo to *Animals,* or the *ſenſitive Life* ; for *Philips* hath with great judgment deſcribed *Wolves* in *England* in his firſt Paſtoral. Nor would I have a Poet ſlaviſhly confine himſelf (as Mr. *Pope* hath done) to one particular *ſeaſon* of the Year, one certain *time* of the *day,* and one *unbroken Scene* in each Eclogue. 'Tis plain *Spencer* neglected this Pedantry, who in his Paſtoral of *November* mentions the mournful ſong of the *Nightingale :*

Sad Philomel *her ſong in Tears doth ſteep.*

And Mr. *Philips,* by a poetical Creation, hath raiſed up finer beds of Flowers than the moſt induſtrious Gardiner ; his Roſes, Endives, Lillies, Kingcups and Daffadils blow *all in the ſame ſeaſon.*

7. But the better to diſcover the merits of our two contemporary Paſtoral Writers, I ſhall endeavour to draw a Parallel of them, by ſetting ſeveral of their particular thoughts in the ſame light, whereby it will be obvious how much *Philips* hath the advantage. With what Simplicity he introduces two Shepherds ſinging alternately ?

Hobb. *Come,* Roſalind, *O come, for without thee*
        What Pleaſure can the Country have for me :
        Come, Roſalind, *O come ; my brinded Kine,*
        My ſnowy Sheep, my Farm, and all, is thine.

Lanq. *Come* Roſalind, *O come ; here ſhady Bowers*
        Here are cool Fountains, and here ſpringing Flow'rs.
        Come, Roſalind ; *Here ever let us ſtay,*
        And ſweetly waſt, our live-long time away.

Our other Paſtoral Writer, in expreſſing the ſame thought, deviates into
downright Poetry.

Streph. *In Spring the Fields, in Autumn Hills I love,*
At Morn the Plains, at Noon the ſhady Grove,
But Delia *always ; forc'd from* Delia's *ſight,*
Nor Plains at Morn, nor Groves at Noon delight.

Daph. Sylvia's *like Autumn ripe, yet mild as May,*
More bright than Noon, yet freſh as early Day ;
Ev'n Spring diſpleaſes, when ſhe ſhines not here,
But bleſt with her, 'tis Spring throughout the Year.

In the firſt of theſe Authors, two Shepherds thus *innocently* deſcribe the
Behaviour of their Miſtreſſes.

Hobb. *As* Marian *bath'd, by chance I paſſed by,*
She bluſh'd, and at me caſt a ſide-long Eye :
Then ſwift beneath the cryſtal Wave ſhe try'd
Her beauteous Form, but all in vain, to hide.

Lanq. *As I to cool me bath'd one ſultry day,*
Fond Lydia *lurking in the Sedges lay.*
The wanton laugh'd, and ſeem'd in haſte to fly ;
Yet often ſtopp'd, and often turn'd her Eye.

The other Modern (who it muſt be confeſſed hath a *knack of verſifying)*
hath it as follows.

Streph. *Me gentle* Delia *beckons from the Plain,*
Then, hid in Shades, eludes her eager Swain ;
But feigns a Laugh, to ſee me ſearch around,
And by that Laugh the willing Fair is found.

Daph. *The ſprightly* Sylvia *trips along the Green,*
She runs, but hopes ſhe does not run unſeen ;
While a kind glance at her Purſuer flyes,
How much at variance are her Feet and Eyes !

There

There is nothing the Writers of this kind of Poetry are fonder of, than defcriptions of Paftoral Prefents. *Philips* fays thus of a Sheep-hook.

Of feafon'd Elm ; where ftuds of Brafs appear,
To fpeak the Giver's name, the month and year.
The book of polifh'd Steel, the handle turn'd,
And richly by the Graver's skill adorn'd.

The other of a Bowl emboffed with Figures,

———where wanton Ivy twines,
And fwelling Clufters bend the curling Vines ;
Four Figures rifing from the work appear,
The various Seafons of the rolling year ;
And What is that which binds the radiant Sky,
Where twelve brig ht Signs in beauteous order lie.

The fimplicity of the Swain in this place, who forgets the name of the *Zodiack*, is no ill imitation of *Virgil* ; but how much more plainly and unaffectedly would *Philips* have dreffed this Thought in his *Doric ?*

And what that hight, which girds the Welkin fheen,
Where twelve gay Signs in meet array are feen.

If the Reader would indulge his curiofity any farther in the comparifon of Particulars, he may read the firft Paftoral of *Philips* with the fecond of his Contemporary, and the fourth and fixth of the former with the fourth and firft of the latter ; where feveral parallel places will occur to every one.

Having now fhown fome parts, in which thefe two Writers may be compared, it is a juftice I owe to Mr. *Philips*, to difcover thofe in which *no man can compare with him*. Firft, That *beautiful Rufticity*, of which I fhall only produce two Inftances, out of a hundred not yet quoted.

O woful day ! O day of Woe, quoth he,
And woful I, who live the day to fee !

The fimplicity of Diction, the melancholy flowing of the Numbers, the folemnity of the Sound, and the eafie turn of the Words, in this *Dirge*, (to make ufe of our Author's Expreffion) are extreamly elegant.

In

In another of his Paftorals, a Shepherd utters a *Dirge* not much inferior to the former, in the following lines.

Ah me the while! ah me! the luckleſs day,
Ah luckleſs Lad! the rather might I ſay;
Ah ſilly I! more ſilly than my Sheep,
Which on the flowry Plains I once did keep.

How he ftill charms the ear with theſe *artful Repetitions* of the Epithets; and how *ſignificant* is the laſt verſe! I defy the moſt common Reader to re-peat them, without feeling ſome *motions of compaſſion.*

In the next place I ſhall rank his *Proverbs,* in which I formerly obſerved he excells : For example,

A rolling Stone *is ever bare of* Moſs;
And to their coſt, green years old proverbs *croſs.*
——*He that* late lyes down, *as* late will riſe,
And Sluggard-like, till noon-day ſnoaring lyes.
Againſt Ill-Luck *all cunning* Fore-ſight *fails;*
Whether we ſleep or wake, it nought avails.
——*Nor fear, from* upright *Sentence,* wrong.

Laftly, his *elegant Dialect,* which alone might prove him the eldeſt born of *Spencer,* and our only true *Arcadian.* I ſhould think it proper for the ſeve-ral writers of Paftoral, to confine themſelves to their ſeveral *Counties.* *Spencer* ſeems to have been of this opinion : for he hath laid the ſcene of one of his Paftorals in *Wales,* where with all the Simplicity natural to that part of our Iſland, one Shepherd bids the other *good morrow* in an unuſual and elegant manner.

Diggon Davy, *I bid hur God-day:*
Or Diggon *hur is, or I miſ-ſay.*
Diggon anſwers,
Hur was hur, while it was day-light;
But now hur is a moſt wretched wight, &c.

But the moſt beautiful example of this kind that I ever met with, is in a very valuable Piece, which I chanced to find among ſome old Manuſcripts,

U   en

entituled, *A Pastoral Ballad:* which I think, for its nature and simplicity, may (notwithstanding the modesty of the Title) be allowed a perfect Pastoral: It is composed in the *Somersetshire* Dialect, and the names such as are proper to the Country People. It may be observed, as a further beauty of this Pastoral, the words *Nymph, Dryad, Naiad, Fawn, Cupid,* or *Satyr,* are not once mentioned through the whole. I shall make no Apology for inserting some few lines of this excellent Piece. *Cicily* breaks thus into the subject, as she is going a Milking:

Cicily. Rager *go vetch tha (b) Kee, or else tha Zun*
Will quite be go, be vore c'have half a don.

Roger. *Thou shouldst not ax ma tweece, but I've a be*
To dreave our Bull to bull tha Parson's Kee.

It is to be observed, that this whole Dialogue is formed upon the *Passion of Jealousie*; and his mentioning the Parson's Kine naturally revives the Jealousie of the Shepherdess *Cicily*, which she expresses as follows:

Cicily. *Ah* Rager, Rager, *chez was zore avraid*
When in yond Vield you kiss'd tha Parsons Maid:
Is this tha Love that once to me you zed,
When from tha Wake thou brought'st me Gingerbread?

Roger. Cicily *thou charg'st me valse,——I'll zwear to thee,*
Tha Parson's Maid is still a Maid for me.

In which Answer of his are express'd at once that *Spirit of Religion,* and that *Innocence of the Golden Age,* so necessary to be observed by all Writers of Pastoral.

At the conclusion of this piece, the Author reconciles the Lovers, and ends the Eclogue the most *simply* in the world.

So Rager *parted vor to vetch tha Kee,*
And vor her Bucket in went Cicily.

I am loath to show my fondness for Antiquity so far as to prefer this ancient *British* Author to our present *English* Writers of Pastoral; but I can-

---

(b) That is the *Kine* or *Cow.*

not

not avoid making this obvious Remark, that *Philips* hath hit into the *same Road* with this old *West Country* Bard of ours.

After all that hath been said, I hope none can think it any Injustice to Mr. *Pope*, that I forbore to mention him as a Pastoral Writer; since upon the whole, he is of the same class with *Moschus* and *Bion*, whom we have excluded that rank; and of whose Eclogues, as well as some of *Virgil*'s, it may be said, that (according to the description we have given of this sort of Poetry) they are by no means *Pastorals*, but *something better*.

VI.

A PARALLEL

OF THE

CHARACTERS

OF

Mr. DRYDEN and Mr. POPE,

As drawn by certain of their Cotemporaries.

Mr. DRYDEN.

His POLITICKS, RELIGION, MORALS.

MR. *Dryden* is a mere Renegado from *Monarchy, Poetry,* and *good Senſe. (a)* A true *Republican* Son of a *monarchical* Church. *(b)* A Republican *Atheiſt. (c) Dryden* was from the beginning an αλλοπροſαλλϴ, and I doubt not will continue ſo to the laſt. *(d)*

In the Poem call'd *Abſalom and Achitophel* are notoriouſly traduced, The KING, the QUEEN, the LORDS and GENTLEMEN, not only their Honourable Perſons expoſed, but the WHOLE NATION and its RE-PRESENTATIVES notoriouſly libell'd ; It is *Scandalum Magnatum,* yea of MAJESTY itſelf. *(e)*

He looks upon *God's Goſpel* as a *fooliſh Fable,* like the *Pope,* to whom he is a pitiful Purveyor. *(f)* His very *Chriſtianity* may be queſtioned. *(g)* He ought to expect more Severity than other men, as he is *moſt unmerciful* in his own *Reflections* on others. *(h)* With as good right as his *Holineſs,* he ſets up for *Poetical Infallibility. (i)*

(a) Milbourn on Dryden's Virgil, 8°. 1698. *p.* 6. *(b) pag.* 38. *(c) pag.* 192. *(d) pag.* 8. *(e) Whip and Key,* 4°. *printed for R. Janeway* 1682. *Preface. (f) ibid. (g) Milbourn, p.* 9. *(h) ibid. p.* 175. *(i) pag.* 39.

A

VI.

A PARALLEL

OF THE

CHARACTERS

OF

Mr. DRYDEN and Mr. POPE,

Mr. POPE.

His POLITICKS, RELIGION, MORALS.

MR. *Pope* is an open and mortal *Enemy* to his *Country*, and the *Commonwealth* of *Learning*. *(a)* Some call him a Popish *Whig*, which is directly inconsistent. *(b)* *Pope* as a Papist must be a *Tory* and *High-flyer*. *(c)* He is *both* a *Whig* and a *Tory*. *(d)* He hath made it his custom to cackle to more than one Party in their own Sentiments. *(e)*

In his *Miscellanies*, the Persons abused are, The KING, the QUEEN, His late MAJESTY, both Houses of PARLIAMENT, the *Privy-Council*, the Bench of *Bishops*, the Establish'd CHURCH, the present MINISTRY, *&c.* To make sense of some passages, they must be constru'd into ROYAL SCANDAL. *(f)*

He is a *Popish* Rhymester, bred up with a *Contempt* of the *Sacred Writings*. *(g)* His *Religion* allows him to *destroy Hereticks*, not only with his pen, but with fire and sword; and such were all those *unhappy Wits* whom he sacrificed to his *accursed Popish Principles*. *(h)* It deserved Vengeance to suggest, that Mr. *Pope* had less *Infallibility* than his *Namesake at Rome*. *(i)*

(a) Dennis, Remarks on the Rape of the Lock, pref. p. 12. *(b)* Dunciad dissected. *(c)* Preface to *Gulliveriana*. *(d) Denn.* and *Gill.* Character of Mr. *P.* *(e) Theobald,* Letter in *Mist's* Journal, *June* 22, 1728. *(f)* List, at the end of a Collection of Verses, Letters, Advertisements, 8°. Printed for *A. Moore,* 1728. and the Preface to it, pag. 6. *(g) Dennis's* Remarks on *Homer,* p. 27. *(h)* Preface to *Gulliveriana,* p. 11. *(i)* Dedication to the Collection of Verses, Letters, pag. 9.

Mr. DRY-

Mr. DRYDEN only a Verſifyer.

His whole Libel is all *bad matter,* beautify'd (which is *all* that can be ſaid of it) with *good metre.* (k) Mr. *Dryden's* Genius did not appear in any thing more than his *Verſification,* and whether he is to be ennobled for *that only,* is a queſtion? (l)

Mr. DRYDEN's VIRGIL.

Tonſon calls it *Dryden's Virgil,* to ſhow that this is not that *Virgil* ſo admired in the Auguſtæan age, but a *Virgil* of another ſtamp, a *ſilly, impertinent, nonſenſical* Writer. (m) None but a *Bavius,* a *Mævius,* or a *Bathyllus* carp'd at *Virgil,* and none but ſuch unthinking Vermin *admire* his Tranſlator. (n) It is true, *ſoft and eaſy lines* might become *Ovid's* Epiſtles or Art of Love——But *Virgil* who is all great and majeſtic, *&c.* requires ſtrength of lines, weight of words, and cloſeneſs of expreſſions, not an *ambling Muſe* running on a Carpet-ground, and ſhod as lightly as a *Newmarket* racer.——He has numberleſs faults in his *Engliſh,* in *Senſe,* in his *Author's meaning,* and in propriety of *Expreſſion.* (o)

Mr. DRYDEN underſtood no *Greek* or *Latin.*

Mr. *Dryden* was *once,* I have heard, at *Weſtminſter School :* Dr. *Busby* wou'd have *whipt him* for ſo childiſh a Paraphraſe. (p) The meaneſt Pedant in *England* wou'd *whip* a *Lubber* of twelve for *conſtruing ſo abſurdly.* (q) The Tranſlator is *mad, every line* betrays his Stupidity. (r) The faults are innumerable, and convince me that Mr. *Dryden* did not, or would not *underſtand his Author.* (s) This ſhows how fit Mr. *D.* may be to *tranſlate Homer !* A miſtake in a ſingle letter might fall on the *Printer* well enough. but Είχωϛ for Ίχωϛ muſt be the error of the *Author :* Nor had he art enough to correct it at the Preſs. (t) Mr. *Dryden* writes for the *Court Ladies*——He writes for the *Ladies,* and not for uſe. (u)

The Tranſlator puts in a little *Burleſque* now and then into *Virgil,* for a Ragout to his *cheated Subſcribers.* (w)

(k) *Whip and Key,* pref. (l) *Oldmixon, Eſſay on Criticiſm,* p. 84. (m) *Milbourn,* pag. 2. (n) Pag. 35. (o) Pag. 22, and 192. (p) *Milbourn,* pag. 72. (q) Pag. 203. (r) Pag. 78. (s) Pag. 206. (t) Pag. 19. (u) Pag. 124, 190. (w) Pag. 67.

Mr. POPE

Mr. POPE only a Verfifyer.

The *smooth numbers* of the Dunciad are *all* that recommend it, nor has it *any other merit.* (*k*) It muſt be own'd that he hath got a notable *Knack* of rhymeing, and writing *smooth verse.* (*l*)

Mr. POPE's HOMER.

The *Homer* which *Lintot* prints, does not talk like *Homer*, but like *Pope*; and he who tranſlated him one wou'd ſwear had a Hill in *Tipperary* for his *Parnaſſus*, and a puddle in ſome Bog for his *Hippocrene.* (*m*) He has no *Admirers* among thoſe that can diſtinguiſh, diſcern, and judge. (*n*)

He hath a knack at *smooth verse*, but without either *Genius* or **good** *Senſe*, or any tolerable knowledge of *Engliſh*. The qualities which diſtinguiſh *Homer* are the beauties of his Diction and the *harmony of his Verſification*——But this little Author who is ſo much in vogue, has neither *Senſe* in his *Thoughts*, nor *Engliſh* in his *Expreſſions.* (*o*)

Mr. POPE underſtood no *Greek.*

He hath undertaken to tranſlate *Homer* from the *Greek*, of which he knows not *one word*, into *Engliſh*, of which he underſtands *as little.* (*p*) I wonder how this Gentleman wou'd look ſhould it be diſcover'd, that he has not tranſlated *ten verſes* together in any book of *Homer* with juſtice to the Poet, and yet he dares reproach his fellow-writers with *not underſtanding Greek.* (*q*) He has ſtuck ſo little to his Original, as to have his *knowledge in Greek* called in queſtion. (*r*) I ſhould be glad to know which it is of all *Homer's* Excellencies, which has ſo delighted the *Ladies*, and the Gentlemen who judge like *Ladies ?* (*s*)

But he has a notable talent at *Burleſque* ; his genius ſlides ſo naturally into it, that he hath burleſqu'd *Homer* without deſigning it. (*t*)

(*k*) *Miſt's Journal*, of *June* 8, 1728. (*l*) *Character of Mr. P.* and *Dennis on Homer.* (*m*) *Dennis's* Remarks on *Pope's Homer*, pag. 12. (*n*) Ibid, (*o*) *Character of Mr. P.* pag. 17. and Remarks on *Homer*, p. 91. (*p*) *Dennis's* Remarks on *Homer*, p. 12. (*q*) Daily Journal of *April* 23, 1728. (*r*) Supplement to the Profund. Pref. (*s*) *Oldmixon*, Eſſay on Criticiſm, p. 66. (*t*) *Dennis's* Remarks, p. 28.

Mr. DRY-

Mr. DRYDEN trick'd his Subſcribers.

I wonder that any man who cou'd not but be conſcious of his own *unfitneſs* for it, ſhou'd go to amuſe the learned world with ſuch an *Undertaking!* A man ought to value his *Reputation* more than *Money*; and not to hope that thoſe who can read for themſelves, will be *Impoſed upon*, merely by a *partially and unſeaſonably-celebrated Name.* (x) *Poetis quidlibet audendi* ſhall be Mr. *Dryden*'s Motto, tho' it ſhould extend to *Picking of Pockets.* (y)

Names beſtow'd on Mr. DRYDEN.

An APE.] A crafty *Ape* dreſt up in a gaudy Gown——Whips put into an *Ape*'s paw, to play pranks with——None but *Apiſh* and *Papiſh* Brats will heed him. *Whip and Key, Pref.*

An ASS.] A Camel will take upon him no more burden than is ſufficient for his ſtrength, but there is *another Beaſt* that crouches under all: Mr. *Dryden*, &c. *Milb.* p. 105.

A FROG.] Poet *Squab* indued with Poet *Maro*'s Spirit! an ugly, *croaking* kind of *Vermine*, which would ſwell to the bulk of an *Oxe.* Pag. 11.

A COWARD.] A *Clinias* or a *Damætas*, or a man of Mr. *Dryden*'s *own Courage.* Pag. 176.

A KNAVE.] Mr. *Dryden* has heard of *Paul, the Knave of Jeſus Chriſt*: And if I miſtake not, I've read ſomewhere of *John Dryden Servant to his Majeſty.* Pag. 57.

A FOOL.] Had he not been ſuch a ſelf-conceited *Fool—Whip and Key, pref.* Some great Poets are poſitive *Blockheads. Milbourn*, p. 34.

A THING.] So little a *Thing* as Mr. *Dryden. Ibid.* pag. 35.

(x) *Milbourn*, p. 192. (y) *Ibid.* p. 125.

Mr. POPE

Mr. POPE trick'd his Subfcribers.

'Tis indeed fomewhat *bold*, and almoſt *prodigious*, for *a ſingle man* to un-dertake ſuch a work ! But 'tis too late to diſſuade by demonſtrating the *mad-neſs* of your Project : The Subfcribers expectations have been rais'd, in pro-portion to what their *Pockets have been drain'd of.* (*u*) *Pope* has been con-cern'd in Jobbs, and hired out his *Name* to Bookſellers. (*x*)

Names beſtow'd on Mr. POPE.

An APE.] Let us take the initial letter of his chriſtian name, and the initial and final letters of his ſurname, *viz.* A. P. E. and they give you the ſame Idea of an *Ape*, as his face, *&c.* *Dennis*, Daily Journal, *May* 11, 1728.

An ASS.] It is my duty to pull off the Lions ſkin from this little *Aſs.* *Dennis's* Rem. on *Homer*, pref.

A FROG.] A *ſquab* ſhort Gentleman—a little creature that like the *Frog* in the Fable, ſwells and is angry that it is not allow'd *to be as big as an Oxe.* *Dennis's Remarks on the Rape of the Lock, pref. p. 9.*

A COWARD.] A lurking, way-laying *Coward.* *Char. of Mr. P. pag. 3.*

A KNAVE.] He is one whom God and nature have mark'd for *want* of common *honeſty.* *Ibid.*

A FOOL.] Great *Fools* will be chriſten'd by the names of great Poets, and *Pope* will be called *Homer.* *Dennis's* Rem. on *Homer, p. 37.*

A THING.] A little, abject, *Thing.* *Ibid. p. 8.*

(*u*) Burnet, Homerides. *p.* 1, &c.   *x* Britiſh Journal, Nov. 25, 1727.

VII.

A

LIST

OF

All our AUTHOR's Genuine Works.

THE Works of Mr. ALEXANDER POPE, in quarto and folio. Printed for *Jacob Tonſon* and *Bernard Lintot*, in the year 1717. This Edition contains whatſoever is his, except theſe few following, which have been written ſince that time.

INSCRIPTION to Dr. *Parnel's* Poems; To the Right Honourable ROBERT Earl of OXFORD and Earl MORTIMER.

VERSES on Mr. ADDISON's Treatiſe of *Medals*, firſt printed after his death in Mr. *Tickel's* Edition of his Works.

EPITAPHS: On the Honourable *Simon Harcourt :* on the Honourable *Robert Digby :* on Mrs. *Corbett* ; and another intended for Mr. *Rowe.*

The WHOLE ILIAD of HOMER, with the PREFACE, and the NOTES, (except the *Extracts from Euſtathius* in the four laſt volumes, made by Mr. *Broome* ; and the *Eſſay* on the *Life* and *Writings* of· *Homer*, which tho' collected by our Author, was put together by Dr. *Parnell.*)

TWELVE BOOKS of the ODYSSEY, with ſome parts of other Books ; and the *Diſſertation* by way of *Poſtſcript* at the end.

The *Preface* to Mr. *Tonſon's* Edition of SHAKESPEAR.

MISCELLANIES, by Dr. *Swift* and our Author, *&c.* Printed for *B. Motte.*

And ſome *Spectators* and *Guardians.*

INDEX

INDEX

Of THINGS (including AUTHORS) to be found in the NOTES, &c. The firſt Number denotes the BOOK, the ſecond the VERSE. Teſt. Teſtimonies. Ap. Appendix.

A.

ADDISON (Mr.) written againſt with vehemence, by *J. Dennis*. Book ii. verſe 273. Railed at by *A. Philips*. iii. 322.

Abuſed by *J. Oldmixon*, in his Proſe-Eſſay on Criticiſm, *&c*. ii. 201.

——by *J. Ralph*, in a London Journal, iii. 159.

——Celebrated by our Author——Upon his Diſcourſe of Medals——In his Prologue to *Cato*——and in this Poem. ii. 132.

Falſe Facts concerning him and our Author related by anonymous Perſons in *Miſt*'s Journals, *&c*. Teſt. *pag*. 9, 10, 11.

Diſprov'd by the Teſtimonies of

——The Earl of *Burlington*, 12.

——Mr. *Tickel*, 10.

——Mr. *Addiſon* himſelf, *Ibid*. and 9.

Anger, one of the Characteriſtics of Mr. *Dennis*'s Critical Writings, i. 104.]

——*Affirmation*, another : Teſt. p. 5. [To which are added by Mr. *Theobald*, *Ill-nature, Spite, Revenge*, i. 104.]

Altar of *Tibbald*'s Works, how built, and how founded? i. 135, *&c*.

Æſchylus, How long he was *about* him, i. 210.

In what reſpect like him, iii. 311.

Aſſes, at a Citizens gate in a morning, ii. 239.

Appearances, that we are never to judge by them, eſpecially of Poets and Divines, ii. 395.

Alehouſe, The Birth-place of many Poems, i. 202.

——And of ſome Poets, ii. 130.

——One kept by *Taylor* the Water-poet, ii. 325.

——and by *Edward Ward*, i. 200.

B.

BAVIUS, Book iii. verſe 16. Mr. *Dennis* his great opinion of him, *ibid*.

Bawdry, in Plays, not diſapprov'd of by Mr. *Dennis*, iii. 174.

BLACKMORE, (Sir *Rich*.) his Impiety and Irreligion, proved by Mr. *Dennis*, ii. v. 258.

His Quantity of Works, and various Opinions of them.——His abuſe of Mr. *Dryden* and Mr. *Pope*, *ibid*.

Bray, a word much belov'd by Sir *Richard*, ii. 250.

Braying, deſcribed, ii. 245.

Birch, by no means proper to be apply'd to young Noblemen, iii. 330.

BROOME, (Rev. Mr. *Will*.) His Sentiments of our Author's Virtue, Teſt. p. art.

——Our Author's of his abilities, iii. 328.

——And how he rewarded them, *ibid*.

Billingsgate language, how to be uſed by learned Authors, ii. 134.

K 2　　　　BOND,

FINIS.

ADDENDA.

M. SCRIBLERUS Lectori.

ONCE more, gentle reader I appeal unto thee, from the shameful ignorance of the Editor, by whom Our own Specimen of *Virgil* hath been mangled in such miserable manner, that scarce without tears can we behold it. At the very entrance, Instead of προλεγόμενα, lo! π͵ολεγόμενα with an Omega! and in the same line *consulâs*, with a circumflex! In the next page thou findest *leviter perlabere*, which his ignorance took to be the infinitive mood of *perlabor*, but ought to be *perlabi*.——*Alter* lectio, for *altera*, a false Concord!——*Jamque fæces*, for *Iam fæces*——for so certainly the Author of the Emendation made it.——And again, *ad discubitum*, for *ad discumbendum!*——In pag. 102. Not. *c. plusquam*, for *potius quam*, ibid. Not. *g. casus nostras*, for *nostros*. So it is in the Text, so in the Note. See you not, that the Editor thought *casus*, being of the fourth declension, was of the fœminine gender, like *manus?*——Lastly, in pag. 103. Not. i. *utero gestiunt*, for *gerunt*, or *gestant*; Alas! *Gestio* signifies quite another thing. Wipe away all these monsters, Reader, with thy quill.

Publisht Janu. 2. 1734/5.

AN
EPISTLE
FROM
Mr. *POPE,*
TO
Dr. *ARBUTHNOT.*

Neque sermonibus Vulgi *dederis te, nec in* Præmiis *humanis spem posueris rerum tuarum: suis te oportet illecebris* ipsa Virtus *trahat ad verum decus. Quid de te alii loquantur, ipsi videant, sed loquentur tamen.*

TULLY.

LONDON:
Printed by *J.* Wright for LAWTON GILLIVER
at *Homer's* Head in *Fleetstreet,* 1734.

ADVERTISEMENT.

THIS *Paper is a Sort of Bill of Complaint, begun many years since, and drawn up by snatches, as the several Occasions offer'd.* I had no thoughts of publishing it, *till it pleas'd some Persons of Rank and Fortune* ⎣*the Authors of* Verses to the Imitator of Horace, *and of an* Epistle to a Doctor of Divinity from a Nobleman at Hampton Court,⎦ *to attack in a very extraordinary manner, not only my* Writings *(of which being publick the Publick judge)* but my Person, Morals, *and* Family, *whereof to those who know me not, a truer Information may be requisite.* Being divided between the Necessity to say something of Myself, *and my own Laziness to undertake so awkward a Task,* I thought it the shortest way to put the last hand to this Epistle. *If it have any thing pleasing, it will be That by which I am most desirous to please, the* Truth *and the* Sentiment ; *and if any thing offensive, it will be only to those I am least sorry to offend, the* Vicious *or the* Ungenerous.

Many will know their own Pictures in it, there being not a Circumstance but what is true ; but I have, for the

ADVERTISEMENT.

the most part spar'd their Names, and they may escape being laugh'd at, if they please.

I would have some of them know, it was owing to the Request of the learned and candid Friend to whom it is inscribed, that I make not as free use of theirs as they have done of mine. However I shall have this Advantage, and Honour, on my side, that whereas by their proceeding, any Abuse may be directed at any man, no Injury can possibly be done by mine, since a Nameless Character can never be found out, but by its Truth and Likeness.

AN
EPISTLE
TO
Dr. *ARBUTHNOT*.

SHUT, shut the door, good *John!* fatigu'd I said,
Tye up the knocker, say I'm sick, I'm dead,
The Dog-star rages! nay 'tis past a doubt,
All *Bedlam*, or *Parnaſſus*, is let out :
Fire in their eye, and Papers in their hand, 5
They rave, recite, and madden round the land.

What Walls can guard me, or what Shades can hide?
They pierce my Thickets, thro' my Grot they glide,
By land, by water, they renew the charge,
They stop the Chariot, and they board the Barge. 10

B   No

No place is facred, not the Church is free,
Ev'n *Sunday* fhines no *Sabbath-day* to me :
Then from the *Mint* walks forth the Man of Ryme,
Happy ! to catch me, juft at Dinner-time.

Is there a Parfon, much be-mus'd in Beer, 15
A maudlin Poetefs, a ryming Peer,
A Clerk, foredoom'd his Father's foul to crofs,
Who pens a Stanza when he fhould *engrofs* ?
Is there, who lock'd from Ink and Paper, fcrawls
With defp'rate Charcoal round his darken'd walls ? 20
All fly to *Twit'nam*, and in humble ftrain
Apply to me, to keep them mad or vain.

Arthur moore *Arthur*, whofe giddy Son neglects the Laws,
Imputes to me and my damn'd works the caufe :
Poor *Cornus* fees his frantic Wife elope, 25
And curfes Wit, and Poetry, and *Pope*.

Friend to my Life, (which did not you prolong,
The World had wanted many an idle Song)
wards famous What *Drop* or *Noftrum* can this Plague remove ?
drop Or which muft end me, a Fool's Wrath or Love ? 30
A dire Dilemma ! either way I'm fped,
If Foes, they write, if Friends, they read me dead.

Seiz'd

Seiz'd and ty'd down to judge, how wretched I !
Who can't be silent, and who will not lye ;
To laugh, were want of Goodnefs and of Grace,   35
And to be grave, exceeds all Pow'r of Face.
I fit with fad Civility, I read
With honeft anguifh, and an aking head ;
And drop at laft, but in unwilling ears,
This faving counfel, "Keep your Piece nine years."   40
       Nine years ! cries he, who high in *Drury-lane*
Lull'd by foft Zephyrs thro' the broken Pane,
Rymes e're he wakes, and prints before *Term* ends,
Oblig'd by hunger and Requeft of friends :
"The Piece you think is incorrect ? why take it,   45
"I'm all fubmiffion, what you'd have it, make it."
       Three things another's modeft wifhes bound,
My Friendfhip, and a Prologue, and ten Pound.   *Tibbald*
                                                 × Welfted
Pitholeon fends to me : "You know his Grace,   *& the Duke of Argile*
"I want a Patron ; ask him for a Place."   52
Pitholeon libell'd me — "but here's a Letter
"Informs you Sir, 'twas when he knew no better.
"Dare you refufe him ? *Curl* invites to dine,
"He'll write a *Journal*, or he'll turn *Divine*."
                                        Blefs

Blefs me! a Packet. — "'Tis a ftranger fues,   55
"A Virgin Tragedy, an Orphan Mufe."
If I diflike it, "Furies, death and rage!
If I approve, "Commend it to the Stage."
There (thank my Stars) my whole Commiffion ends,
The Play'rs and I are, luckily, no friends.   60
Fir'd that the Houfe reject him, "'Sdeath I'll print it
"And fhame the Fools—your Int'reft, Sir, with *Lintot*."
Lintot, dull rogue! will think your price too much.
"Not Sir, if you revife it, and retouch."
All my demurrs but double his attacks,   65
At laft he whifpers "Do, and we go fnacks."
Glad of a quarrel, ftrait I clap the door,
Sir, let me fee your works and you no more.

'Tis fung, when *Midas*' Ears began to fpring,
(*Midas*, a facred Perfon and a King)   70
His very Minifter who fpy'd them firft,
(Some fay his * Queen) was forc'd to fpeak, or burft.
And is not mine, my Friend, a forer cafe,
When ev'ry Coxcomb perks them in my face?

* The Story is told by fome of his Barber, but by *Chaucer* of his Queen. See
Wife of Bath's Tale in *Dryden*'s Fables.

"Good

"Good friend forbear! you deal in dang'rous things,
"I'd never name Queens, Minifters, or Kings;
"Keep clofe to Ears, and thofe let Affes prick,
"Tis nothing"—Nothing? if they bite and kick?   76
Out with it, *Dunciad!* let the fecret pafs,
That Secret to each Fool, that he's an Afs:
The truth once told, (and wherefore fhou'd we lie?)
The Queen of *Midas* flept, and fo may I.   80
    You think this cruel? take it for a rule,
No creature fmarts fo little as a Fool.
Let Peals of Laughter, *Codrus!* round thee break,
Thou unconcern'd canft hear the mighty Crack.
Pit, Box and Gall'ry in convulfions hurl'd,   85
Thou ftand'ft unfhook amidft a burfting World.
Who fhames a Scribler? break one cobweb thro',
He fpins the flight, felf-pleafing thread anew;
Deftroy his Fib, or Sophiftry; in vain,
The Creature's at his dirty work again;
Thron'd in the Centre of his thin defigns;
Proud of a vaft Extent of flimzy lines.   90
Whom have I hurt? has Poet yet, or Peer,
Loft the arch'd eye-brow, or *Parnaffian* fneer?

C   And

And has not *C—lly* still his Lord, and Whore?

His Butchers *H—ley*, his Free-masons *M—r*?

Does not one Table *Bavius* still admit?   95

Still to one <u>Bishop</u> *Ph—ps* seem a Wit?

the ſrs common phraſe

Still *Sapho*—"Hold! nay ſee you, you'll offend:

"No Names—be calm—learn Prudence of a Friend:

"I too could write, and I am twice as tall,

"But Foes like theſe!—One Flatt'rer's worſe than all;

Of all mad Creatures, if the Learn'd are right,   101

It is the Slaver kills, and not the Bite.

A Fool quite angry is quite inn———

Truſt me, 'tis ten times worſe when they ———t.

One dedicates, in high Heroic proſe,

And ridicules beyond a hundred foes;   105

One from all *Grubſtreet* will my fame defend,

And, more abuſive, calls himſelf my friend.

This prints my <u>Letters</u>, that expects a Bribe,

And others roar aloud, "Subſcribe, ſubſcribe.

There are, who to my Perſon pay their court,   110

I cough like *Horace*, and tho' lean, am ſhort,

Am-

Ammon's great Son one shoulder had too high,
Such *Ovid*'s nose, and "Sir! you have an *Eye* —
Go on, obliging Creatures, make me see
All that disgrac'd my Betters, met in me: 115
Say for my comfort, languishing in bed,
"Just so immortal *Maro* held his head:
And when I die, be sure you let me know
Great *Homer* dy'd three thousand years ago.

      Why did I write? what sin to me unknown 120
Dipt me in Ink, my Parent's, or my own?
As yet a Child, nor yet a Fool to Fame,
I lisp'd in Numbers, for the Numbers came.
I left no Calling for this idle trade,
No Duty broke, no Father dif-obey'd.   125
The Muse but serv'd to ease some Friend, not Wife,
To help me thro' this long Disease, my Life,
To second, ARBURTHNOT! thy Art and Care,
And teach, the Being you preserv'd, to bear.

      But why then publish? *Granville* the polite,   130
And knowing *Walsh*, would tell me I could write;

                                        Well-

Well-natur'd *Garth* inflam'd with early praife,
And *Congreve* lov'd, and *Swift* endur'd my Lays;
The Courtly *Talbot, Somers, Sheffield* read,
Ev'n mitred *Rochefter* would nod the head,
And *St. John*'s felf (great *Dryden*'s friends before †)
With open arms receiv'd one Poet more.
Happy my Studies, when by thefe approv'd!
Happier their Author, when by thefe belov'd!
From thefe the world will judge of Men and Books,
Not from the * *Burnets, Oldmixons*, and *Cooks*. 141
   Soft were my Numbers, who could take offence
While pure Defcription held the place of Senfe?
Like gentle ~~*Damon*~~'s was my flow'ry Theme,
A painted Miftrefs, or a purling Stream. 145
Yet then did *Gildon* draw his venal quill;
I wifh'd the man a dinner, and fate ftill:
Yet then did *Dennis* rave in furious fret;
I never anfwer'd, I was not in debt:
If want provok'd, or madnefs made them print, 150
I wag'd no war with *Bedlam* or the *Mint*.

fanny

† All thefe were Patrons or Admirers of Mr. *Dryden*, tho' a fcandalous Libel againft him, entituled, *Dryden's Satyr to his Mufe*, has been printed in the Name of the Lord *Somers*, of which he was wholly ignorant.

* Authors of fecret and fcandalous Hiftory.

Did

Did some more sober Critics come abroad?
If wrong, I smil'd; if right, I kiss'd the rod.
Pains, reading, study, are their just pretence,
And all they want is spirit, taste, and sense.   155
Comma's and points they set exactly right,
And 'twere a sin to rob them of their Mite.
Yet ne'r one sprig of Laurel grac'd these ribalds,
From flashing *B—ley* down to pidling *T—ds*.
The Wight who reads not, and but scans and spells, 160
The Word-catcher that lives on syllables,
Such piece-meal Critics some regard may claim,
Preserv'd in *Milton*'s or in *Shakespear*'s name.
Pretty! in Amber to observe the forms
Of hairs, or straws, or dirt, or grubs, or worms; 156
The things, we know, are neither rich nor rare,
But wonder how the Devil they got there?

Were others angry? I excus'd them too;
Well might they rage; I gave them but their due.
A man's true merit 'tis not hard to find,   170
But each man's secret standard in his mind,
That Casting-weight Pride adds to Emptiness,
This, who can gratify? for who can *guess*?

The Bard whom pilf'red Paſtorals renown,
Who turns a *Perſian* Tale for half a crown,   175
Juſt writes to make his barrenneſs appear,
And ſtrains from hard-bound brains eight lines a-year:
He, who ſtill wanting tho' he lives on theft,
Steals much, ſpends little, yet has nothing left:
And he, who now to ſenſe, now nonſenſe leaning,   180
Means not, but blunders round about a meaning:
And he, whoſe Fuſtian's ſo ſublimely bad,
It is not Poetry, but Proſe run mad:
All theſe, my modeſt Satire bid *tranſlate*,
And own'd, that nine ſuch Poets made a *Tate*. 185
How did they fume, and ſtamp, and roar, and chafe?
How did they ſwear, not *Addiſon* was ſafe.

Peace to all ſuch! but were there One whoſe fires
True Genius kindles, and fair Fame inſpires,
Bleſt with each Talent and each Art to pleaſe,   190
And born to write, converſe, and live with eaſe:
Shou'd ſuch a man, too fond to rule alone,
Bear, like the *Turk*, no brother near the throne,
View him with ſcornful, yet with jealous eyes,
And hate for Arts that caus'd himſelf to riſe; 195

Damn

Damn with faint praise, assent with civil leer,
And without sneering, teach the rest to sneer;
Willing to wound, and yet afraid to strike,
Just hint a fault, and hesitate dislike;
Alike reserv'd to blame, or to commend,   200
A tim'rous foe, and a suspicious friend,
Dreading ev'n fools, by Flatterers besieg'd,
And so obliging that he ne'er oblig'd;
Like *Cato*, give his little Senate laws,
And sit attentive to his own applause;   205
While Wits and Templers ev'ry sentence raise,
And wonder with a foolish face of praise.
Who but must laugh, if such a man there be?
Who would not weep, if †*Atticus* were he!

What tho' my Name stood rubric on the walls?
Or plaister'd posts, with Claps in capitals?   211
Or smoaking forth, a hundred Hawkers load,
On Wings of Winds came flying all abroad?
I sought no homage from the Race that write;
I kept, like *Asian* Monarchs, from their sight: 215
Poems I heeded (now be-rym'd so long)
No more than Thou, great GEORGE! a Birth-day Song.

I

† The assertion of some anonymous authors that Mr P. writ this character after the gentleman's death, was utterly untrue; it having been sent him several years before, ~~~~ ~~~~ ~~~~ ~~~~ and then shown to Mr Secretary Craggs, & present Earl of Burlington; who ~~~~ our author's conduct on an occasion ~~~~ he has too much regard to that gentleman's memory willingly to make public. ~~~~ it came into print, he never ~~~~ but ~~~~ now ~~~~ to omit the name.

I ne'r with Wits and Witlings paſt my days,

To ſpread about the Itch of Verſe and Praiſe;

Nor like a Puppy daggled thro' the Town,   220

To fetch and carry Sing-ſong up and down;

Nor at Rehearſals ſweat, and mouth'd, and cry'd,

With Handkerchief and Orange at my ſide:

But ſick of Fops, and Poetry, and Prate,

To *Buſo* left the whole *Caſtalian* State.   225

Proud, as *Apollo* on his forked hill,

Sate full-blown *Buſo*, puff'd by ev'ry quill;

Fed with ſoft Dedication all day long,

Horace and he went hand in hand in ſong.

His Library, (where Buſts of Poets dead   230

And a true *Pindar* ſtood without a head)

Receiv'd of Wits an undiſtinguiſh'd race,

Who firſt his Judgment ask'd, and then a Place:

Much they extoll'd the Pictures, much the Seat,

And flatter'd ev'ry day, and ſome days eat: 235

Till grown more frugal in his riper days,

He pay'd ſome Bards with Port, and ſome with Praiſe,

To ſome a dry Rehearſal was aſſign'd,

And others (harder ſtill) he pay'd in kind.

May

May some choice Patron bless each gray goose quill!
May ev'ry *Bavius* have his *Bufo* still!
So, when a Statesman wants a Day's defence,   240
Or Envy holds a whole Week's war with Sense,
Or simple Pride for Flatt'ry makes demands;
May Dunce by Dunce be whistled off my hands!
Blest be the *Great!* for those they take away,
And those they leave me – For they left me GAY,
Left me to see neglected Genius bloom,   246
Neglected die! and tell it on his Tomb;
Of all thy blameless Life the sole Return
My Verse, and QUEENSB'RY weeping o'er thy Urn!

    Give me on *Thames*'s Banks, in honest Ease,   250
To see what Friends, or read what Books I please;
There let me live my own, and die so too,
"To live and die is all I have to do!"
Above a Patron, tho' I condescend
Sometimes to call a Minister my Friend: 255
I was not born for Courts or great Affairs,
I pay my Debts, believe, and go to Pray'rs,
Can sleep without a Poem in my head,
Nor know, if *Dennis* be alive or dead.

    Why am I ask'd, what next shall see the light?
Heav'ns! was I born for nothing but to write? 260

E   Has

Gay] he was neglected by the court & had no place though often promised, He lived with the Duke of Queensberry & died at his House Dec. 4. 1732. He was buried at the Duks expence and will set up a monument for him

Has Life no Joys for me? or (to be grave)
Have I no Friend to ferve, no Soul to fave?
"I found him clofe with *Swift* — Indeed? no doubt
(Cries prating *Balbus*) "fomething will come out."
'Tis all in vain, deny it as I will.   266
"No, fuch a Genius never can lye ftill,"
And then for mine obligingly miftakes
The firft Lampoon Sir *Will.* or *Bubo* makes.
Poor guiltlefs I! and can I chufe but fmile, 270
When ev'ry Coxcomb knows me by my *Style?*

Curft be the Verfe, how well foe'er it flow,
That tends to make one worthy Man my foe,
Give Virtue fcandal, Innocence a fear,
Or from the foft-ey'd Virgin fteal a tear! 275
But he, who hurts a harmlefs neighbour's peace,
Infults fal'n Worth, or Beauty in diftrefs,
Who loves a Lye, lame flander helps about,
Who writes a Libel, or who copies out:
The Fop whofe pride affects a Patron's name, 280
Yet abfent, wounds an Author's honeft fame;
Who can your Merit felfifhly approve,
And fhow the Senfe of it, without the Love;
Who has the Vanity to call you Friend,
Yet wants the Honour injur'd to defend; 285

Who

sr will, sr william
young. as great Scribler
of Libels & Lampoons.
Bubo, Bubb Dorington
of the same stamp.

Who tells whate'er you think, whate'er you say,
And, if he lyes not, muſt at leaſt betray:
Who to the * *Dean* and *ſilver Bell* can ſwear,
And ſees at *Cannons* what was never there:
Who reads but with a Luſt to miſ-apply,   290
Make Satire a Lampoon, and Fiction, Lye.
A Laſh like mine no honeſt man ſhall dread,
But all ſuch babling blockheads in his ſtead.
P   Let *Paris* tremble — ᵒʳ "What? that Thing of ſilk,
"*Paris*, that mere white Curd of Aſs's milk?   295
"Satire or Shame alas! can *Paris* feel?
"Who breaks a Butterfly upon a Wheel?"
P Yet let me flap this Bug with gilded wings,
This painted Child of Dirt that ſtinks and ſtings;
Whoſe Buzz the Witty and the Fair annoys,   300
Yet Wit ne'er taſtes, and Beauty ne'er enjoys,
So well-bred Spaniels civilly delight
In mumbling of the Game they dare not bite.
Eternal Smiles his Emptineſs betray,
As ſhallow ſtreams run dimpling all the way. 305
Whether in florid Impotence he ſpeaks,
And, as the Prompter breathes, the Puppet ſqueaks;

* See the Epiſtle to the Earl of *Burlington*.

Marginal notes (handwritten):

cannons, the ſeat of his Grace the Duke of Chandos.

Paris] It ſo happens that this is generally apply'd to lord Harvey, and as he deſerved it of mr pope, it is very proper for him & is very juſtly drawn. In a late edition the name is changed to Sporus a more proper name.

Sporus was a youth whom Nero had a mind to make a woman of by gelding him.

Or

Or at the Ear of * *Eve*, familiar Toad,

Half Froth, half Venom, spits himself abroad,

In Puns, or Politicks, or Tales, or Lyes,   310

Or Spite, or Smut, or Rymes, or Blasphemies.

Did ever Smock-face act so vile a Part?

A trifling Head, and a corrupted Heart!

Eve's Tempter thus the Rabbins have exprest,

A Cherub's face, a Reptile all the rest;

Beauty that shocks you, Parts that none will trust,

Wit that can creep, and Pride that licks the dust. 315

    Not Fortune's Worshipper, nor Fashion's Fool,

Nor Lucre's Madman, nor Ambition's Tool,

Nor proud, nor servile, be one Poet's praise

That, if he pleas'd, he pleas'd by manly ways;

That Flatt'ry, ev'n to Kings, he held a shame,   320

And thought a Lye in Verse or Prose the same:

In Fancy's Maze that wand'ring not too long,

He stoop'd to Truth, and moraliz'd his song:

That not for Fame, but Virtue's better end,

He stood the furious Foe, the timid Friend,   325

The damning Critic, half-approving Wit,

The Coxcomb hit, or fearing to be hit;

* In the fourth Book of *Milton*, the Devil is represented in this Shape & Posture. It is but justice to own, that the Hint of *Eve* and the *Serpent* was taken from the *Verses on the Imitator of* Horace.

Laugh'd

Laugh'd at the loſs of Friends he never had,
The dull, the proud, the wicked, and the mad;
The Tales of Vengeance; Lyes ſo oft o'erthrown;
The imputed Traſh, the Dulneſs not his own;
The Morals blacken'd when the Writings ſcape;
The libel'd Perſon, and the pictur'd Shape;   335
Th' Abuſe on all he lov'd, or lov'd him, ſpread,
A Friend in Exile, or a Father, dead;
The Whiſper that to Greatneſs ſtill too near,
Perhaps, yet vibrates on his SOVEREIGN's Ear —
Welcome for thee, fair Virtue! all the paſt: 340
For thee, fair Virtue! welcome ev'n the _laſt!_

"But why inſult the Poor, affront the Great?"
A Knave's a Knave, to me, in ev'ry State,
Alike my ſcorn, if he ſucceed or fail,
Glencus at Court, or _Japhet_ in a Jayl,   345
A hireling Scribler, or a hireling Peer,
Knight of the Poſt corrupt, or of the Shire,
If on a Pillory, or near a Throne,
He gain his Prince's Ear, or loſe his own.

Lies ſo oft o'erthrown.] Such as thoſe in relation to Mr. _A——_, that Mr. _P._ writ his Character after his death, _&c._ that he ſet his Name to Mr. _Broom_'s Verſes, that he receiv'd Subſcriptions for _Shakeſpear_, &c. which tho' publickly diſprov'd by the _Teſtimonies_ prefix'd to the _Dunciad_, were nevertheleſs ſhameleſly repeated in the Libels, and even in the Paper call'd, _The Nobleman's Epiſtle._

Th' imputed Traſh.] Profane _Pſalms, Court Poems_, and many Libellous Things in his Name, printed by _Curl_, &c.

Abuſe on all he lov'd, or lov'd him ſpread.] Namely on the Duke of _Buckingham_, Earl of _Burlington_, Biſhop _Atterbury_, Dr. _Swift_, Mr. _Gay_, Dr. _Arbuthnot_, his Friends, his Parents, and his very _Nurſe_, aſpers'd in printed Papers.

Yet

Yet soft by Nature, more a Dupe than Wit, 350
Sapho can tell you how this Man was bit:
This dreaded Sat'rist *Dennis* will confess
Foe to his Pride, but Friend to his Distress:
So humble, he has knock'd at *T—b—ld*'s door,
Has drank with *C—r*, nay has rym'd for *M—r*. 395
Full ten years slander'd, did he once reply?
Three thousand Suns went down on *Welsted*'s Lye:
To please a *Mistress*, One aspers'd his life;
He lash'd him not, but let her be his *Wife*:
Let *Budgel* charge low *Grubstreet* on his quill, 360
And write whate'er he pleas'd, except his *Will*;
Let the *Two Curls* of Town and Court, abuse
His Father, Mother, Body, Soul, and Muse.

Yet

Ten Years.] It was so long, before the Author of the *Dunciad* published that Poem, till when, he never writ a word of the many Scurrilities and Falsehoods concerning him.

Welsted's Lye.] This Man had the Impudence to tell in print, that Mr. *P.* had occasion'd a *Lady's death*, and to *name* a person he never heard of. He also publish'd that he had libell'd the Duke of *Chandos*; with whom (it was added) that he had liv'd in familiarity, and receiv'd from him a Present of *five hundred pounds*: The Falsehood of which is known to his Grace, whom Mr. *P.* never had the honour to see but *twice*, and never receiv'd any Present farther than the Subscription for *Homer*, from him, or from Any Great Man whatsoever.

Budgel in a Weekly Pamphlet call'd the *Bee*, bestow'd much abuse on him, in the imagination that he writ some things about the *Last Will* of Dr. *Tindal*, in the *Grubstreet Journal*; a *Paper* wherein he never had the least *Hand*, *Direction*, or *Supervisal*, nor the least *knowledge of its Authors*. He took no notice of so frantick an Abuse; and expected that any man who knew himself Author of what he was slander'd for, would have justify'd him on that Article.

His Father, Mother, &c.] In some of *Curl's* and other Pamphlets, Mr. *Pope's* Father was said to be a Mechanic, a Hatter, a Farmer, nay a Bankrupt. But, what is stranger, a *Nobleman* (if such a Reflection can be thought to come

from

Yet why? that Father held it for a rule
It was a Sin to call our Neighbour Fool,   370
That harmless Mother thought no Wife a Whore,—
Hear this! and spare his Family, *James Moore*
Unspotted Names! and memorable long,
If there be Force in Virtue, or in Song.

Of gentle Blood (part shed in Honour's Cause, 370
While yet in *Britain* Honour had Applause)
Each Parent sprung—"What Fortune, pray?—Their own,
And better got than *Bestia*'s from a Throne.
Born to no Pride, inheriting no Strife,
Nor marrying Discord in a Noble Wife,   375
Stranger to Civil and Religious Rage,
The good Man walk'd innoxious thro' his Age.
No Courts he saw, no Suits would ever try,
Nor dar'd an Oath, nor hazarded a Lye:
Un-learn'd, he knew no Schoolman's subtle Art, 380
No Language, but the Language of the Heart.

from a Nobleman) has dropt an Allusion to this pitiful Untruth, in his *Epistle
to a Doctor of Divinity:* And the following Line,
      Hard as thy Heart, and as thy Birth Obscure,
had fallen from a like Courtly pen, in the *Verses to the Imitator of Horace.* p 4 line 10
Mr. *Pope*'s Father was of a Gentleman's Family in *Oxfordshire,* the Head of
which was the Earl of *Downe,* whose sole Heiress married the Earl of *Lind-
sey.*—His Mother was the Daughter of *William Turnor,* Esq; of *York:* She
had three Brothers, one of whom was kill'd, another died in the Service of
King *Charles,* the eldest following his Fortunes, and becoming a General Of-
ficer in *Spain,* left her what Estate remain'd after the Sequestrations and For-
feitures of her Family —— Mr. *Pope* died in 1717, aged 75; She in 1733,
aged 93, a very few Weeks after this Poem was finished.

By

By Nature honeſt, by Experience wiſe,
Healthy by Temp'rance and by Exerciſe:
His Life, tho' long, to ſickneſs paſt unknown,
His Death was inſtant, and without a groan.   385
Oh grant me thus to live, and thus to die!
Who ſprung from Kings ſhall know leſs joy than I.
   O Friend! may each Domeſtick Bliſs be thine!
Be no unpleaſing Melancholy mine:
Me, let the tender Office long engage   390
To rock the Cradle of repoſing Age,
With lenient Arts extend a Mother's breath,
Make Languor ſmile, and ſmooth the Bed of Death,
Explore the Thought, explain the asking Eye,
And keep a while one Parent from the Sky!   395
On Cares like theſe if Length of days attend,
May Heav'n, to bleſs thoſe days, preſerve my Friend,
Preſerve him ſocial, chearful, and ſerene,
And juſt as rich as when he ſerv'd a QUEEN!
Whether that Bleſſing be deny'd, or giv'n,   410
Thus far was right, the reſt belongs to Heav'n.

EPISTLE VII TO DR. ARBUTHNOT

FROM

THE WORKS, VOLUME II

1735

EPISTLE VII.

TO

Dr. ARBUTHNOT.

SHUT, shut the door good *John*! fatigu'd I said,
Tye up the knocker, say I'm sick, I'm dead.
The Dogstar rages! nay 'tis past a doubt,
All Bedlam, or Parnassus, is let out:
Fire in their eye, and Papers in their hand,   5
They rave, recite, and madden round the land.

What walls can guard me, or what shades can hide?
They pierce my thickets, thro' my Grot they glide,
By land, by water, they renew the charge,
They stop the chariot, and they board the barge.   10

N

No place is sacred, not the Church is free,
Ev'n Sunday shines no Sabbath-day to me:
Then from the Mint walks forth the man of Ryme,
Happy! to catch me, just at dinner-time.

Is there a Parson much be-mus'd in beer?　　15
A maudlin Poetess? a ryming Peer?
A Clerk, foredoom'd his father's soul to cross,
Who pens a Stanza when he should *engross?*
Is there, who lock'd from pen and paper, scrawls
With desp'rate charcoal round his darken'd walls?　20
All fly to Twit'nam, and in humble strain
Apply to me, to keep them mad or vain.
Arthur, whose giddy Son neglects the Laws,
Imputes to me and my damn'd works the cause:
Poor Cornus sees his frantic Wife elope,　　25
And curses Wit, and Poetry, and *Pope.*

Friend thro' my life, (which did'st not thou prolong,
The world had wanted many an idle song)
Dear Doctor! tell me, is not this a curse?
Say, is their Anger, or their Friendship worse?　30
A dire Dilemma! either way I'm sped,
My Foes will write, my Friends will read me dead.

Seiz'd and ty'd down to judge, how wretched I!
I can't be filent, and I will not lye,
To laugh, were want of goodnefs and of Grace,   35
And to be grave, exceeds all Pow'r of Face.
I fit with fad Civility, I read
With honeft anguifh, and an aking head;
And drop at laft, but in unwilling ears,
This faving counfel, "Keep your piece nine years."

 Nine years! cries he, who high in Drury-lane   41
Lull'd by foft Zephyrs thro' the broken pane,
Rymes e're he wakes, and prints before Term ends,
Oblig'd by hunger and Requeft of friends:
"The piece you think is incorrect? why take it,   45
"I'm all fubmiffion, what you'd have it, make it."

 Three things another's modeft wifhes bound;
My Friendfhip, and a Prologue, and ten pound.

 Pitholeon greets me thus: "You know his Grace,
"I want a Patron — afk him for a Place."   50
Pitholeon libell'd me — "but here's a Letter
"Informs you Sir, 'twas when he knew no better.
"Dare you refufe him? *Curl* invites to dine,
"He'll write a Journal, or he'll turn Divine."

Bleſs me! a Packet! — "'Tis a ſtranger ſues, 55
" A Virgin Tragedy, an Orphan Muſe."
If I diſlike it, "Furies, death and rage!
If I approve, "Commend it to the Stage."
There (thank my ſtars) my whole commiſſion ends,
Cibber and I are, luckily, no friends. 60
Fir'd that the Houſe reject him, "'Sdeath I'll print it
" And ſhame the Fools —your Int'reſt Sir with Lintot."
Lintot, dull rogue! will think your price too much.
" Not Sir if you reviſe it, and retouch."
All my demurrs but double his attacks, 65
At laſt he whiſpers "Do, and we go ſnacks."
Glad of a quarrel, ſtrait I clap the door,
Sir, let me ſee your works and you no more.

　　'Tis ſung, when *Midas*' Ears began to ſpring,
(Midas, a ſacred Perſon and a King) 70
His very Miniſter who ſpy'd them firſt,
(Some ſay his * Queen) was forc'd to ſpeak, or burſt.
And is not mine, my Friend, a ſorer caſe,
When ev'ry Coxcomb perks them in my face?

---

* The Story is told by ſome of his Barber, by *Chaucer* of his Queen. See the Wife of Bath's
Tale in *Dryden's* Fables.

" Good friend forbear! you deal in dang'rous things!

" I'd never name Queens, Minifters, or Kings;

" Keep clofe to Ears, and thofe let Affes prick,

" Tis nothing"—Nothing, if they bite and kick?   76

Out with it, *Dunciad!* let the fecret pafs,

That Secret to each Fool, that he's an Afs:

The truth once told (and wherefore fhou'd we lie?)

The Queen of Midas flept, and fo may I.   80

 You think this cruel? take it for a rule,

No creature fmarts fo little as a Fool.

Let Peals of Laughter, **Codrus!** round thee break,

Thou unconcern'd canft hear the mighty Crack;

Pit, Box and Gall'ry in convulfions hurl'd,   85

Thou ftand'ft unfhook amidft a burfting World.

Scriblers like Spiders, break one cobweb thro',

Still fpin the flight, felf-pleafing thread anew,

Thron'd in the centre of their thin defigns!

Proud of a vaft extent of flimzy lines!   90

Whom have I hurt? has Poet yet, or Peer,

Loft the arch'd eye-brow, or Parnaffian fneer?

And has not Colly ftill his Lord, and Whore?

His Butchers Henley, his Free-mafons Moor?

Does not one Table Arnall still admit? 95
Still to one Bishop Philips seem a Wit?
Still Sapho — "Hold! nay see you, you'll offend:
" Wit makes you foes, learn Prudence of a friend.
" I too could write — and sure am twice as tall,
" But all these foes! — One Flatt'rer's worse than all;
A Wit quite angry is quite innocent; 101
The only danger is, when they *repent*.

   One dedicates, in high Heroic prose,
And ridicules beyond a hundred foes;
One from all Grubstreet will my fame defend, 105
And, more abusive, calls himself my friend.
For song, for silence, some expect a bribe,
And others roar aloud, "Subscribe, subscribe.
Time, Praise, or Money, is the least they crave,
Yet each declares the other, fool or knave.

   There are, who to my Person pay their court,
I cough like Horace, and tho' lean, am short, 110
Ammon's great Son one shoulder had too high,
Such Ovid's nose, and "Sir! you have an *Eye* —
Go on, obliging creatures, make me see
All that disgrac'd my Betters, met in me:

Say for my comfort, languishing in bed, 115
" Just so immortal Maro held his head;
And when I die, be sure you let me know,
" Great Homer dy'd three thousand years ago.

Why did I write? what sin to me unknown
Dipt me in Ink? my Parent's, or my own? 120
As yet a Child, nor yet a fool to Fame,
I lisp'd in Numbers, for the numbers came.
I left no calling for this idle trade,
No duty broke, no father dis-obey'd.
The Muse but serv'd to ease some friend, not Wife,
To help me thro' this long Disease, my Life, 126
To second, ARBUTHNOT! thy Art and Care,
And teach, the Being you preserv'd, to bear.

But why then publish? Granville the polite,
And knowing Walsh, would tell me I could write; 130
Well-natur'd Garth inflam'd with early praise,
And Congreve lov'd, and Swift endur'd my Lays;
The courtly Talbot, Somers, Sheffield read,
Ev'n mitred Rochester would nod the head,

And St. John's self (great Dryden's friends before) 135
With open arms receiv'd one Poet more.
Happy my Studies, when by thefe approv'd!
Happier their Author, when by thefe belov'd!
From thefe the world will judge of Men and Books,
Not from the * Burnets, Oldmixons, and Cooks.   140

    Soft were my numbers, who could take offence
While pure defcription held the place of fenfe?
Like gentle Fanny's was my flowry Theme,
A painted Miftrefs, or a purling Stream.
Yet then did Gildon draw his venal quill;
I wifh'd the man a dinner, and fate ftill:
Yet then did Dennis rave in furious fret;   145
I never anfwer'd, I was not in debt:
Hunger provok'd, or madnefs made them print;
I wag'd no war with Bedlam or the Mint.

    Did fome more fober Critic come abroad?
If wrong, I fmil'd; if right, I kifs'd the rod.   150
Pains, reading, ftudy, are their juft pretence,
And all they want is fpirit, tafte, and fenfe.
Comma's and points they fet exactly right,
And 'twere a fin to rob them of their Mite.

      * Authors of fecret and fcandalous Hiftory.

Yet ne'r one fprig of Laurel grac'd thefe ribalds, 155
From daring Bentley down to pidling Tibalds.
Each wight, who reads not, and but fcans and fpells,
Each Word-catcher that lives on fyllables,
Ev'n fuch fmall Critics fome regard may claim,
Preferv'd in Milton's or in Shakefpear's name. 160
Pretty! in Amber to obferve the forms
Of hairs, or ftraws, or dirt, or grubs, or worms;
Not that the things are either rich or rare,
But all the wonder is, how they got there?

Were others angry? I excus'd them too; 165
Well might they rage, I gave them but their due.
A man's true merit 'tis not hard to find,
But each man's fecret ftandard in his mind,
That cafting-weight Pride adds to emptinefs,
This, who can gratify? for who can guefs? 170
The Bard whom pilf'red Paftorals renown,
Who turns a Perfian Tale for half a crown,
Juft writes to make his barrennefs appear,
And ftrains from hard-bound brains eight lines a-year:
He, who ftill wanting tho' he lives on theft, 175
Steals much, fpends little, yet has nothing left:

P

And he, who now to fenfe, now nonfenfe leaning,
Means not, but blunders round about a meaning:
And he, whofe Fuftian's fo fublimely bad,
It is not Poetry, but Profe run mad: 180
All thefe my modeft Satire bade tranflate,
And own'd, that nine fuch Poets made a Tate.
How did they fume, and ftamp, and roar, and chafe?
And fwear, not Addifon himfelf was fafe.

Peace to all fuch! but were there One whofe fires
True Genius kindles, and fair Fame infpires,   186
Bleft with each talent and each art to pleafe,
And born to write, converfe, and live with eafe:
Shou'd fuch a man, too fond to rule alone,
Bear, like the Turk, no brother near the throne, 190
View him with fcornful, yet with jealous eyes,
And hate for Arts that caus'd himfelf to rife;
Damn with faint praife, affent with civil leer,
And without fneering, teach the reft to fneer;
Willing to wound, and yet afraid to ftrike,   195
Juft hint a fault, and hefitate diflike;
Alike referv'd to blame, or to commend,
A tim'rous foe, and a fufpicious friend,

Dreading ev'n fools, by Flatterers befieg'd,   200
And fo obliging that he ne'er oblig'd;
Like **Cato**, give his little Senate laws,
And fit attentive to his own applaufe;
While Wits and Templers ev'ry fentence raife,
And wonder with a foolifh face of praife.   205
Who but muft laugh, if fuch a man there be?
Who would not weep, if Atticus were he!

    What tho' my Name ftood rubric on the walls?
Or plaifter'd pofts, with claps in capitals?
Or fmoaking forth, a hundred hawkers load,   210
On wings of winds came flying all abroad?
I fought no homage from the race that write;
I kept, like Afian Monarchs, from their fight;
Poems I heeded (now be-rym'd fo long)
No more than thou, great **George**! a Birth-day Song.
I ne'r with Wits or Witlings paft my days,   216
To fpread about the itch of Verfe and Praife;
Nor like a puppy dagled through the town,
To fetch and carry Sing-fong up and down;
Nor at Rehearfals fweat, and mouth'd, and cry'd,   220
With handkerchief and orange at my fide;

But fick of Fops, and Poetry, and Prate,
To Bufo left the whole Caftalian State.

Proud, as Apollo on his forked hill,
Sate full-blown Bufo, puff'd by ev'ry quill;   225
Fed with foft Dedication all day long,
Horace and he went hand in hand in fong.
His Library, (where Bufts of Poets dead
And a true Pindar ftood without a head)
Receiv'd of Wits an undiftinguifh'd race,   230
Who firft his judgment ask'd, and then a Place:
Much they extol'd his pictures, much his feat,
And flatter'd ev'ry day, and fome days eat:
Till grown more frugal in his riper days,
He pay'd fome Bards with Port, and fome with Praife,
To fome a dry Rehearfal was affign'd,   236
And others (harder ftill) he pay'd in kind.
Dryden alone (what wonder?) came not nigh,
Dryden alone efcap'd this judging eye:
But ftill the Great have kindnefs in referve,
He help'd to bury him he help'd to ftarve.

May fome choice Patron blefs each gray goofe quill!
May ev'ry Bavius have his Bufo ftill!

So, when a Statesman wants a Day's defence,   240
Or Envy holds a whole Week's war with sense,
Or simple Pride for flatt'ry makes demands,
May dunce by dunce be whistled off my hands!
Blest be the Great! for those they take away,
And those they leave me — For they left me GAY:
Left me to see neglected Genius bloom,
Neglected die, and tell it on his Tomb:
Of all thy blameless Life the sole return
My Verse, and QUEENSB'RY weeping o'er thy Urn!

Oh let me live my own! and die so too!
("To live and die is all I have to do:)
Maintain a Poet's Dignity, and Ease,
And see what friends, and read what books I please. 245
I was not born for Courts or great Affairs,
I pay my debts, believe, and say my pray'rs,
Can sleep without a Poem in my head,
Nor know, if Dennis be alive or dead.

Why will the Town imagine still I write?   250
Why ask, when this or that shall see the light?
"I found him close with Swift — Indeed? no doubt
"(Cries prating Balbus) something will come out."

Q

'Tis all in vain, deny it as I will:
"No, ſuch a Genius never can lye ſtill,"   255
And then for mine obligingly miſtakes
The firſt Lampoon Sir Will. or Bubo makes.
Poor guiltleſs I! and can I chuſe but ſmile,
When ev'ry Coxcomb knows me by my *Style?*

    Curſt be the Verſe, how well ſoe'er it flow,   260
That tends to make one worthy man my foe,
Give Virtue ſcandal, Innocence a fear,
Or from the ſoft-ey'd Virgin ſteal a tear!
But he, who hurts a harmleſs neighbour's peace,
Inſults fal'n Worth, or Beauty in diſtreſs,   265
Who loves a lye, lame ſlander helps about,
Who writes a Libel, or who copies out:
That Fop whoſe pride affects a Patron's name,
Yet abſent, wounds an Author's honeſt fame;
Who can your merit ſelfiſhly approve,   270
And ſhow the Senſe of it without the Love;
Who has the Vanity to call you friend,
Yet wants the Honour injur'd to defend;
Who to the * Dean and ſilver Bell can ſwear,
And ſees at Cannons what was never there;   275

* See the Epiſtle to the Earl of Burlington.

Who tells whate'er you think, whate'er you fay,
And, if he lye not, muft at leaft betray :
Let never honeft Man my fatire dread,
But all fuch babling blockheads in his ftead.

 Let Sporus tremble——"What? that thing of filk,
" Sporus, that mere white curd of Afs's milk ?   281
" Satire or fenfe alas! he cannot feel,
" Who breaks a Butterfly upon a Wheel?"
Yet let me flap this Bug with gilded wings,
This painted child of dirt, that ftinks and ftings ;
Whofe buzz the witty and the fair annoys,   286
Yet wit ne'er taftes, and beauty ne'er enjoys,
So well-bred Spaniels civilly delight
In mumbling of the Game they dare not bite.
Eternal fmiles his emptinefs betray,   290
As fhallow ftreams run dimpling all the way.
Whether in florid Impotence he fpeaks,
And, as the Prompter breathes, the Puppet fqueaks :
Or at the ear of Eve, familiar Toad,
Half froth, half venom, fpits himfelf abroad,   295
In Puns, or Politicks, or Tales, or Lyes,
Or Spite, or Smut, or Rymes, or Blafphemies.

His Wit all fee-faw between *that* and *this*, }
Now high, now low, now Mafter up, now Mifs, }
And he himfelf one vile Antithefis : }
Amphibious Thing ! that acting either part,
The trifling head, or the corrupted heart,
Fop at the Toilet, Flatt'rer at the Board,   320
Now trips a Lady, and now ftruts a Lord.
Eve's Tempter thus the Rabbins have expreft,
A Cherub's face, a Reptile all the reft ;
Beauty that fhocks you, Parts that none will truft,
Wit that can creep, and Pride that licks the duft. 325

Oh keep me what I am ! not Fortune's fool,
Nor Lucre's madman, nor Ambition's tool :
Not proud, nor fervile, be one Poet's praife,
That, if he pleas'd, he pleas'd by manly ways,
That Flatt'ry, ev'n to Kings, he held a fhame,   330
And thought a Lye in Verfe or Profe the fame.
That not in Fancy's maze he wander'd long,
But ftoop'd to Truth, and moraliz'd his fong.
That not for Fame, but Virtue's better end,
He ftood the furious Foe, the timid Friend,   335
The damning Critic, half-approving Wit,
The Coxcomb hit, or fearing to be hit :

Laugh'd at the lofs of Friends he never had,
The dull, the proud, the wicked, and the mad;
The diftant Threats of Vengeance on his head,   340
The Blow unfelt, the Tear he never fhed;
The Tale reviv'd, the Lye fo oft o'erthrown,
Th' imputed Trafh, and Dulnefs not his own,
The Morals blacken'd when the Writings fcape,
The libel'd Perfon, and the pictur'd Shape,   345
Th' Abufe on all he lov'd or lov'd him fpread,
A Friend in Exile, or a Father, dead;
The Whifper, that to Greatnefs ftill too near,
Perhaps, yet vibrates on his Sovereign's Ear—
Welcome for thee, fair Virtue! all the paft: 350
For thee, fair Virtue! welcome ev'n the *laft!*

" But why infult the Poor, affront the Great? "
A Knave's a Knave, to me, in ev'ry State,
Alike my fcorn if he fucceed or fail,
Sporus at Court, or Japhet in a Jayl,   355
A hireling Scribler, or a hireling Peer,
Knight of the Poft corrupt, or of the Shire,
If on a Pillory, or near a Throne,
He gain his Prince's ear, or lofe his own.

R

Yet soft by nature, more a Dupe than Wit, 360
Sapho can tell you how this Man was bit:
This dreaded Sat'rist Dennis will confess
Foe to his Pride, but Friend to his Distress:
So humble, he has knock'd at Tibbald's door,
Has drank with Cibber, nay has rym'd for Moor: 365
Full ten years slander'd, did he once reply?
Three thousand Suns went down on Welsted's Lye:
To please a Mistress, One aspers'd his life;
He lash'd him not, but let her be his Wife:
Let Budgel charge low Grubstreet on his quill, 370
And write whate'er he pleas'd, except his *Will*;
Let the two Curls of Town and Court, abuse
His Father, Mother, Body, Soul, and Muse.
Yet why? that Father held it for a rule
It was a Sin to call our Neighbour Fool; 375
That harmless Mother thought no Wife a Whore,
Hear this! and spare his Family, James M * ,
Unspotted Names! and memorable long,
If there be force in Virtue, or in Song.

Of gentle Blood (part shed in Honour's cause, 380
While yet in Britain Honour had applause)

Each Parent fprung–"What Fortune, pray?–their own,

And better got than Clodio's from the Throne.

Born to no Pride, inheriting no Strife,

Nor marrying Difcord in a Noble Wife,   385

Stranger to Civil and Religious Rage,

The good Man walk'd innoxious thro' his Age:

No Courts he faw, no Suits would ever try,

Nor dar'd an Oath, nor hazarded a Lye:

Un-learn'd, he knew no fchoolman's fubtle Art, 390

No Language, but the Language of the Heart.

By Nature honeft, by Experience wife,

Healthy by Temp'rance and by Exercife,

His Life, tho' long, to ficknefs paft unknown,

His Death was inftant, and without a groan.   395

Oh grant me thus to live, and thus to die!

Who fprung from Kings fhall know lefs joy than I.

O Friend! may each domeftick Blifs be thine!

Be no unpleafing Melancholy mine:

Me, let the tender office long engage   400

To rock the Cradle of repofing Age,

With lenient arts extend a Mother's breath,

Make Languor fmile, and fmooth the Bed of Death,

Explore the Thought, explain the asking Eye,
And keep a while one Parent from the Sky!   405
On cares like thefe if length of days attend,
May Heav'n, to blefs thofe days, preferve my Friend,
Preferve him focial, chearful, and ferene,
And juft as rich as when he ferv'd a QUEEN.
Whether that Blefling be deny'd, or giv'n,   410
Thus far was right, the reft belongs to Heav'n.

AN
ESSAY
ON
MAN.

A N
ESSAY on MAN,

Being the FIRST BOOK of

ETHIC EPISTLES.

T O

HENRY St. JOHN, L. BOLINGBROKE.

L O N D O N:

Printed by JOHN WRIGHT, for LAWTON GILLIVER,
MDCCXXXIV.

THE
DESIGN.

HAVING *proposed to write some Pieces on Human Life and Manners, such as (to use my Lord Bacon's expression)* come home to Men's Business and Bosoms, *I thought it more satisfactory to begin with considering* Man *in the Abstract, his* Nature *and his* State : *since to prove any moral* Duty, *to inforce any moral* Precept, *or to examine the Perfection or Imperfection of any Creature whatsoever, it is necessary first to know what* Condition *and* Relation *it is placed in, and what is the proper* End *and* Purpose *of its* Being.

The Science of Human Nature is, like all other Sciences, reduced to a few, clear Points : There are not many certain Truths in this World. It is therefore in the Anatomy of the Mind as in that of the Body ; more Good will accrue to mankind by attending to the large, open, and perceptible parts, than by studying too much such finer nerves and vessels as will for ever escape our observation. The Disputes are all upon these last, and I will venture

ture

The DESIGN.

ture to say, they have less sharpen'd the Wits *than the*
Hearts of Men against each other, and have diminished
the Practise, more than advanced *the Theory,* of Mora-
lity.   *If I could flatter my self that this Essay has any*
Merit, it is in steering betwixt Doctrines seemingly op-
posite, in passing over Terms utterly un-intelligible, and
in forming out of all a temperate yet not inconsistent,
and a short *yet not imperfect System of Ethics.*

This I might have done in Prose; but I chose Verse,
and even Rhyme, for two reasons. The one will ap-
pear obvious; that Principles, Maxims, or Precepts
so written, both strike the reader more strongly at first,
and are more easily retained by him afterwards. The
other may seem odd but is true; I found I could ex-
press them more shortly this way than in Prose itself,
and nothing is more certain than that much of the Force
as well as Grace of Arguments or Instructions depends
on their Conciseness. I was unable to treat this part
of my subject more in detail, *without becoming dry and*
tedious; or more poetically, *without sacrificing Perspi-*
cuity to Ornament, without wandring from the Precision,
or breaking the Chain of Reasoning. If any man can unite
all these, without diminution of any of them, I freely con-
fess he will compass a thing above my capacity.

What is now published, is only to be considered as a ge-
neral Map of MAN, *marking out no more than the* Greater
Parts,

The DESIGN.

Parts, *their* Extent, *their* Limits, *and their* Connection, *but leaving the Particular to be more fully delineated in the Charts which are to follow. Consequently, these Epistles in their progress will become less dry, and more susceptible of Poetical Ornament.   I am here only opening the Fountains, and clearing the passage ; To deduce the* Rivers, *to follow them in their Course, and to observe their Effects, will be a task more agreeable.*

THE
CONTENTS
OF THE
FIRST BOOK.

EPISTLE I.

Of the NATURE and STATE of MAN, with reſpect to the UNIVERSE.

OF *Man* in the *Abſtract*. We can judge only with regard to our *own Syſtem*, being ignorant of the *Relations* of Syſtems and Things, VER. 17, *&c.* to 68. Man is not therefore to be deem'd *Imperſect*, but a Being ſuited to his *Place* and *Rank* in the Creation, agreeable to the *General Order* of Things, and conformable to *Ends* and *Relations* to him unknown. 69, *&c.* It is partly upon this *Ignorance* of future Events, and partly upon the *Hope* of a Future State, that all his Happineſs in the preſent depends, 73, *&c.* His *Pride*, in aiming at more *Knowledge* and pretending to more *Perfection*, the cauſe of his Error and Miſery, 109. 119. The *Impiety* of putting himſelf in the

A

The CONTENTS.

EPISTLE II.

Of the NATURE and STATE of MAN, with refpect to HIMSELF as an Individual.

THE bufinefs of man not to pry into *God,* but to ftudy *himfelf.* His *Middle Nature*; his *powers* and *frailties,* and the Limits of his *capacity,* VER. 3 *to* 43. His two Principles, *Self-*

The CONTENTS.

EPISTLE III.

Of the NATURE and STATE of MAN, with reſpect to SOCIETY.

THE *whole Univerſe* one ſyſtem of *Society*, VER. 7, &c. Nothing is made wholly for *itſelf*, nor yet wholly for *another*, 27. The happineſs of animals mutual, 53. *Reaſon* or *Inſtinct* operate alike to the good of each individual, 83. *Reaſon* or *inſtinct* operate to *ſociety*, in all animals, 109. How far *Society* carry'd by Inſtinct, 119. How much farther by Reaſon, 132. Of that which is call'd the *State* of *Nature*, 148. Reaſon inſtructed by Inſtinct in the invention of *Arts*, 170. and in the *Forms* of ſociety, 180. Origin of *political* Societies, 199. Origin of *Mo-*

The CONTENTS.

EPISTLE IV.

Of the NATURE and STATE of MAN, with respect to HAPPINESS.

The CONTENTS.

EPISTLE I.

WAKE! my ST. JOHN! leave
all meaner things
To low Ambition and the Pride
of Kings.
Let Us (since Life can little
more supply
Than juſt to look about us, and to die)
Expatiate free, o'er all this *Scene of Man*,⠀⠀⠀⠀5
A mighty Maze! but not without a Plan;
A Wild, where weeds and flow'rs promiſcuous ſhoot,
Or Garden, tempting with forbidden fruit.

Together let us beat this ample field,
Try what the open, what the covert yield;   10
The latent tracts or giddy heights explore,
Of all who blindly creep, or sightless soar;
Eye Nature's walks, shoot Folly as it flies,
And catch the manners living as they rise;
Laugh where we *must*, be candid where we *can*,   15
But vindicate the Ways of GOD to Man.

　　Say first, of *God* above, or *Man* below,'
What can we *reason*, but from what we *know?*
Of Man, what see we but his Station here,
From which to reason, or to which refer?   20
Thro' Worlds unnumber'd tho' the God be known,
'Tis ours to trace him, only in our own.
He who thro' vast Immensity can pierce,
See worlds on worlds compose one Universe,
Observe how System into System runs,   25
What other Planets, and what other Suns?
What vary'd Being peoples ev'ry Star?
May tell, why Heav'n has made us as we are.

But of this frame the bearings, and the Ties,
The ſtrong connections, nice dependencies,   30
Gradatïons juſt, has thy pervading ſoul
Look'd thro'? or can a Part contain the Whole?

　　Is the great Chain that draws all to agree,
And drawn ſupports, upheld by God, or thee?

　　Preſumptuous Man! the Reaſon would'ſt thou find
Why form'd ſo weak, ſo little, and ſo blind?   36
Firſt, if thou can'ſt, the harder reaſon gueſs
Why form'd no weaker, blinder, and no leſs?
Ask of thy mother Earth, why oaks are made
Taller or ſtronger than the weeds they ſhade?   40
Or ask of yonder argent fields above,
Why Jove's Satellites are leſs than Jove?

　　Of Syſtems poſſible, if 'tis confeſt
That Wiſdom infinite muſt form the beſt,
Where all muſt full, or not coherent be,   45
And all that riſes, riſe in due degree;
Then, in the ſcale of life and ſenſe, 'tis plain
There muſt be, ſome where, ſuch a rank as Man;

B

Varied to
"reaſoning life"

And all the queſtion (wrangle 'ere ſo long)
Is only this, if God has plac'd him wrong?   50
   Reſpecting Man whatever wrong we call,
May, muſt be right, as relative to All.
In human works, though labour'd on with pain,
A thouſand movements ſcarce one purpoſe gain;
In God's, one ſingle can its End produce,   55
Yet ſerves to ſecond too ſome other Uſe.
So Man, who here ſeems principal alone,
Perhaps acts ſecond to a Sphere unknown,
Touches ſome wheel, or verges to ſome gole;
'Tis but a part we ſee, and not a whole.   60
   When the proud Steed ſhall know,why Man reſtrains
His fiery courſe, or drives him o'er the plains;
When the dull Ox, why now he breaks the clod,
Now wears a Garland, an Ægyptian God;
Then ſhall Man's pride and dulneſs comprehend   65
His action's, paſſion's, being's, Uſe and End;
Why doing, ſuff'ring, check'd, impell'd; and why
This hour a Slave, the next a Deity?

Then fay not Man's imperfect, Heav'n in fault;
Say rather, Man's as perfect as he ought;   70
His being meafur'd to his State, and Place,
His time a moment, and a point his fpace.

Heav'n from all Creatures hides the book of Fate,
All but the page prefcrib'd, their prefent ftate,
From Brutes what Men, from Men what Spirits know,
Or who could fuffer Being here below?   76
The Lamb thy riot dooms to bleed to day,
Had he thy Reafon, would he skip and play?
Pleas'd to the laft, he crops the flow'ry food,
And licks the hand juft rais'd to fhed his blood.   80
Oh blindnefs to the future! kindly giv'n,
That each may fill the Circle mark'd by Heav'n,
Who fees with equal eye, as God of All,
A Hero perifh, or a Sparrow fall,
Atoms, or Syftems, into ruin hurl'd,   85
And now a Bubble burft, and now a World!

Hope humbly then; with trembling pinions foar;
Wait the great teacher, Death, and God adore!

What future blifs, he gives not thee to know,
But gives that *Hope* to be thy blefling now. 90
Hope fprings eternal in the human breaft ;
Man never is, but always to be bleft ;
The foul uneafy, and confin'd at home,
Refts, and expatiates, in a life to come.

Lo ! the poor Indian, whofe untutor'd mind 95
Sees God in clouds, or hears him in the wind ;
His foul, proud Science never taught to ftray
Far as the Solar walk, or Milky way ;
Yet fimple Nature to his Hope has giv'n
Behind the cloud-topt hill an humbler heav'n, 100
Some fafer world in depth of woods embrac'd,
Some happier Ifland in the watry wafte,
Where Slaves once more their native land behold,
No Fiends torment, no Chriftians thirft for Gold.
To be, contents his natural defire, 105
He asks no Angel's wing, or Seraph's fire,
But thinks, admitted to that equal sky,
This faithful Dog fhall bear him company.

His

Go, wiſer thou! and in thy ſcale of ſenſe
Weigh thy Opinion againſt Providence : 110
Call Imperfection what thou fancy'ſt ſuch ;
Say, here he gives too little, there too much
Deſtroy all Creatures for thy ſport or guſt,
Yet cry, if Man's unhappy, God's unjuſt,
If Man, alone, engroſs not Heav'ns high care, 115
Alone, made perfect here, immortal there ;
Snatch from his hand the Balance and the Rod,
Re-judge his Juſtice, Be the GOD of GOD!

In reas'ning Pride (my Friend) our error lies ;
All quit their ſphere, and ruſh into the Skies. 120
Pride ſtill is aiming at the bleſt abodes,
Men would be Angels, Angels would be Gods.
Aſpiring to be Gods, if Angels fell,
Aſpiring to be Angels, Men rebell :
And who but wiſhes to invert the Laws 125
Of ORDER, ſins againſt th' Eternal Cauſe.

Ask for what end the heav'nly Bodies ſhine ?
Earth for whoſe uſe ? Pride anſwers, "'Tis for mine :

" For me kind Nature wakes her genial pow'r,

" Suckles each herb, and fpreads out ev'ry flow'r; 130

" Annual for me the grape, the rofe renew

" The juice nectareous, and the balmy dew;

" For me the mine a thoufand treafures brings,

" For me health gufhes from a thoufand fprings;

" Seas roll to waft me, funs to light me rife,   135

" My footftool earth, my canopy the skies.

    But errs not Nature from this gracious end,

From burning Suns when livid deaths defcend,

When Earthquakes fwallow, or when Tempefts fweep

Towns to one grave, and Nations to the Deep?   140

No ('tis reply'd) the firft Almighty Caufe

" Acts not by partial, but by gen'ral Laws;

" Th' Exceptions few; fome Change fince all began;

" And what created, perfect?" — Why then Man?

If the great End be human Happinefs,   145

And Nature deviates, how can Man do lefs?

As much that End a conftant courfe requires

Of fhow'rs and funfhine, as of Man's Defires,

As much eternal fprings and cloudlefs skies,

As men for ever temp'rate, calm, and wife.   150

If Plagues or Earthquakes break not heav'ns defign,

Why then a Borgia or a Catiline?

From Pride, from Pride, our very reas'ning fprings;

Account for moral, as for nat'ral things:

Why charge we heav'n in thofe, in thefe acquit? 155

In both, to reafon right, is to fubmit.

Better for us, perhaps, it might appear,

Were there all harmony, all virtue here;

That never air or ocean felt the wind;

That never paffion difcompos'd the mind: 160

But *All* fubfifts by elemental ftrife;

And Paffions are the Elements of life.

The gen'ral Order, fince the whole began,

Is kept in Nature, and is kept in Man.

What would this Man? now upward will he foar,

And little lefs than Angel, would be more;   166

Now looking downward, juft as griev'd appears

To want the ftrength of Bulls, the fur of Bears.

152. A beautiful infertion was subsequently made by Pope.
      Who knows but he, whose hand the lightning forms,
      Who heaves old Ocean, and who wings the storms,
      Pours fierce ambition in a Casar's mind,
      Or turns young Ammon loose to scourge mankind?

Made for his ufe all Creatures if he call,
Say what their ufe, had he the pow'rs of all? 170
   Nature to thefe without profufion kind,
The proper organs, proper pow'rs affign'd,
Each feeming want compenfated of courfe,
Here, with degrees of Swiftnefs, there, of Force;
All in exact proportion to the ftate, 175
Nothing to add, and nothing to abate.
Each Beaft, each Infect, happy in its own,
Is Heav'n unkind to Man, and Man alone?
Shall he alone, whom rational we call,
Be pleas'd with nothing, if not blefs'd with all? 180
   The blifs of Man (could Pride that blefling find)
Is, not to think, or act, beyond Mankind;
No pow'rs of Body or of Soul to fhare,
But what his Nature and his State can bear.
Why has not Man a microfcopic eye? 185
For this plain reafon, Man is not a Fly.

VER. 174. *Here with degrees of Swiftnefs, there of Force.*] It is a certain Axiom in the Anatomy of Creatures, that in proportion as they are form'd for Strength their Swiftnefs is leffen'd; or as they are form'd for Swiftnefs, their Strength is abated.

Say what the ufe, were finer opticks giv'n,
T' infpect a Mite, not comprehend the Heav'n?
Or Touch, if tremblingly alive all o'er,
To fmart, and agonize at ev'ry pore? 190
Or keen Effluvia darting thro' the brain,
Die of a Rofe, in aromatic pain?
If Nature thunder'd in his opening ears,
And ftunn'd him with the mufic of the Spheres,
How would he wifh that Heav'n had left him ftill 195
The whifp'ring Zephyr, and the purling rill?
Who finds not Providence all-good and wife,
Alike in what it gives, and what denies?

Far as Creation's ample range extends,
The fcale of fenfual, mental pow'rs afcends; 200
Mark how it mounts to Man's imperial race,
From the green myriads in the peopled grafs!
What modes of Sight, betwixt each wide extreme,
The Mole's dim curtain, and the Lynx's beam:

C

Of fmell, the headlong Lionefs between,   205

And hound, fagacious on the tainted green:

Of hearing, from the Life that fills the flood,

To that which warbles through the vernal wood:

The fpider's touch, how exquifitely fine!

Feels at each thread, and lives along the line: 210

In the nice bee, what fenfe fo fubtly true

From pois'nous herbs extracts the healing dew.

How Inftinct varies! in the groveling fwine,

Compar'd, half-reas'ning Elephant! with thine;

'Twixt that, and Reafon, what a nice Barrier, 215

For ever fep'rate, yet for ever near:

Remembrance, and Reflection, how ally'd;

What thin partitions Senfe from Thought divide:

And middle natures, how they long to join,

Yet never pafs th' infuperable line! 220

Without this juft Gradation, could they be

Subjected thefe to thofe, or all to thee?

VER. 205.— *the headlong Lionefs* —] The manner of the Lions hunting their Prey in the Deferts of Africa is this; at their firft going out in the night-time they fet up a loud Roar, and then liften to the Noife made by the Beafts in their Flight, purfuing them by the Ear, and not by the Noftril. It is probable, the ftory of the Jackall's hunting for the Lion was occafion'd by obfervation of the Defect of Scent in that terrible Animal.

The pow'rs of all fubdu'd by thee alone,
Is not thy Reafon all thofe pow'rs in one?
  See, thro' this air, this ocean, and this earth,   225
All Matter quick, and burfting into birth.
Above, how high progreffive life may go?
Around how wide? how deep extend below?
Vaft Chain of Being! which from God began,
Natures Ethereal, human, Angel, Man,   230
Beaft, bird, fifh, infect; what no Eye can fee,
No Glafs can reach: from Infinite to thee,
From thee to Nothing! — On fuperior pow'rs
Were we to prefs, inferior might on ours;
Or in the full Creation leave a Void,   235
Where, one ftep broken, the great Scale's deftroy'd:
From Nature's Chain whatever link you ftrike,
Tenth or ten thoufandth, breaks the chain alike.
  And if each Syftem in gradation roll,
Alike effential to th' amazing Whole;
The leaft confufion but in one, not all
That Syftem only, but the whole muft fall.

Let Earth unbalanc'd from her Orbit fly,
Planets and Suns rush lawlefs thro' the sky,
Let ruling Angels from their fpheres be hurl'd,   245
Being on Being wreck'd, and World on World,
Heav'ns whole foundations to their Centre nod,
And Nature tremble, to the Throne of God.
All this dread ORDER break — For whom? for thee,
Vile Worm!— O Madnefs! Pride! Impiety!   250

What if the foot ordain'd the duft to tread,
Or hand to toil, afpir'd to be the Head?
What if the head, the eye or ear, repin'd
To ferve mere Engines to the ruling Mind?
Juft as abfurd, for any Part to claim   255
To be Another, in this gen'ral Frame:
Juft as abfurd, to mourn the tasks, or pains,
The great directing *Mind* of *All* ordains.

All are but parts of one ftupendous Whole,
Whofe Body Nature is, and God the Soul;   260
That, chang'd thro' all, and yet in all the fame,
Great in the Earth as in th' Æthereal frame,

Warms in the Sun, refreſhes in the Breeze,

Glows in the Stars, and bloſſoms in the Trees,

Lives thro' all Life, extends thro' all Extent, 265

Spreads undivided, operates unſpent,

Breathes in our ſoul, informs our mortal part,

As full, as perfect, in a hair, as heart,

As full, as perfect, in vile Man that mourns,

As the rapt Seraphim that ſings and burns ; 270

To Him no high, no low, no great, no ſmall ;

He fills, he bounds, connects, and equals all.

Ceaſe then, nor ORDER *Imperfection* name :

Our proper bliſs depends on what we blame.

Know thy own *Point* : This kind, this due degree 275

Of blindneſs, weakneſs, Heav'n beſtows on thee.

Submit — in this, or any other Sphere,

Secure to be as bleſt as thou canſt bear ;

Safe in the hand of one diſpoſing Pow'r,

Or in the natal, or the mortal Hour. 280

All Nature is but Art, unknown to thee ;

All Chance, Direction which thou canſt not ſee ;

Greatly improved, thus.
"As the rapt seraph that adores and burns."

All Difcord, Harmony not underftood ;
All partial Evil, univerfal Good :
And fpight of Pride, in erring Reafon's fpight,   285
One truth is clear ; " Whatever Is, is Right."

EPISTLE II.

Now then thy-self, prefume not God to
    fcan;
The proper ftudy of mankind is *Man.*
Plac'd on this Ifthmus of a middle ftate,
A Being darkly wife, and rudely great;
With too much knowledge for the Sceptic fide,   5
With too much weaknefs for a Stoic's pride,
He hangs between; in doubt to act, or reft,
In doubt to deem himfelf a God, or Beaft,
In doubt his mind or body to prefer,
Born but to die, and reas'ning but to err;   10
Alike in ignorance, his Reafon fuch,
Whether he thinks too little, or too much.

Chaos of Thought and Paſſion, all confus'd;
Still by himſelf abus'd, or diſ-abus'd;
Created half to riſe, and half to fall;   15
Great Lord of all things, yet a Prey to all;
Sole Judge of Truth, in endleſs Error hurl'd;
The Glory, Jeſt, and Riddle of the world!
Go, wond'rous Creature! mount where Science guides,
Go meaſure Earth, weigh Air, and ſtate the Tydes, 20
Inſtruct the Planets in what Orbs to run,
Correct old Time, and regulate the Sun.
Go, ſoar with Plato to th' empyreal ſphere,
To the firſt Good, firſt Perfect, and firſt Fair;
Or tread the mazy round his Follow'rs trod,   25
And quitting Senſe call Imitating God,
As Eaſtern Prieſts in giddy circles run,
And turn their heads, to imitate the Sun.
Go, teach Eternal Wiſdom how to rule;
Then drop into thy-ſelf, and be a Fool!   30
    Superior Beings, when of late they ſaw
A mortal Man unfold all Nature's Law,

Admir'd ſuch Wiſdom in an earthly ſhape,
And ſhow'd a NEWTON, as we ſhow an *Ape*.

Could He who taught each Planet where to roll, 35
Deſcribe, or fix, one Movement of the Soul?
Who mark'd their points, to riſe and to deſcend,
Explain, or his Beginning, or his End?
Alas what wonder! Man's ſuperior part
Uncheck'd may riſe, and climb from Art to Art; 40
But when his own great work is but begun,
What Reaſon weaves, by Paſſion is undone.

An inſertion of 10 lines.

Two Principles in human Nature reign;
Self-Love, to urge; and *Reaſon*, to reſtrain;
Nor this a good, nor that a bad we call, 45
Each works its end, to move, or govern all:
And to their proper operation ſtill
Aſcribe all Good; to their improper, Ill.

Self-Love, the Spring of motion, acts the ſoul;
Reaſon's comparing Balance rules the whole; 50
Man, but for that, no *Action* could attend,
And but for this, were active to no *End*.

D

Fix'd like a Plant, on his peculiar fpot,
To draw nutrition, propagate, and rot ;
Or Meteor-like, flame lawlefs through the void, 55
Deftroying others, by himfelf deftroy'd.

    Moft ftrength the *moving* Principle requires,
Active its task, it prompts, impels, infpires :
Sedate and quiet the *comparing* lies,
Form'd but to check, delib'rate, and advife.   50
Self-Love yet ftronger, as its objects nigh ;
Reafon's at diftance and in profpect lye ;
That fees immediate Good, by prefent fenfe,
Reafon the future, and the confequence ;
Thicker than Arguments, Temptations throng, 65
At beft more watchful this, but that more ftrong.
The action of the ftronger to fufpend,
Reafon ftill ufe, to Reafon ftill attend :
Attention, Habit and Experience gains,
Each ftrengthens Reafon, and Self-love reftrains. 70

    Let fubtile Schoolmen teach thefe Friends to fight,
More ftudious to divide, than to unite,

And Grace and Virtue, Senfe and Reafon fplit,
With all the rafh dexterity of Wit.
Wits, juft like fools, at war about a Name, 75
Have full as oft, no meaning, or the fame.
Self-love and Reafon to one end afpire,
Pain their averfion, Pleafure their defire;
But greedy that its object would devour,
This tafte the honey, and not wound the flower. 80
Pleafure, or wrong or rightly underftood,
Our greateft Evil, or our greateft Good.

Modes of Self-love the PASSIONS we may call;
'Tis real Good, or feeming, moves them all:
But fince not every Good we can divide, 85
And Reafon bids us for our own provide,
Paffions tho' felfifh, if their Means be fair,
Lift under *Reafon,* and deferve her care:
Thofe that imparted, court a nobler aim,
Exalt their kind, and take fome *Virtue*'s name. 90

In lazy *Apathy* let Stoics boaft
Their Virtue fix'd; 'tis fix'd as in a Froft:

Contracted all, retiring to the breaſt:
But Strength of Mind is Exerciſe, not Reſt:
The riſing tempeſt puts in act the ſoul,   95
Parts it may ravage, but preſerves the whole.
On Life's vaſt Ocean diverſely we ſail,
Reaſon the Card, but Paſſion is the Gale:
Nor GOD alone in the ſtill Calm we find,
He mounts the Storm, and *walks upon the Wind.* 100

    Paſſions, like Elements, tho' born to fight,
Yet mix'd and ſoften'd, in his work unite:
Theſe, 'tis enough to temper and employ;
But what compoſes Man, can Man deſtroy?
Suffice that Reaſon keep to Nature's road,   105
Subject, compound them, follow her, and God.

    Love, Hope, and Joy, fair Pleaſure's ſmiling train,
Hate, Fear, and Grief, the Family of Pain;
Theſe mix'd with art, and to due bounds confin'd,
Make, and maintain, the Balance of the Mind: 110
The Lights and Shades, whoſe well-accorded ſtrife
Gives all the Strength and Colour of our life.

Pleafures are ever in our hands, or eyes,
And when in Act they ceafe, in Profpect rife;
Prefent to grafp, and future ftill to find,   115
The whole employ of Body and of Mind.
All fpread their charms, but charm not all alike;
On diff'rent Senfes diff'rent Objects ftrike:
Hence diff'rent Paffions more or lefs inflame,
As ftrong, or weak, the Organs of the Frame; 120
And hence one Mafter Paffion in the breaft,
Like Aaron's Serpent, fwallows up the reft.

As Man perhaps, the moment of his breath,
Receives the lurking Principle of death,
The young Difeafe that muft fubdue at length, 125
Grows with his growth, and ftrengthens with his
So, caft and mingled with his very Frame,   [ftrength:
The Mind's difeafe, its *ruling Paffion* came:
Each vital humour which fhould feed the whole,
Soon flows to this, in Body and in Soul.   130
Whatever warms the heart, or fills the head,
As the mind opens, and its functions fpread,

Imagination plies her dang'rous art,
And pours it all upon the peccant part.

Nature its Mother, Habit is its Nurfe;   135
Wit, Spirit, Faculties, but make it worfe;
Reafon itfelf but gives it edge and pow'r,
As Heav'n's bleft Beam turns Vinegar more fow'r.

Omitted afterwards. The ruling Paffion, be it what it will,
The ruling Paffion conquers Reafon ftill.
We, wretched fubjects tho' to lawful fway,
In this weak Queen, fome Fav'rite ftill obey.   140
Ah! if fhe lend not Arms as well as Rules,
What can fhe more, than tell us we are Fools?
Teach us to mourn our nature, not to mend,
A fharp Accufer, but a helplefs Friend?
Or from a Judge turn Pleader, to perfuade   145
The choice we make, or juftify it made?
Proud of imagin'd Conquefts all along,
She but removes weak Paffions for the ftrong;
So, when fmall Humours gather to a Gout,
The Doctor fancies he has driv'n them out.   150

Yes; *Nature*'s Road muſt ever be prefer'd;
Reaſon is here no Guide, but ſtill a Guard;
'Tis her's to rectify, not overthrow,
And treat this Paſſion more as Friend than Foe:
A Mightier Pow'r the ſtrong Direction ſends,
And ſev'ral Men impells to ſev'ral Ends:
Like varying Winds, by other paſſions toſt,   155
This drives them conſtant to a certain Coaſt.
Let Pow'r or Knowledge, Gold, or Glory pleaſe,
Or (oft more ſtrong than all) the Love of eaſe,
Thro' life 'tis follow'd, ev'n at life's expence;
The Merchant's toil, the Sage's indolence,   160
The Monk's humility, the Hero's pride,
All, all alike find Reaſon on their ſide.

Th' Eternal Art, educing Good from Ill,
Grafts on this Paſſion our beſt Principle:
'Tis thus, the Mercury of Man is fix'd,   165
Strong grows the Virtue with his Nature mix'd;
The Droſs cements what elſe were too refin'd,
And in one int'reſt Body acts with Mind.

As Fruits ungrateful to the Planter's care
On favage ftocks inferted, learn to bear;   170
The fureft Virtues thus from Paffions fhoot,
Wild Nature's Vigour working at the root.
What Crops of Wit and Honefty appear,
From Spleen, from Obftinacy, Hate or Fear!
See Anger, Zeal and Fortitude fupply;   175
Ev'n Av'rice Prudence; Sloth Philofophy;
Envy, to which th' ignoble mind's a flave,
Is Emulation in the Learn'd and Brave:
Luft, thro' fome certain Strainers well refin'd,
Is gentle Love, and charms all Womankind.   180
Nor Virtue, male or female, can we name,
But what will grow on Pride, or grow on Shame.

  Thus Nature gives us (let it check our pride)
The Virtue neareft to our Vice ally'd;
Reafon the Byas turns to Good from Ill,   185
And Nero reigns a Titus, if he will.
The fiery foul abhorr'd in Catiline
In Decius charms, in Curtius is divine.

The fame Ambition can deftroy or fave,

And makes a Patriot, as it makes a Knave.

This Light and Darknefs, in our Chaos join'd, 195

What fhall divide? The God within the Mind.

Extremes in nature equal ends produce,

In man, they join to fome myfterious ufe;

Tho' oft fo mix'd, the diff'rence is too nice

Where ends the virtue, or begins the vice,   200

Now this, now that the other's bound invades,

As in fome well-wrought Picture, lights and fhades.

Fools! who from hence into the notion fall,

That Vice or Virtue there is none at all.

If white and black, blend, foften, and unite   205

A thoufand ways, is there no black or white?

Ask your own Heart, and nothing is fo plain;

'Tis to *miftake* them, cofts the time and pain.

Vice is a monfter of fo frightful mien,

As, to be hated, needs but to be feen;   210

Yet feen too oft, familiar with her face,

We firft endure, then pity, then embrace.

E

But where th' Extreme of Vice, was ne'er agreed;
Ask, where's the *North?* at York 'tis on the Tweed,
In Scotland at the Orcades, and there   215
At Greenland, Zembla, or the Lord knows where.
No creature owns it, in the firſt degree,
But thinks his Neighbour farther gone than he.
Ev'n thoſe who dwell beneath her very Zone,
Or never feel the rage, or never own;   220
What happier Natures ſhrink at with affright,
The hard Inhabitant contends is right.

Virtuous and vicious ev'ry man muſt be,
Few in th' Extreme, but all in the Degree:
The Rogue and Fool by fits is fair and wiſe,   225
And ev'n the beſt by fits what they deſpiſe,
'Tis but by *Parts* we follow Good or Ill,
For, Vice or Virtue, *Self* directs it ſtill;
Each Individual ſeeks a ſev'ral goal:
But HEAV'N's great view is *One,* and that the WHOLE:
That counter-works each Folly and Caprice;   231
That diſappoints th' Effect of ev'ry Vice:

That, happy Frailties to all ranks apply'd,
Shame to the Virgin, to the Matron Pride,
Fear to the Statefman, Rafhnefs to the Chief, 235
To Kings Prefumption, and to Crowds Belief.
That, Virtue's Ends from Vanity can raife,
Which feeks no int'reft, no reward but Praife;
And build on Wants, and on Defects of mind,
The Joy, the Peace, the Glory of Mankind. 240
　　Heav'n forming each on other to depend,
A Mafter, or a Servant, or a Friend,
Bids each on other for affiftance call,
'Till one man's weaknefs grows the ftrength of all.
Wants, Frailties, Paffions, clofer ftill allye 245
The common int'reft, or endear the tye:
To thefe we owe true Friendfhip, Love fincere,
Each home-felt joy that Life inherits here:
Yet from the fame we learn, in its decline,
Thofe joys, thofe loves, thofe int'refts to refign; 250
Taught half by reafon, half by mere decay,
To welcome Death, and calmly pafs away.

Whate'er the Paſſion, Knowledge, Fame, or Pelf,
Not one will change his Neighbour with himſelf.
The learn'd are happy, Nature to explore;   255
The fool is happy, that he knows no more;
The rich are happy in the plenty giv'n;
The poor contents him with the care of Heav'n.
See the blind Beggar dance, the Cripple ſing,
The Sot a Hero, Lunatic a King,   260
The ſtarving Chymiſt in his golden Views
Supreamly bleſt, the Poet in his Muſe.

See! ſome ſtrange Comfort ev'ry *State* attend,
And *Pride* beſtow'd on all, a common Friend;
See! ſome fit Paſſion ev'ry *Age* ſupply,   265
Hope travels thro', nor quits us when we die.

'Till then, *Opinion* gilds with varying rays
Thoſe painted clouds that beautify our days;
Each want of Happineſs by Hope ſupply'd,
And each vacuity of Senſe by Pride.   270
Theſe build up all that Knowledge can deſtroy;
In Folly's cup ſtill laughs the bubble, Joy;

— He made here a most delightful addition of 8 lines
Behold the Child, by nature's kindly law,
Pleas'd with a rattle, tickled with a ſtraw:
Some livelier play-thing gives his Youth delight,
A little louder, but as empty quite:

One Prospect loft, another ftill we gain,
And not a Vanity is giv'n in vain :
Ev'n mean *Self-Love* becomes, by force divine, 275
The Scale to meafure others wants by thine.
See! and confefs, one comfort ftill muft rife,
'Tis this, tho' *Man's a Fool*, yet GOD IS WISE.

W.K.jn.   P.F.fc.

Scarfs, garters, gold, amuse his riper Stage,
And beads and pray'r-books are the toys of Age;
Pleas'd with this bauble still, as that before,
Till tir'd he sleeps, and life's poor play is oer.

EPISTLE III.

Earn Dulneſs, learn! "The *Univerſal Cauſe*
"Acts to *one End*, but acts by various Laws."
In all the Madneſs of ſuperfluous Health,
The Trim of Pride, and Impudence of Wealth,
Let that great Truth be preſent night and day;   5
But moſt be preſent, if thou *preach*, or *pray*.
View thy own World: behold the Chain of Love
Combining all below, and all above.
See, plaſtic Nature working to this End,
The ſingle Atoms each to other tend,   10
Attract, attracted to, the next in place,
Form'd, and impell'd, its *Neighbour* to embrace.

See Matter next, with various life endu'd,
Prefs to one Centre ftill, the *Gen'ral Good.*
See dying Vegetables Life fuftain,   15
See Life diffolving vegetate again.
All Forms that perifh other forms fupply,
By turns they catch the vital breath, and die;
Like Bubbles on the Sea of Matter born,
They rife, they break, and to that Sea return.   20
Nothing is foreign: Parts relate to Whole:
One all-extending, all-preferving Soul
Connects each Being, greateft with the leaft;
Made Beaft in aid of Man, and Man of Beaft;
All ferv'd, and ferving, nothing ftands alone;   25
The Chain holds on, and *where* it ends, unknown!

    Has GOD, thou Fool! work'd folely for thy good,
Thy joy, thy paftime, thy attire, thy food?
Who for thy Table feeds the wanton Fawn,
For him as kindly fpreads the flow'ry Lawn.   30
Is it for thee the Lark afcends and fings?
Joy tunes his voice, Joy elevates his wings:

Is it for thee the Linnet pours his throat?
Loves of his own, and raptures fwell the note.
The bounding Steed you pompoufly beftride,   35
Shares with his Lord the pleafure and the pride.
Is thine alone the Seed that ftrows the plain?
The Birds of heav'n fhall vindicate their grain:
Thine the full Harveft of the golden year?
Part pays, and juftly, the deferving Steer.   40
The Hog that plows not, nor obeys thy call,
Lives on the labours of this Lord of all.

   Know, Nature's Children all divide her care;
The Furr that warms a Monarch, warm'd a Bear.
While Man exclaims, "fee all things for my ufe!   45
"See Man for mine," replies a pamper'd Goofe:
What care to tend, to lodge, to cram, to treat him,
All this he knew; but not that 'twas to eat him.
As far as Goofe could judge, he reafon'd right,
But as to Man, miftook the matter quite: 50
And juft as fhort of Reafon, Man will fall,
Who thinks *All* made for *One*, not *One* for *All.*

These he omitted as too ludicrous for the gravity of the subject.

Grant, that the pow'rful ftill the weak controul,
Be Man the Wit and Tyrant of the whole.
Nature that Tyrant checks; He only knows   55
And feels, another creature's wants and woes.
Say will the falcon, ftooping from above,
Smit with her varying plumage, fpare the dove?
Admires the jay the infect's gilded wings,
Or hears the hawk, when *Philomela* fings?   60
Man cares for All: to birds he gives his woods,
To beafts his paftures, and to fifh his floods;
For fome his Int'reft prompts him to provide,
For more his Pleafure, yet for more his Pride:
All feed on one vain Patron, and enjoy   65
Th' extenfive blessing of his Luxury.
That very life his learned hunger craves,
He faves from famine, from the favage faves;
Nay, feafts the Animal he dooms his feaft,
And 'till he ends the Being, makes it bleft: 70

F

Which fees no more the ftroke, or feels the pain,
Than favour'd Man, by Touch ætherial flain.
The Creature had his feaft of life before;
Thou too muft perifh, when thy feaft is o'er!

To each unthinking being Heav'n a friend,　75
Gives not the ufelefs knowledge of its End;
To Man imparts it; but with fuch a View,
As while he dreads it, makes him hope it too:
The hour conceal'd, and fo remote the fear,
Death ftill draws nearer, never feeming near.　80
Great ftanding Miracle! that Heav'n affign'd
Its only thinking thing, this turn of mind.

Whether with *Reafon*, or with *Inftinct* bleft,
Know, all enjoy that pow'r which fuits 'em beft,
To Blifs, alike, by that direction tend,　　85
And find the means proportion'd to their end.
Say, where full *Inftinct* is th' unerring guide,
What Pope or Council can they need befide?

VER. 72.] Several of the Ancients, and many of the Orientals at this day, efteem'd thofe who were ftruck by Lightning as facred Perfons, and the particular Favourites of Heaven.

Reaſon, however able, cool at beſt,
Cares not for ſervice, or but ſerves when preſt,　90
Stays till we call, and then not often near;
But honeſt Inſtinct comes a Volunteer.
This too ſerves always, Reaſon never long;
One *muſt* go right, the other *may* go wrong.
See then the *acting* and *comparing* pow'rs　95
One in their nature, which are two in ours,
And Reaſon raiſe o'er Inſtinct, as you can;
In this 'tis *God* directs, in that 'tis *Man*.

Who taught the Nations of the field and wood,
To ſhun their Poiſon, and to chuſe their Food?　100
Preſcient, the Tydes or Tempeſts to withſtand,
Build on the Wave, or arch beneath the Sand?
Who made the Spider Parallels deſign,
Sure as *De-Moivre*, without rule or line?
Who bid the Stork, *Columbus*-like, explore　105
Heav'ns not his own, and worlds unknown before?
Who calls the Council, ſtates the certain day,
Who forms the Phalanx, and who points the way?

God, in the Nature of each being, founds
Its proper bliſs, and ſets its proper bounds: 110
But as he fram'd a Whole, the whole to bleſs
On mutual *Wants* built mutual *Happineſs:*
So from the firſt Eternal ORDER ran,
And Creature link'd to Creature, Man to Man.
What'ere of Life all-quickening Æther keeps, 115
Or breathes thro' Air, or ſhoots beneath the Deeps,
Or pours profuſe on Earth ; one Nature feeds
The vital flame, and ſwells the genial ſeeds.
Not Man alone, but all that roam the wood,
Or wing the sky, or roll along the flood,   120
Each loves Itſelf, but not itſelf alone,
Each Sex deſires alike, till two are one:
Nor ends the pleaſure with the fierce embrace ;
They love themſelves, a third time, in their Race.
Thus beaſt and bird their common charge attend, 125
The mothers nurſe it, and the ſires defend ;
The young diſmiſs'd to wander earth or air,
There ſtops the Inſtinct, and there ends the care,

The link diffolves, each feeks a frefh embrace, 130
Another love fucceeds, another race.
A longer care Man's helplefs kind demands;
That longer care contracts more lafting bands:
Reflection, Reafon, ftill the ties improve,
At once extend the Int'reft, and the Love: 135
With Choice we fix, with Sympathy we burn,
Each Virtue in each Paffion takes its turn;
And ftill new Needs, new Helps, new Habits rife,
That graft Benevolence on Charities.
Still as one brood, and as another rofe, 140
Thefe nat'ral Love maintain'd, habitual thofe;
The laft fcarce ripen'd into perfect Man,
Saw helplefs Him from whom their life began:
Mem'ry, and Forecaft, juft returns engage,
That pointed back to Youth, this on to Age; 145
While Pleafure, Gratitude, and Hope combin'd,
Still fpread the Int'reft, and preferv'd the Kind.
　　Nor think, in *Nature's State* they blindly trod;
The *State* of NATURE was the *Reign* of GOD:

Self-Love, and Social, at her birth began,　　150
Union the Bond of all things, and of Man.
Pride then was not; nor Arts, that Pride to aid;
Man walk'd with Beaſt, joint Tenant of the Shade;
The ſame his Table, and the ſame his Bed;
No murder cloath'd him, and no murder fed.　155
In the ſame Temple, the reſounding Wood,
All vocal Beings hymn'd their equal God:
The Shrine with Gore unſtain'd, with Gold undreſt,
Unbrib'd, unbloody, ſtood the blameleſs Prieſt.
Heav'ns Attribute was Univerſal Care,　　160
And Man's Prerogative to rule, but ſpare.
Ah how unlike the man of times to come!
Of half that live, the Butcher, and the Tomb;
Who, foe to Nature, hears the gen'ral groan,
Murders their ſpecies, and betrays his own.　165
But juſt diſeaſe to luxury ſucceeds,
And ev'ry death its own Avenger breeds;
The Fury-Paſſions from that blood began,
And turn'd on Man a fiercer ſavage, Man.

See him from Nature rising slow to Art! 170
To copy *Instinct* then was *Reason's* part;
Thus then to Man the Voice of Nature spake ——
" Go! from the Creatures thy instructions take;
" Learn from the Birds, what food the thickets yield;
" Learn from the Beasts, the Physick of the field:
" Thy Arts of building from the Bee receive; 176
" Learn of the Mole to plow, the Worm to weave;
" Learn of the little * Nautilus to sail,
" Spread the thin oar, and catch the driving gale.
" Here too all Forms of social Union find, 180
" And hence let Reason, late, instruct mankind:
" Here subterranean Works and Cities see,
" There Towns aerial on the waving Tree.
" Learn each small people's Genius, Policies;
" The Ants Republick, and the Realm of Bees; 185
" How those in common all their stores bestow,
" And Anarchy without confusion know,

VER. 178.] Oppian. Halieut. Lib. I. describes this Fish in the following manner.
They swim on the surface of the Sea, on the back of their Shells, which exactly re-
semble the Hulk of a Ship; they raise two Feet like Masts, and extend a Membrane
between which serves as a Sail; the other two Feet they employ as Oars at the side.
They are usually seen in the Mediterranean.

" And thefe for ever, tho' a Monarch reign,
" Their fep'rate Cells and Properties maintain.
" Mark what unvary'd Laws preferve their State,
" Laws wife as Nature, and as fix'd as Fate.   191
" In vain thy Reafon finer webs fhall draw,
" Entangle Juftice in her Net of Law,
" And Right too rigid harden into Wrong,
" Still for the ftrong too weak, the weak too ftrong.
" Yet go! and thus o'er all the Creatures fway, 196
" Thus let the wifer make the reft obey,
" Who for thofe Arts they learn'd of Brutes before,
" As Kings fhall crown them, or as Gods adore.
 Great *Nature* fpoke; obfervant Men obey'd; 200
Cities were built, Societies were made :
Here rofe one little State; another near
Grew by like means, and join'd thro' Love, or Fear.
Did here the Trees with ruddier burdens bend,
And there the Streams in purer rills defcend?   205
What War could ravifh, Commerce could beftow,
And he return'd a friend, who came a foe.

Converse and Love mankind might strongly draw,
When Love was Liberty, and Nature Law.
Thus States were form'd; the name of *King* unknown,
'Till common Int'rest plac'd the sway in One.   211
Then VIRTUE ONLY (or in Arts, or Arms,
Diffusing blessings, or averting harms)
The same which in a Sire the Sons obey'd,
A Prince the Father of a People made.   251
        'Till then, by Nature crown'd, each Patriarch sate,
King, Priest, and Parent of his growing State:
On him, their second Providence, they hung,
Their Law, his Eye; their Oracle, his Tongue.
He, from the wond'ring furrow call'd their food,   220
Taught to command the Fire, controul the Flood,
Draw forth the Monsters of th' Abyss profound,
Or fetch th' aerial Eagle to the ground.
Till drooping, sick'ning, dying, they began
Whom they rever'd as God, to mourn as Man.   225
Then, looking up from Sire to Sire, explor'd
One great, first Father, and that *first* ador'd.

G

Or plain Tradition that this All *begun*,
Convey'd unbroken Faith from Sire to Son,
The Workman from the Work diftinct was known, 230
And fimple Reafon never fought but One :
E're Wit oblique had broke that fteady light,
Man, like his Maker, faw, that *all was right*,
To Virtue in the paths of Pleafure trod,
And own'd a Father when he own'd a God.   235
Love all the Faith, and all th' Allegiance then ;
For Nature knew no Right Divine in Men,
No Ill could fear in God ; and underftood
A Sovereign Being but a Sovereign Good.
True Faith, true Policy, united ran,   240
That was but Love of God, and this of Man.

   Who firft taught fouls enflav'd, and realms undone,
Th' enormous Faith of Many made for One ?
That proud Exception to all Nature's laws,
T'invert the World, and counter-work its Caufe ? 245
Force firft made Conqueft, and that Conqueft, Law ;
Till Superftition taught the Tyrant Awe,

Then fhar'd the Tyranny, and lent it aid,
And Gods of Conqu'rors, Slaves of Subjects made:
She, midft the Light'ning's blaze and Thunder's found,
When rock'd the Mountains, and when groan'd the
She taught the weak to bend, the proud to pray [ground,
To Pow'r unfeen, and mightier far than they.
She, from the rending earth, and burfting skies,
Saw Gods defcend, and Fiends infernal rife;   255
Here fix'd the dreadful, there the bleft abodes;
Fear made her Devils, and weak Hope her Gods:
Gods partial, changeful, paffionate, unjuft,
Whofe Attributes were Rage, Revenge, or Luft:
Such as the fouls of Cowards might conceive,   260
And form'd *like* Tyrants, Tyrants would believe.
Zeal then, not Charity, became the guide,
And Hell was built on Spite, and Heav'n on Pride.
Then facred feem'd th' Æthereal Vault no more;
Altars grew marble then, and reek'd with gore: 265
Then firft the Flamen tafted living food;
Next his grim Idol fmear'd with human blood;

With Heav'ns own Thunders shook the world below,
And play'd the God an Engine on his foe.
 So drives *Self-love*, thro' just and thro' unjust, 270
To One man's Pow'r, Ambition, Lucre, Lust:
The same Self-love, in All, becomes the cause
Of what restrains him, Government and Laws.
For what one likes if others like as well,
What serves one Will when many Wills rebel? 275
How shall he keep, what sleeping or awake
A weaker may surprize, a stronger take?
His Safety must his Liberty restrain;
All join to guard what each desires to gain.
Forc'd into Virtue thus by Self-defence, 280
Ev'n Kings learn'd Justice and Benevolence:
Self-love forsook the path it first pursu'd,
And found the private in the public Good.
 'Twas then, the studious Head, or gen'rous Mind,
Follo'wer of God, or Friend of Humankind, 285
Poet or Patriot rose, but to restore
The Faith and Moral, *Nature* gave before:

Re-lum'd her ancient light, not kindled new;
If not God's Image, yet his Shadow drew;
Taught Pow'rs due ufe to People and to Kings,   290
Taught, not to flack nor ftrain its tender ftrings;
The Lefs, and Greater, fet fo juftly true,
That touching one muft ftrike the other too,
And jarring Int'refts of themfelves create
Th' according Mufic of a well-mix'd State.   295
Such is the WORLD's great Harmony, that fprings
From Union, Order, full Confent of things!
Where fmall and great, where weak and mighty made
To ferve, not fuffer, ftrengthen, not invade,
More pow'rful each as needful to the reft,   300
And in proportion as it bleffes, bleft,
Draw to one point, and to one Centre bring
Beaft, Man, or Angel, Servant, Lord, or King.

For Forms of Government let fools conteft,
Whate'er is beft adminiftred, is beft:
For Modes of Faith let gracelefs Zealots fight,
His can't be wrong whofe Life is in the right:

He added here a couplet—
   In faith and hope the world will disagree,
   But all mankind's concern is charity.

All muſt be falſe, that thwart this *One, great End*,
And all of God, that bleſs Mankind, or mend.   310
   Man, like the gen'rous Vine, ſupported lives,
The Strength he gains is from th'Embrace he gives.
On their own Axis as the Planets run,
Yet make at once their Circle round the Sun;
So two conſiſtent Motions act the ſoul,   320
And one regards *Itſelf*, and one the *Whole*.
   Thus God and Nature link'd the gen'ral Frame,
And bade Self-Love and Social be the ſame.

EPISTLE IV.

O HAPPINESS! our Being's End and Aim!
Good, Pleafure, Eafe, Content! whate'er
    thy name :
That Something ftill, which prompts th'eternal figh,
For which we bear to live, nor fear to die ;
Which ftill fo near us, yet beyond us lies,   5
O'erlook'd, feen double, by the fool — and wife.
Plant of Cæleftial feed ! if dropt below,
Say, in what mortal foil thou deign'ft to grow?
Fair-opening to fome Court's propitious Shine,
Or deep with diamonds in the flaming Mine,
Twin'd with the wreaths Parnaffian Laurels yield,
Or reap'd in Iron Harvefts of the Field?

Where grows – where grows it not?– If vain our toil,
We ought to blame the Culture, not the Soil :
Fix'd to no ſpot is Happineſs ſincere ;   15
'Tis no where to be found, or ev'ry where ;
'Tis never to be bought, but always free,
And fled from Monarchs, ST. JOHN! dwells with thee.

  Ask of the Learn'd the way, the Learn'd are blind,
This bids to ſerve, and that to ſhun mankind :   20
Some place the bliſs in Action, ſome in Eaſe,
Thoſe call it Pleaſure, and Contentment theſe :
Who thus define it, ſay they more or leſs
Than this, that Happineſs is Happineſs?
One grants his Pleaſure is but Reſt from pain,   25
One doubts of All, one owns ev'n Virtue vain.

  Take *Nature*'s path, and mad Opinion's leave,
All States can reach it, and all Heads conceive ;
Obvious her goods, in no Extreme they dwell,
There needs but thinking right, and meaning well ;
And mourn our various portions as we pleaſe,   31
Equal is *common Senſe*, and *common Eaſe*.

Remember Man! "the Univerſal Cauſe
" Acts not by partial, but by gen'ral Laws;
And makes what Happineſs we juſtly call,   30
Subſiſt not in the Good of one, but all.
There's not a bleſſing Individuals find,
But ſome way leans and hearkens to the Kind.
No Bandit fierce, no Tyrant mad with pride,
No cavern'd Hermit, reſt ſelf-ſatisfy'd;   40
Who moſt to ſhun or hate mankind pretend,
Seek an Admirer, or wou'd fix a Friend.
Abſtract what others feel, what others think,
All Pleaſures ſicken, and all Glories ſink;
Each has his ſhare, and who wou'd more obtain   45
Shall find, the pleaſure pays not half the pain.

    ORDER is Heav'n's firſt Law; and this confeſt,
Some are, and muſt be, greater than the reſt,
More rich, more wiſe: but who infers from hence
That ſuch are *happier*, ſhocks all common ſenſe.   50
Heav'n to mankind impartial we confeſs
If all are equal in their happineſs:

H

But mutual wants this happiness increase,
All Nature's diff'rence keeps all Nature's peace.
Condition, Circumstance is not the thing: 55
Bliss is the same, in Subject or in King;
In who obtain defence, or who defend;
In him who is, or him who finds, a friend.
Heav'n breathes thro' ev'ry member of the whole
One common Blessing, as one common Soul: 60
But Fortune's gifts if each alike possest,
And each were equal, must not all contest?
If then to all men Happiness was meant,
God in Externals could not place Content.

Fortune her gifts may variously dispose, 65
And these be call'd unhappy, happy those;
But Heav'n's just balance equal will appear,
While those are plac'd in Hope, and these in Fear:
Not present Good or Ill, the joy or curse,
But future views, of Better, or of Worse. 70

Oh Sons of Earth! attempt ye still to rise
By mountains pil'd on mountains, to the Skies?

Heav'n ſtill with laughter the vain toil ſurveys,
And buries Madmen in the Heaps they raiſe.

Know, all the Good that Individuals find, 75
Or God and Nature meant to meer mankind,
Reaſon's whole pleaſures, all the joys of Senſe,
Lie in three words, *Health, Peace,* and *Competence.*
But Health conſiſts with Temperance alone,
And Peace, fair Virtue! Peace is all thy own; 80
The gifts of Fortune good or bad may gain;
But theſe leſs taſte them, as they worſe obtain.
Say, in purſuit of Profit or Delight,
Who riſque the moſt, that take wrong means, or right?
Of Vice or Virtue, whether bleſt or curſt, 85
Which meets Contempt, or which Compaſſion firſt?
Count all th' advantage proſp'rous Vice attains,
'Tis but what Virtue flies from, and diſdains;
And grant the bad what happineſs they wou'd,
One they muſt want, which is, to paſs for good. 90

Oh blind to Truth, and God's whole Scheme be-
Who fancy Bliſs to Vice, to Virtue Woe: [low!

H 2

Who fees and follows that great Scheme the beft,
Beft knows his blefling, and will moft be bleft.
But Fools the *Good* alone unhappy call,   95
For Ills or Accidents that chance to *All.*
See FALKLAND falls, the virtuous and the juft!
See godlike TURENNE proftrate on the duft!
See SIDNEY bleeds amid the martial ftrife!
Was this their *Virtue,* or Contempt of life?   100
Say was it Virtue, more tho' Heav'n ne'er gave,
Lamented DIGBY! funk thee to the Grave?
Tell me, if Virtue made the Son expire,
Why, full of Days and Honour, lives the Sire?
Why drew *Marfeilles* good Bifhop purer breath,   105
When Nature ficken'd, and each gale was death?
Or why fo long (in Life if long can be)
Lent Heav'n a *Parent* to the Poor and Me?
    What makes all Phyfical or Moral Ill?
There deviates Nature, and here wanders Will.   110
God fends not Ill, 'tis Nature lets it fall
Or Chance efcape, and Man improves it all.

We juſt as wiſely might of Heav'n complain,
That righteous Abel was deſtroy'd by Cain,
As that the virtuous Son is ill at eaſe,   115
When his lewd Father gave the dire diſeaſe.
Think we like ſome weak Prince th' Eternal Cauſe,
Prone for his Fav'rites to reverſe his Laws?

     Shall burning Ætna, if a Sage requires,
Forget to thunder, and recall her fires?   120
On Air or Sea new motions be impreſt,
O blameleſs Bethel! to relieve thy breaſt?
When the looſe Mountain trembles from on high,
Shall Gravitation ceaſe, if you go by?
Or ſome old Temple nodding to its fall,   125
For Chartres head reſerve the hanging Wall?

     But ſtill this World (ſo fitted for the Knave)
Contents us not.   A better ſhall we have?
A Kingdom of the Juſt then let it be:
But firſt conſider how thoſe Juſt agree?   130
The Good muſt merit God's peculiar care;
But who but God can tell us, who they are?

One thinks on Calvin Heav'n's own spirit fell,
Another deems him Instrument of Hell;
If Calvin feel Heav'n's Blessing, or its Rod,   135
This cries there is, and that, there is no God.
What shocks one part will edify the rest,
Nor with one System can they all be blest.
Give each a System, all must be at strife;
What diff"rent Systems for a man and wife?   140
The very best will variously incline,
And what rewards your Virtue, punish mine.
" Whatever *is*, is *right*." — This world, 'tis true,
Was made for Cæsar — but for Titus too:
And which more *blest?* who chain'd his Country, say,
Or he, whose Virtue sigh'd to lose a day?   146
   " But sometimes Virtue starves while Vice is fed."
What then? is the reward of Virtue, Bread?
That, Vice may merit; 'tis the price of Toil:
The Knave deserves it when he tills the Soil,   150
The Knave deserves it when he tempts the Main,
Where Madness fights, for Tyrants, or for Gain.

The good man may be weak, be indolent,

Nor is his claim to Plenty, but Content.

But grant him Riches, your demand is o'er?   155

" No — fhall the good want health, the good want

Add health and pow'r, and ev'ry earthly thing: [Pow'r?

" Why bounded pow'r? why private? why no King?

Nay, why external for internal giv'n,

Why is not Man a God, and Earth a Heav'n?   160

Who ask and reafon thus, will fcarce conceive

God gives enough while he has more to give:

Immenfe the Pow'r, immenfe were the demand;

Say, at what part of Nature will they ftand?

What nothing earthly gives, or can deftroy, 165

The Soul's calm fun-fhine, and the heart-felt joy,

Is Virtue's Prize: A better would you fix,

And give Humility a Coach and fix?

Juftice a Conqu'ror's fword, or Truth a Gown,

Or Publick Spirit, its great cure, a Crown?   170   xx

Rewards that either would to Virtue bring

No joy, or be deftructive of the thing.

xx —

He made an insertion of little moment as to its beauty, and clashing
with his argument. "What Heaven may give us there" is beyond our know-
ledge, and therefore admits no inference. It is better as it stands here
But see Warburton's Edition 8vo. 3 Vol. p. 140.

How oft by thefe at fixty are undone
The Virtues of a Saint at twenty-one!

For *Riches,* can they give but to the Juft,   175
His own Contentment, or another's Truft?
Judges and Senates have been bought for gold,
Efteem and Love were never to be fold.
O Fool! to think, God hates the worthy Mind,
The Lover, and the Love, of Human kind,   180
Whofe Life is healthful, and whofe Confcience clear;
Becaufe he wants a thoufand pounds a year!

Honour and *Shame* from no Condition rife;
Act well your part, there all the Honour lies.
Fortune in men has fome fmall diff'rence made,   185
One flaunts in Rags, one flutters in Brocade,
The Cobler apron'd, and the Parfon gown'd,
The Fryar hooded, and the Monarch crown'd.
" What differ more (you cry) than Crown and Cowl?"
I'll tell you, friend: a Wife man and a Fool.   190
You'll find, if once the Monarch acts the Monk,
Or Cobler-like, the Parfon will be drunk,

Worth makes the Man, and want of it the Fellow ;
The reft, is all but Leather or Prunella.

 Stuck o'er with *Titles*, and hung round with Strings,
That thou may'ft be, by Kings, or Whores of Kings.
Thy boafted Blood, a thoufand years or fo,
May from Lucretia to Lucretia flow ;
But by your Father's worth if yours you rate,
Count me thofe only who were good and great. 205
Go ! if your ancient but ignoble blood
Has crept thro' Scoundrels ever fince the Flood,
Go ! and pretend your Family is young ;
Not own your Fathers have been fools fo long. 210
What can ennoble Sots, or Slaves, or Cowards?
Alas ! not all the blood of all the HOWARDS.

 Look next on *Greatnefs*, fay where Greatnefs lies?
" Where, but among the Heroes, and the Wife?"
Heroes are much the fame, the point's agreed, 215
From Macedonia's Madman to the Suede ;
The whole ftrange purpofe of their lives, to find
Or make, an Enemy of all Mankind :

I

Not one looks backward, onward ſtill he goes,
Yet ne'er looks foreward, further than his noſe. 220
No leſs alike the Politick and wiſe,
All ſly ſlow things, with circumſpective eyes;
Men in their looſe, unguarded hours they take,
Nor that themſelves are wiſe, but others weak.
But grant that thoſe can *conquer*, theſe can *cheat*, 225
'Tis phraſe abſurd to call a Villain *great*.
Who wickedly is wiſe, or madly brave,
Is but *the more* a fool, *the more* a knave.
Who noble ends by noble means obtains,
Or failing, ſmiles in Exile or in Chains,   230
Like good Aurelius let him reign, or bleed
Like Socrates, that Man is great indeed.

What's *Fame?* that fancy'd Life in others breath!
A thing beyond us ev'n before our death.
Juſt what you *hear* you have, and what's unknown 235
The ſame (my Lord) if Tully's, or your own.
All that we feel of it begins and ends
In the ſmall circle of our foes or friends;

To all beſide as much an empty Shade
An Eugene living, as a Cæſar dead, 240
Alike or when or where, they ſhone or ſhine,
Or on the Rubicon, or on the Rhine.
A Wit's a *Feather*, and a Chief a *Rod*;
An honeſt man's the nobleſt Work of God:
Fame but from death a Villain's name can ſave, 245
As Juſtice tears his body from the grave;
When what t' oblivion better were reſign'd,
Is hung on high, to poiſon half mankind.
All Fame is foreign, but of true deſert,
Plays round the head, but comes not to the heart.
One ſelf-approving hour whole years out-weighs 251
Of ſtupid Starers, and of loud huzza's;
And more true joy Marcellus exil'd feels
Than Cæſar with a Senate at his heels.

In Parts ſuperior what advantage lies! 255
Tell (for *You* can) what is it to be wiſe?
'Tis but to know, how little can be known;
To ſee all others faults, and feel our own;

I 2

Condemn'd in Bufinefs or in Arts to drudge
Without a Second, or without a Judge: 260
Truths would you teach, or fave a finking Land?
All fear, none aid you, and few underftand.
Painful Preheminence! yourfelf to view
Above Life's Weaknefs, and its Comforts too.

Bring then thefe Bleflings to a ftrict account, 265
Make fair deductions, fee to what they mount?
How much of other each is fure to coft?
How each for other oft is wholly loft?
How inconfiftent greater Goods with thefe?
How fometimes Life is rifqu'd, and always Eafe? 270
Think, and if ftill the Things thy envy call,
Say, would'ft thou be the Man to whom they fall?
To figh for Ribbands if thou art fo filly,
Mark how they grace Lord Umbra, or Sir Billy.
Is yellow Dirt the paffion of thy life?   275
Look but on Gripus, or on Gripus' wife.
If Parts allure thee, think how Bacon fhin'd,
The wifeft, brighteft, meaneft of Mankind:

Or ravifh'd with the whiftling of a Name,

See Cromwell, damn'd to everlafting Fame!   280

If all, united, thy ambition call,

From ancient Story learn to fcorn them all.

There, in the rich, the honour'd, fam'd, and great,

See the falfe Scale of Happinefs compleat! ·

In hearts of Kings or arms of Queens who lay,   285

(How happy!) thofe to ruin, thefe betray,

Mark by what wretched fteps their Glory grows,

From dirt and fea-weed as proud Venice rofe;

In each, how Guilt and Greatnefs equal ran,

And all that rais'd the Hero funk the Man.   290

Now Europe's Lawrels on their brows behold,

But ftain'd with Blood, or ill exchang'd for Gold:

Then fee them broke with Toils, or loft in Eafe,

Or infamous for plunder'd Provinces.

Oh Wealth ill-fated! which no Act of fame   295

E'er taught to fhine, or fanctify'd from fhame!

What greater blifs attends their clofe of life?

Some greedy Minion, or imperious Wife,

The trophy'd Arches, ftory'd Halls invade,
And haunt their flumbers in the pompous Shade.
Alas! not dazled with their Noontide ray,   300
Compute the Morn and Evening to the Day:
The whole amount of that enormous Fame
A Tale! that blends their Glory with their Shame!
   Know then this Truth (enough for man to know)
VIRTUE alone *is* Happinefs below.   305
The only point where human blifs ftands ftill,
And taftes the Good without the fall to Ill:
Where only, Merit conftant pay receives,
Is blefs'd in what it takes and what it gives:
The joy unequal'd, if its end it gain,   310
And if it lofe, attended with no pain:
Without fatiety, tho' e'er fo blefs'd,
And but more relifh'd as the more diftrefs'd:
The broadeft Mirth unfeeling Folly wears,
Lefs pleafing far than Virtue's very Tears: 315
Good, from each object, from each place acquir'd,
For ever exercis'd, yet never tir'd;

Never elated, while one Man's opprefs'd ;
Never dejected, while another's blefs'd :
And where no wants, no wifhes can remain,   320
Since but to wifh more Virtue, is to gain.

See ! the fole Blifs Heav'n could on *all* beftow,
Which who but feels, can tafte, but thinks, can know :
Yet, poor with Fortune and with Learning blind,
The Bad muft mifs, the Good untaught will find, 352
Slave to no Sect, who takes no private road,
But looks thro' *Nature* up to *Nature's* GOD,
Purfues that *Chain* which links th' immenfe Defign,
Joyns Heav'n, and Earth, and mortal, and divine ;
Sees, that no Being any Blifs can know   330
But touches fome above, and fome below ;
Learns, from this Union of the rifing *Whole*,
The firft, laft Purpofe of the human Soul ;
And knows, where Faith, Law, Morals all began,
All end, in LOVE *of* GOD and LOVE *of* MAN.   335

For him alone, *Hope* leads from gole to gole,
And opens ftill, and opens, on his Soul,

Till lengthen'd on to *Faith*, and unconfin'd,
It pours the blifs that fills up all the mind.
He fees, why Nature plants in Man alone   340
Hope of known blifs, and Faith in blifs unknown?
(Nature, whofe dictates to no other Kind
Are giv'n in vain, but what they feek they find)
Wife is the Prefent: fhe connects in this
His greateft *Virtue* with his greateft *Blifs*,   345
At once his own bright Profpect to be bleft,
And ftrongeft Motive to aflift the reft.
   Self-Love thus pufh'd to Social, to Divine,
Gives thee to make thy Neighbour's blefling thine:
Is this too little for the boundlefs heart?   350
Extend it, let thy Enemies have part!
Grafp the whole Worlds, of Reafon, Life, and Senfe,
In one clofe Syftem of Benevolence!
Happier, as kinder! in whate'er degree;
And height of *Blifs* but height of CHARITY.   355
   GOD loves from whole to parts: but human Soul
Muft rife from individual to the whole.

Self-love but ferves the virtuous Mind to wake,
As the fmall pebble ftirs the peaceful Lake;
The Centre mov'd, a Circle ftrait fucceeds,　　360
Another ftill, and ftill another fpreads;
Friend, Parent, Neighbour, firft it will embrace,
His Country next, and next all Human-race;
Wide, and more wide, th' O'erflowings of the mind
Take ev'ry Creature in, of every kind;　　365
Earth fmiles around, with boundlefs bounty bleft,
And Heav'n beholds its Image in his Breaft,

　　Come then, my Friend! my Genius come along,
Oh Mafter of the Poet, and the Song!
And while the Mufe now ftoops, or now afcends,　370
To Man's low Paffions or their glorious Ends,
Teach me like thee, in various Nature wife,
To fall with Dignity, with Temper rife,
Form'd by thy Converfe, happily to fteer
From grave to gay, from lively to fevere,　　375
Correct with fpirit, eloquent with eafe,
Intent to reafon, or polite to pleafe.

K

O! while along the ſtream of Time, thy Name
Expanded flies, and gathers all its fame,
Say, ſhall my little Bark attendant ſail,　　380
Purſue the Triumph, and partake the Gale?
When Stateſmen, Heroes, Kings, in duſt repoſe,
Whoſe Sons ſhall bluſh their Fathers were thy foes,
Shall then this Verſe to future age pretend
Thou wert my Guide, Philoſopher, and Friend? 385
That urg'd by thee, I turn'd the tuneful Art
From Sounds to Things, from Fancy to the Heart;
For Wit's falſe Mirror held up Nature's Light;
Shew'd erring Pride, *Whatever Is,* is *Right*;
That *Reaſon, Paſſion,* anſwer *one great Aim*;　　390
That true *Self-love* and *Social* are the *ſame*;
That *Virtue* only makes our *Bliſs below*;
And all our *Knowledge* is, *Ourſelves to know.*

APPENDIX

The following pair of leaves is reproduced from a fine-paper copy in the possession of Mr. H. B. Forster. This pair of leaves appears to have been replaced in ordinary copies by a reset K1 containing the last two pages of text with only accidental changes; the real purpose seems to have been to suppress beyond hope of recovery the 'Index to the Ethic Epistles', and the resetting of K1 was only incidental to this. Normally fine-paper copies contain the original K1 but not the Index, which is only known to survive in this copy. Clearly Pope was unwilling to commit himself to this detailed plan, and it is possible that he only intended it to be printed in those fine-paper copies he intended for his friends; in that case the cancellation was made necessary by the printer's error.

Self-love but ferves the virtuous Mind to wake,
As the fmall pebble ftirs the peaceful Lake;
The Centre mov'd, a Circle ftrait fucceeds,   360
Another ftill, and ftill another fpreads;
Friend, Parent, Neighbour, firft it will embrace,
His Country next, and next all Human-race;
Wide, and more wide, th' O'erflowings of the mind
Take ev'ry Creature in, of ev'ry kind;   365
Earth fmiles around, with boundlefs bounty bleft,
And Heav'n beholds its Image in his Breaft.

  Come then, my Friend! my Genius come along,
Oh Mafter of the Poet, and the Song!
And while the Mufe now ftoops, or now afcends,   370
To Man's low Paffions, or their glorious Ends,
Teach me like thee, in various Nature wife,
To fall with Dignity, with Temper rife,
Form'd by thy Converfe, happily to fteer
From grave to gay, from lively to fevere,   375
Correct with fpirit, eloquent with eafe,
Intent to reafon, or polite to pleafe.

K

O! while along the ſtream of Time, thy Name
Expanded flies, and gathers all its fame,
Say, ſhall my little Bark attendant ſail,   380
Purſue the Triumph, and partake the Gale?
When Stateſmen, Heroes, Kings, in duſt repoſe,
Whoſe Sons ſhall bluſh their Fathers were thy foes,
Shall then this Verſe to future age pretend
Thou wert my Guide, Philoſopher, and Friend? 385
That urg'd by thee, I turn'd the tuneful Art
From Sounds to Things, from Fancy to the Heart;
For Wit's falſe Mirror held up Nature's Light;
Shew'd erring Pride, *Whatever Is, is Right*;
That *Reaſon, Paſſion,* anſwer *one great Aim*;   390
That true *Self-love* and *Social* are the *ſame*;
That *Virtue* only makes our *Bliſs below*;
And all our *Knowledge* is, *Ourſelves to know.*

INDEX

TO THE

ETHIC EPISTLES.